FROM HERMENEUTICS TO ETHICAL CONSENSUS AMONG CULTURES

South Florida-Rochester-Saint Louis
Studies on Religion and the Social Order

EDITED BY

Jacob Neusner   William Scott Green   William M. Shea

FROM HERMENEUTICS TO ETHICAL
CONSENSUS AMONG CULTURES

by
Pier Cesare Bori

FROM HERMENEUTICS TO ETHICAL CONSENSUS AMONG CULTURES

Pier Cesare Bori

*Translations by Patrick Leech,
Charles Hindley and David Ward*

Scholars Press
Atlanta, Georgia

From Hermeneutics to Ethical
Consensus Among Cultures
by
Pier Cesare Bori

Published by Scholars Press
for the University of South Florida, University of Rochester,
and Saint Louis University

Library of Congress Cataloging in Publication Data
Bori, Pier Cesare.
    From hermeneutics to ethical consensus among cultures / Pier
Cesare Bori.
        p.   cm. — (South Florida-Rochester-Saint Louis studies on
religion and the social order ; v.7)
    Includes index.
    ISBN 1-55540-977-6 (alk. paper)
    1. Hermeneutics. 2. Ethics, Comparative. 3. Ethics.
4. Civilization—Philosophy. 5. Bible—Influence. 6. Civilization,
Classical. I. Title. II. Series.
B3613.B57F76   1994
121'.68—dc20   94-10779
                                      CIP

Printed in the United States of America
on acid-free paper

Table of contents

Foreword

Foreword

The first part of this work, which gives its name to the whole book, contains the translation of my *Per un consenso etico tra culture. Tesi per la lettura secolare delle Scritture ebraico-cristiane* (Genova: Marietti, 1991). Although expanded in comparison with this first Italian edition, this first section of the book still preserves its synthetic, thesis-like structure, drawing essentially on my previous analytical research.

To acquaint the reader with this research, this American edition presents a translation of some of my most recent essays, collected in the second section ("An idea of reading").

A series of lectures and talks at Yale University, in various departments and on various occasions, is at the origin of this book. I would therefore like to thank Yale's Cyrus Hamlin for providing that opportunity.

I am also indebted to Jacob Neusner, from South Florida University, for having accepted my book for the series of "South-Florida-Rochester-St. Louis Studies in Religion and the Social Order".

P.C.B.

I

FROM HERMENEUTICS
TO ETHICAL CONSENSUS

Preface

Generally speaking, Italy has never offered a favourable terrain to multi-culturalism. Our Italian, Catholic tradition is monocultural, with traditional external antagonists: Judaism, Islam and Protestantism. This mono-culture has done considerable damage down the centuries. In general it has fostered a separation of private ethics from public morality, with a resulting pessimistic and resigned attitude towards social life (sometimes labelled as Machiavellianism). In this culture tolerance and human rights are a rather recent achievement, due to external pressure rather than to internal evolution.

But on the other hand, since the time of the Comunes the contributions made in many fields of art and science by small Italian élites had some relevance to the encounter between cultures. As a late offspring of the Classical heritage, and perhaps of a secondary but essential spiritual tradition (in which I would include figures as different as Gregory the Great, Joachim of Fiore and Francis of Assisi), the humanistic tradition succeeded, from Petrarch on, in reading both the Bible and the classics with the same attention and devotion. Among the humanists some had such a broad idea of classicism as to include also Jewish and Islamic cultures (I have in mind in particular Pico della Mirandola).

Italy did not experience either a Reformation, or a religious democratic revolution such as England had (with its expansion into the New World), nor an Enlightenment comparable to that of the French, that led to the Revolution. However, a solitary thinker like Giovanbattista Vico could build a vision of history on religious humanistic foundations in which the different cultures of mankind could find a place and be interpreted in a way that was precluded in general to the Enlightenment, and that foreshadowed the Romantic cult of history and contemporary anthropology. Gramsci's thought was a result of a synthesis between this vision of history, re-enhanced by Italian historicism (Croce, Gentile) and Marxism, and much of his vision of society and culture will probably survive the crisis of the latter.

1

Remarkable social changes have also taken place in Italy recently. The Mediterranean situation of this country is exposing it to a continual immigration from the Maghreb, that is from an Arab-Muslim area, and from the sub-Saharan area. The explosion of the Balkans makes us feel the presence of a highly differentiated population (among whom Muslims) very close to us, pressing on our boundaries, asking for help and mutual understanding. In Italy, economic difficulties and the political crisis is leading a part of the population of the North to ask for more independence from the Centre and the South. This movement contains a potential for violence that I hope will not explode: but in any case there is a widespread, increasing loss of awareness of the reasons for cultural and political Italian unity, developed down the centuries from Dante onwards.

Some years have passed since this all-pervading sense of cultural and ethical non-belonging made us first begin to fear the danger of terrible clashes and made us feel what Simone Weil called, in 1943, *The Need for Roots* (the necessity of *enracinement*): that is, to feel the need to rediscover and read again our sources. I mean "reading" in the widest and most intense possible sense, that is to adhere with all our being to something objective, outside of us, spiritually greater than we are, to find there a vital instruction, a wisdom, without of course leaving on one side our sense of history, our critical, and even suspicious, pluralistic modern consciousness. Thus, we started on an experience of common reading in a small group of young friends. We read Plato, *Bhagavadgita*, the *Katha-upanishad*, the Buddhist *Dhammapada*, Confucius and Lao-tze, Seneca and Marcus Aurelius, Philo *De vita contemplativa*, *Pirque Abot*, various books from the Jewish and the Christian Bible, Augustine (*The Confessions* VIII), the *Coran*, Al Ghazali.

The task and the challenge concerned the possibility of carrying out the simultaneous reading and translation, in the broadest sense, of a plurality of traditions, while maintaining the consciousness of and loyalty to one's own origin and sources. Spurred on by the necessity of replying to the question about the sense of the complex operation we were performing (a question that arises frequently, when we pass from one source to another) I elaborated the following methodological and theoretical "theses".

In this work our attention shifts from ancient and spiritual hermeneutics, which I examined in some previous works, to contemporary problems and requirements for our reading of "classics". Thus a wider pedagogic concern, that is, about our *paideia*, underlies this book. As will become clear, I believe that the most urgent task is neither theoretical nor simply methodological, but rather concerns the possibility of practising the simultaneous reading as I have just said, of a plurality of traditions, which I consider an urgent task that has only marginally been confronted. This has always been, and still is, my main interest and daily commitment. I nevertheless felt it important to outline in an explicit, concise and responsible way the assumptions upon which my work is based. Hence the "Theses" in which I have collected the most important ideas I have elaborated on the necessity and possibility of rediscovering the ancient "spiritual" and "philosophic" model of reading and putting it into a new, critical and creative perspective (Thesis I). This perspective can be described as (II) conscious of the Biblical paradigm but tendentially universalistic; (III) rational in a sapiential sense; (IV) based on a maternal paradigm; (V) oriented towards praxis; (VI) secular, in a positive sense, (VII and VIII) and opening the way to a common project concerning human rights and ethics. I have illustrated these "Theses" succinctly in a way which either makes reference to direct sources or, as is more often the case, to my previous research over the last twenty years, on which I draw considerably.

In its own way, I believe that this work may be considered part of the currently established but also fiercely contested "hermeneutic" tendency. In this sense it shares the conviction that knowledge in the human sciences is above all interpretation, discussion and growth out of past knowledge, and that knowledge is founded on persuasion through the convergence and consensus of authors rather than on the grounds of rigorous proof. However, due to the nature of t he sources with which I deal, I find it necessary to insist on the objective strength of these texts, on their "virtue" or "spirit", which in a certain way guarantees them an accessibility and universality stretching beyond the weakness and limits of the individual interpreter.

The core of the argument can be found at the end, towards the ethical statement (Theses VII and VIII). On the premiss that particularity and universality do not contradict each other, the secular and critical reading of one's own sources, together with a growing consciousness of other cultures, should suggest that a tendential, unexpressed and never fully expressible universality does exist. This would be a fundamental contribution to an "ethical consensus among cultures".

It has been argued that interpretation is to be opposed to creation and that the hermeneutic perspective is a pretext for a refusal to think. I reply to this charge at the end of Thesis I and in more depth when, on the basis of Plato's *Symposium*, I recall that the creation of the beautiful is precisely the result of its contemplation and that therefore creative power passes through obedience and submission. This link between the Eros of the *Symposium* and biblical wisdom is one of the central threads of my own research.

Apropos of the above, Marcel Proust, in his introduction to John Ruskin's *Sesame and Lilies*, discusses with the latter the idea of reading. In the course of their conversation Proust makes what seems to me a crucial remark. Let me conclude my introduction by recommending this passage. What follows (Thesis IV), avails itself of these essential terms: wisdom, desire and beauty.

"We know well that our wisdom begins where the author's ends, and we would like him to give us replies, when he can give us only desires. And he cannot awaken these desires in us except by making us contemplate, too, the supreme beauty that the last effort of his art has allowed him to contemplate. But according to a peculiar and perhaps providential law of the optics of the spirits (a law t hat means perhaps that we cannot receive the truth from anybody, and that we must create it by ourselves), what is the end of his wisdom represents for us only the beginning of ours".[1]

---

[1] "Journées de lecture" (1919), in *Pastiches et mélanges*.

On Reading

A return to the ancient model of reading, something which would appear particularly necessary today, can be proposed and experienced only on the basis of a critical and creative hermeneutic perspective.

1. The Ancient Model of Reading

I mean by this a conception according to which the act of reading is ruled by the objective power of a text to which the reader refers and conforms in an exclusive way, in order to draw on it the knowledge necessary to live a fully human life: wisdom. On the necessity of such a return I shall present further, wider reflections dealing precisely with that "wisdom", which is "the only one worthy to be pursued" (Thesis III).

a) I am thinking first of all of ancient Christian tradition, of the *lectio divina*, of the "spiritual reading". Ancient Christian hermeneutics, with all the differences between the different authors, epochs and traditions, and with many features in common with other religious traditions, and especially the Jewish tradition (*midrash, haggadah*), converge above all in their conception of the sacred text. The Bible evidently transcends all other writing. In it, text and history coincide: *narrat textum, prodit mysterium*, says Gregory the Great, summing up preceding hermeneutic traditions at the end of the sixth century. Animated by the spirit, it constitutes a living, unified and coherent body, which moves with a force, *virtus*, and a *dynamis* of its own, like the chariot in the vision of Ezekiel, according to Gregory's own commentary on the Prophet. Secondly, ancient hermeneutics agree on the definition of the reader of the sacred text. It requires a reader who is also animated by the Spirit, a reader who by reading and interpreting, seeks, through letter and history, knowledge of the "mystery" (as it was then called). Such is the spiritual power, the *virtus* of authentic scriptural contemplation, that it "not

5

only recognizes Sacred Scripture, once it has been created, but would be capable of creating it, if it did not already exist".[1] From this, thirdly, derives the idea of reading as an act which generates infinite meanings, which spring from connections between the texts, and between the texts and the reader. The biblical universe is thus at the same time infinite and closed (symbolic links to the natural world are possible, but only until the twelfth century, in subordination to the Bible and with a biblical basis), the reader himself existing within this universe. The final result of reading will thus be the prolongation of the text until it involves the reader in his own epoch: the text becomes true, it becomes exemplary and normative for the reader and for his community. Its application is not external to its interpretation, but constitutes indeed the necessary final moment of that interpretation: it is *gnosis*, knowledge as the link between contemplation and action, in which contemplation ends.[2]

   b) I am thinking also of the ancient philosophical reading, which in some way seems to represent the secularisation of the *lectio divina*. Pierre Hadot shows that among the essential tasks of ancient philosophy, especially stoic philosophy, side by side with "learning how to live", "how to die" and "how to converse", there was also "learning how to read".[3] He shows how philosophy in the post-Socratic epoch , conceived of as in the preceding period as an art of living, as a spiritual exercise, as spiritual progress, pursues these goals by studying and meditating on the great authors, with a rigorously selective attitude.[4] His conception can be illustrated by referring to Seneca's second *Epistle to Lucilius*:

> The primary indication of a well-ordered mind is an ability to remain in one place and linger in his own company. Be careful, however, lest this

---

1 Gregory the Great: "Contemplatio enim virtus est, non solum per quam Scriptura condita recognoscitur, sed per quam nondum condita conderetur et per quam condita ad Dei voluntatem cotidie disponatur" (*In l. I Reg.* III, 171). Cf. my commentary on the text in *L'interpretazione infinita. L'ermeneutica cristiana antica e le sue trasformazioni* (Bologna: Il Mulino, 1987) p. 67 (see French trans., *L'interprétation infinie* [Paris: Editions du Cerf, 1991]).

2 I am using for this summary my "'Sacred scriptures, or the Bibles of the Nations' in *Walden* by Henry David Thoreau", see below, II, 4.

3 *Exercices spirituels et philosophie antique* (Paris: Etudes augustiniennes, 1987).

4 P. Hadot, "Théologie, exégèse, révélation", in *Les règles de l'interprétation*, M. Tardieu ed. (Paris: Editions du Cerf, 1987). In his later works Michel Foucault paid much attention to this theme: cf. "The Technologies of the Self", in *The Technologies of the Self*, edited by L.H. Martin, H. Gutman, P.H. Hutton (University of Massachusetts Press, 1988) pp. 16 ff.

reading of many authors and books of every sort tends to make you discoursive and unsteady. You must linger among a limited number of master-thinkers, and digest their own works, if you wish to derive ideas which shall win firm hold in your mind. Everywhere means nowhere... Accordingly, since you cannot read all the books which you may possess, it is enough to possess only as many books as you can read. "But" you reply, "I wish to dip first into one book and then into another". I tell you that it is the sign of an overnice appetite to toy with many dishes; for when they are manifold and varied, they cloy but do not nourish. So you should always read standard authors; and when you crave a change, fall back upon those whom you read before.[5]

This letter was used by Tolstoy at the beginning of his *Cycle of Reading*, of which I shall say something later.

2. A Critical and Creative Hermeneutic Perspective

I mean by this that attitude of critical individualism in the interpretation of texts which has been an important feature of modern cultural practice since the Renaissance. This critical attitude includes not only the necessary philological attention to the texts, but also an independence from the theological point of view. This secular attitude is necessarily pluralistic and universalistic, as the absolute normativity of a single text is being lost. But the opening of the canon enables and in some way obliges the reader to bring forth and create his own text. In the following pages I shall present some recent models, starting from that of Simone Weil.

a) One must first of all draw attention to the importance of the hermeneutic perspective in Simone Weil's work in general. Reflection, rather than pure theoretical activity, is for Weil an act of interpretation, a "reading". The notion of reading is given a crucial position in her work, and attains the role of an equivalent, metaphorically, to human knowledge itself. Her *Essay on the notion of reading* remains fully open between the two terms of a contradiction she presents in this way: "In every moment of our life we are seized as it were from the *outside* by the meanings we *ourselves read* in the appearances". Thus, on the one hand, there is reality, or nature, that as a powerful text "seizes the soul, into which the meaning penetrates, together with the black and white in the same irresistible manner". On the other there is the reader, who also has "a certain power, which allows him to change the appearances, but only indirectly, by work, not by mere desire". However, the terms themselves Weil uses show that we are no

---

[5] Seneca, Ep. 1, trans. R.E. Gummere (Loeb Classical Library).

longer in the presence of the ancient hermeneutics, ruled by the objective *virtus* of the text, according to which the interpreter could express his or her power only by establishing connections inside the closed infinity of the text. This power which, when applied to the text and its language, releases from it a multiplicity of objective meanings, reveals the marks of modern subjectivity, the traces of Descartes, of Bacon (whose idea of ruling over nature by obedience she recalls in her *Cahiers*) and of Marx (with her emphasis on reading as "work").

Simone Weil gives a clear outline of the critical character of this hermeneutic attitude with her emphasis, in her *Spiritual Autobiography*, on individuality. She speaks there about the necessity of "a harmonious solution of the problem of the relationships between individuals and society [...] The situation of the intelligence is the touchstone of this harmony, because intelligence is rigorously individual [...] This harmony exists wherever the intelligence, remaining in its own place, exercises its function fully and without hindrance [...] The specific function of intelligence demands total freedom, which implies the right to deny everything, and the absence of any form of predominance".[6] The universalistic character of Simone Weil's hermeneutics appears clearly in her *Last Thoughts*: "We live in an epoch without precedents, and in the present time universality, which could once be implicit, needs to be fully explicit. It must impregnate language and ways of being".[7]

b) Moving beyond these examples, which are all part of the "expanded biblical paradigm" (Thesis II), I would like to recall Gandhi. In 1889 he encountered Erwin Arnold's translation of the *Bhagavadgita*. What struck him most were the last nineteen verses of Chapter II, which he sees as the "centre" of the text, the "essence of the dharma". The content of these nineteen verses is made up of the image of "spiritually stable wisdom", of *sthitaprajna*, which through discipline distances itself from the world yet is also an instrument of liberation for the world: "When it is night for all creatures, a master of restraint is awake; when they are awake, it is night for the sage who sees reality" (v. 69).[8] The *Gita* is considered by Gandhi to be the main source of wisdom for the Hindus, "our Kamadhenu", the mystical cow which satisfies every innocent desire. But according to Gandhi, the

---

6 *Attente de Dieu* (Paris: Fayard, 1966) pp. 55 f.

7 *Attente de Dieu*, p. 81. Cf. my paper on S.Weil and Jewish Scriptures, *Simone Weil e la Bibbia ebraica*, in *Politeia e sapienza. In questione con Simone Weil*, a cura di Adriano Marchetti, (Bologna: Pàtron editore, 1993), 33-46.

8 Trans. B. Stoler Miller, *The Bhagavadgita* (New York-Toronto: Bantam Books, 1986).

nineteen last strophes of the second chapter are the key to understanding the *Gita*, to the point that he suggested rejecting anything that does not agree with these nineteen strophes.[9]

c) I would like to refer also to the idea of interpretation which inspired Lev Tolstoy's later work, which, almost unknown at present, deserves greater attention. This work, which belongs to the gnomic or, I should rather say, sapiential genre, aimed at collecting together and bringing to the attention of the widest possible audience texts from every culture and literature, translated or rather paraphrased, in support of Tolstoy's philosophical and religious convictions. The hermeneutic conception of Tolstoy's *Cycle of Reading* (1904-1906) is the following.

Certain books, in some way inspired, come to us with a special timing and strength, responding to our own vital questions. Although fully accessible, these books must be sharply distinguished from all other books, from the bulk of vulgar production. But these books, in Tolstoy's perspective, are not only the Christian scriptures, but come from many

---

[9] "It was at this time [1889] that, coming into contact with two Englishmen, I was induced to read the *Gita*. I say 'induced' because I had no particular desire to read it. When these two friends asked me to read the *Gita* with them, I felt rather ashamed. The consciousness that I knew nothing about our holy books made me feel miserable. The reason, I think, was my vanity. I did not know Sanskrit well enough to be able to read the *Gita* without help. The two English friends, on their part, did not know Sanskrit at all. They gave me Sir Edwin Arnold's translation of the poem. I went through the whole of it immediately and was fascinated by it. From that time till now, the last nineteen stanzas of Chapter II have ever remained engraved in my heart. For me, they contain the essence of dharma. They embody the highest knowledge. The principles enunciated in them are immutable. The intellect, too, is active in them in the highest degree, but it is intellect disciplined to high purpose. The knowledge which they contain is the fruit of experience. This was my first introduction to the *Gita*. Since then, I have read many other translations and commentaries and listened to many discourses but the impression made by that first reading persists. These stanzas are the key to the understanding of the *Gita*. I would even go so far as to advise people to reject statements in the poem which bear a meaning contrary to that of these nineteen stanzas. For a person who is humble there can be no question of rejecting anything. He will merely reason: 'It is because of the imperfection of my own intellect that today other stanzas seem to me inconsistent with these. In the course of time, I shall be able to see their consistency'. So he will tell himself and others, and leave the matter there. For understanding the meaning of the Shastras, one must have a well-cultivated moral sensibility and experience in the practice of their truths": *Meaning to the "Gita", Collected Works* (The Publications Division, Ministry of Information and Broadcasting, Government of India) pp. xxviii, 316.

different sources, transmitting, with the same intensity as the oral word, the thought of the "wise and holy men" who preceded us. The canon which contains them is always open: it is a library that can be always enriched by new contributions.

These books require a select or enlightened reader who shares their inspiration, a reader able to separate himself from the world and to devote himself to the spiritual exercise of self-knowledge, through the mirror of scripture. But this exercise does not culminate in an act of faith in the text. The relationship with the text — or rather, the texts — is a critical one: it can include historical criticism and in any case leaves the last word to the insight of the independent mind of the reader. Reading is no longer a *lectio divina*, a "sacred action", an act of mystical identification with the text. Rather than being inside the text, the reader assimilates it through conceptual elaboration, in view of his own moral transformation.[10]

d) It may be interesting to recall here the hermeneutic theory underlying the chapter "Reading" in Henry David Thoreau's *Walden*. Even in the hermit's solitude of Walden there is a *lectio divina*, but what are the similarities and the differences with regard to the ancient model?[11]

Above all, there is the notion of the sacred text. This is not denied, although "Scripture" at this point becomes plural, "Scriptures": "the recorded wisdom of mankind, the ancient classics and Bibles", "the sacred Scriptures, or Bibles of mankind". There is no single sacred text: all peoples and all traditions have them, and all are admitted into a sort of canon. One should begin, and then continue to add to a great sacred library, for the sake of humanity:

> That age will be rich indeed when those relics which we call classic, but even less known Scriptures of the nations, shall have further accumulated, when the Vaticans shall be filled with Vedas and Zendavestas and Bibles, with Homers and Dantes and Shakespeares, and all centuries to come shall have successively deposited their trophies in the forum of the world. By such a pile we may hope to scale heaven at last.

With this last comment, the image of a new Vatican is transformed into

---

[10] Cf. my *Tolstoj. Oltre la letteratura (1875-1910)* (Fiesole: Edizioni cultura della pace, 1991) and Leo Tolstoy's *Cycle of Reading*, below, II, 5.

[11] See also "Sunday", in *A Week on the Concord and Merrimack Rivers* : "Read the best books first, or you may not have a chance to read them all" (New York: The Library of America, 1985, p. 78). This text is quoted in the first page of Tolstoy's *Cycle of Reading*.

a biblical reference: the new universal library will be the real Jacob's ladder, and will succeed where the tower of Babel failed, in reaching heaven. While it is true that the expansion of the sacred text, the open unlimited structure of the canon (to the point of including not only the classics and the scriptures of the past, and not only future works, but also the book of nature itself) occurs through an extensive use of sacred terminology, there is no doubt that the general process is one of creative secularisation.[12]

Secondly, as in the ancient model of reading, the reader should have a sympathy with the text, should be animated by the same spirit:

> To read well, that is, to read true books in a true spirit, is a noble exercise and one that will task the reader more than any exercise which the customs of the day esteem. It requires a training such as the athletes underwent, the steady intention almost of the whole life to this object. Books must be read as deliberately and reservedly as they were written.

Here too is a spontaneous restoration of the situation, the *Sitz im Leben* of the ancient *lectio* and "spiritual exercises": the study of scriptures requires conformity to the spirit of the text, a "deliberation", an "intention" which is at the same time an act of isolation from others and a continual exercise. One notes the stoic and monastic terminology, the *askesis* (reading requires "wisdom, generosity and valour"). However, this insistence on the aspect of learning the language presupposes the idea of *claritas Scripturae*, coming from the Reformation, with its notion of the self-evidence and independence of the Bible with regard to the context of ecclesiastical tradition; it supposes also the humanistic upheaval and thus the autonomy of the critical method. It also alludes to early romantic philology, to Friederich Schlegel, for example, for whom philology coexists happily with the interpretation of the textual segment in a wider connotation, because in what is directly meant by the author "the entire world" is present, as a concomitant representation (thus Schleiermacher).[13] We have here once more a secularisation, that is the criticism and rational recovery of the ancient hermeneutical procedure.

And here, thirdly, is the result: reading. With the text thus perceived, and the reader thus prepared, now comes the meeting between the author of the text and his reader. The reader discovers that he is not alone. In the

---

[12] Cf. S. Marchignoli, "La Bibbia come progetto. Esplosione del canone, nuova mitologia, orientalismo in F. Schlegel e nella 'Frühromantik'", *Annali di storia dell'esegesi* 8:1 (1991), pp. 169-191.

[13] Cf. *L'interpretazione infinita*, cit., p. 149.

classics, modern man finds the answers to the questions that he asks: "They are the only oracles which are not decayed, and there are such answers to the most modern inquiry in them as Delphi and Dodona never gave". "These same questions that disturb and puzzle and confound us have in their turn occurred to all wise men". More fully: "There are probably words addressed to our condition exactly, which, if we could read and understand, would be more salutary than the morning or the spring to our lives, and possibly put a new aspect on the face of things for us. How many a man has dated a new era in his life from the reading of a book. The book exists for us perchance which will explain our miracles and reveal new ones. The at present unutterable things we may find somewhere uttered". Thus, in every situation, there is a book "for us". It is difficult not to remember the "for us" with which Christian authors evoke Hebrew texts: for Paul, in *I Corinthians*, the events of Exodus are meant "to admonish us, who have arrived at the end of time". The reward of reading is thus the acquisition of words of wisdom — "wisdom" is here the key term —: "golden words, which the wisest men of antiquity have uttered, and whose worth the wise of every succeeding age have assured us of". Let us return to the fascinating beginning of "Reading": reading, finally, is the appropriation of past experience, to the point of becoming the same person who first had that experience: "The oldest Egyptian or Hindoo philosopher raised a corner of the veil from the statue of the divinity; and still the trembling robe remains raised, and I gaze upon as fresh a glory as he did, since it was I in him that was then so bold, and it is he in me that now reviews the vision".

However, beyond this moment of ecstatic fusion (on the basis of Schiller's poetry), the encounter between text (with its author) and reader occurs as a conceptual construction at a level which is essentially rational and ethical, that is, as the discovery of the permanent validity of certain models, the exemplary nature of certain figures, and the pertinence of certain answers, because the questions are universal, and human nature is fundamentally the same everywhere.

e) The last words of Ralf Waldo Emerson's *Divinity School Address* (delivered in 1838 at Harvard University) should be recalled here.

> I look for the hour when that supreme Beauty which ravished the souls of those Eastern men, and chiefly of those Hebrews, and through their lips spoke oracles to all time, shall speak in the West also. The Hebrew and Greek Scriptures contain immortal sentences, that have been the bread of life for millions. But they have no epical integrity; are fragmentary; are not shown in their order to the intellect. I look for the new Teacher that shall follow so far those shining laws that he shall see them come full circle; shall see their rounding complete grace; shall see the world to be a mirror of the soul; shall

see the identity of the law of gravitation with purity of heart; and shall show that the Ought, that Duty, is one thing with Science, with Beauty, and with Joy.

We are here faced with a real farewell to theology. The ancient "Hebrew and Greek Scriptures" are no longer adequate. Certainly there are in them immortal thoughts, which have been the "bread of life" for the whole Western tradition. Certainly the "supreme beauty" (God is the "all-fair", *Nature*, III) has revealed herself "chiefly" to the Jews. But the Jewish-Christian revelation is only an example of a wider, and continual revelation ("to all time") and has its precedents in the East: "This thought dwelled always deepest in the minds of men in the devout and contemplative East; not alone in Palestine, where it reached its purest expression, but in Egypt, in Persia, in India, in China. Europe has always owed to oriental genius its divine impulses". There are many holy scriptures, the Bibles of the peoples; only those with narrow minds remain tied to one tradition alone.

Notwithstanding their importance, Emerson reproaches the Jewish-Christian Scriptures with a lack of "epic integrity" and of "order". In fact there is only one thing that is really lacking. Emerson suggests by contrast the idea of fullness, of completeness, of circularity: the new Teacher "shall follow so far those shining laws that he shall see them come full circle". In Emerson's language, the "Oversoul" (but one could think also of the Biblical and stoic *pneuma*, or "Wisdom") laid the foundations of this circularity. By this circularity it is possible to acknowledge the essential symmetry between revelation, history, and nature and to recover the "epic" spontaneity of ethical action, whilst the Jewish and Christian traditions conceive morality only in opposition to nature, that is dualistically. From Scripture to scriptures, from scriptures to nature: this should be, according to Emerson, the way that leads from the cavern to the light.[14]

f) "See what strong intellects dare not yet hear God himself unless he speaks the phraseology of I know not what David, or Jeremiah, or Paul" (Emerson, *Self-Reliance*). If Emerson's influence on Thoreau is well known, less known is the influence on Emerson himself of early Quaker writings.[15] From Fox Emerson takes the ancient formula (Boehme's, and still earlier patristic), according to which "Scripture is to be interpreted in the same

---

[14] Cf. my preface to R.W. Emerson, *Teologia e natura* (Genova: Marietti, 1991) and "Emerson and Wisdom" , below II, 3.

[15] Cf. F.B. Tolles, "Emerson ad Quakerism", *American Literature* 10 (1938) pp.142-165.

spirit which gave it forth" (*Nature*, IV),[16] an idea which Emerson correctly took to its most liberal and secular conclusions. Fox would not have followed Emerson up to this point, but his ways of expressing himself, with regard to creativity and autonomous expression, are the most powerful I know in the Christian tradition. Let us conclude with his words as reported by Margaret Fell (she later became his wife, but this was the first time she met him):

> ... and he opened the Scriptures and said: "The Scriptures were the prophets' words and Christ's and the Apostles' words, and what they spoke they enjoyed and possessed and had it from the Lord." And said: "Then what had any to do with the Scriptures, but as they came to the Spirit that gave them forth? You will say, Christ saith this, and the apostles say this; *but what canst thou say?* ...".[17]

---

16 The text continues: "A life in harmony with Nature, the love of truth and of virtue, will purge the eyes to understand her text. By degrees we may come to know the primitive sense of the permanent objects of nature, so that the world will be an open book, and every form significant of its hidden life and final cause". Emerson's source is probably George Fox. Cf. Emerson, *Journal* 1832, IV, p.31: "He [G. Fox] taught that the Ss [Sacred Scriptures] could not be understood but by the same spirit that gave them forth". See *The Journal of George Fox*, in 1648: "I was to direct people to the Spirit that gave forth the Scriptures, by which they might be led into all Truth, and so up to Christ and God, as they had been who gave them forth"; and "These things I did not see by the help of man, nor by the letter, though they were written in the letter, but I saw them in the light of the Lord Jesus Christ, and by his immediate Spirit and power, as did the holy men of God, by whom the Holy Scriptures were written. Yet I had no slight esteem of the Holy Scriptures, but they were very precious to me, for I was in that spirit by which they were given forth, and what the Lord opened in me I afterwards found was agreeable to them": *The Journal of G. Fox*, ed. J.L. Nickalls (Cambridge: University Press, 1952) p. 34. Cf. my "The vision of Paradise in the *Journal* of G. Fox", below, II, 2 and "Emerson and Wisdom", cit.

17 In G. Fox, *Journal*, bicent. ed., 1892, vol. 2, pp. 512-514. One could compare with this Seneca's Epistle 33: "For it is disgraceful even for a man, or one who has sighted old age, to have a note-book knowledge: 'This is what Zeno said'. But what have you yourself said? [*tu quid?*]. This is the opinion of Cleanthes. But what is your own opinion? How long shall you march under another man's orders? Take command and utter some word which posterity will remember. Put forth something from your own stock [*Aliquid et de tuo profer*]. (...) But it is one thing to remember, another to know. Remembering is merely safeguarding something entrusted to the memory; knowing, however, means making everything your own; it means not depending upon the copy and not all the time glancing back at the master. 'Thus said Zeno, thus said Cleanthes, indeed!' Let there be a difference between yourself and your book [*Aliquid inter te intersit et librum*]" (trans. R.E. Gummere).

II

Particularity and Universality

According to this proposal, unlike many enlightenment projects, the task of the interpreter is not that of constructing a meta-language which assimilates and brings together different cultural and religious traditions. Rather, the interpreter's task is to work within the inescapable linguistic-cultural Biblical paradigm, drawing attention to the plurality of languages and cultures, to their translatability, to the historical continuities which link them, and to their potential universality.

1. Not to Build a Meta-Language

a) On the subject of "enlightened projects", here I am not thinking of the anti-religious enlightenment to which Nietzsche (against Schopenhauer) appeals in *Human, All Too Human*, I, § 10, ("Religions have nothing truthful in common, and religion has no truth in itself"). I am thinking, rather, of masonic deism, of Leibnitz, to some extent of Kant, of the religion of the Revolution, of Mazzinian religion, of the later Tolstoy, perhaps also of Capitini in Italy. Beginning with the (correct) intuition that there can be no deep historical changes unless these are based on solid religious foundations, these are examples of religious constructions by means of the synthesis of various "pieces" or of the invention of a new and abstract reality. As well as the enlightenment, the question also touches on romantic philosophies of history which, while projecting themselves beyond Christianity, still see in it the culmination of the religious evolution of humanity and by secularizing it take over and go beyond the Christian conception of history (from Hegel's *Phenomenology of the Spirit* to Benedetto Croce's *Why We Cannot Call Ourselves Christians*).

b) In these constructions there is a presumption, or absence of self-criticism, a flaw in their knowledge of the limitations of culture, which in the name of rationalism and secularisation, leads them to fall into an absolute religious language of their own which they propose as a meta-language, assimilating and unifying different cultural and religious traditions. K. Marx' critique of Bauer is an example of a protest against these proposals of assimilation. According to Marx, in his *Jewish Question*, Bauer argued as follows:

> If they want to free themselves the Jews must not profess Christianity, but a dissolved Christianity, a religion that is dissolved in general. In other words, the Enlightenment, its critique and their result, a free humanity.

To which Marx replied:

> This is once again for the Jews a profession of faith, but no longer a profession of Christianity. Rather, a dissolved Christianity ... The Jew ... to emancipate himself does not have to carry out his own work but also that of the Christian, the *Critique of the Synoptic Gospels, the Life of Jesus* etc. We are trying to break the theological formulation of the question. The question of the ability of the Jew to emancipate himself becomes for us the question of which particular social element is to be overcome [uberwinden] to suppress Judaism [um das Judentum aufzuheben]. In fact, the ability of today's Jew to emancipate himself is the relation of Judaism towards the emancipation of today's world.

2. The Inescapable Linguistic-Cultural Biblical Paradigm

a) "Inescapable " above all as a given. This is a general assumption: we cannot easily escape the Biblical paradigm. Going beyond even the perception of the speaker, the Biblical legacy continues to be the principal source of current language and its metaphors. This presence is the more insidiously to the fore the more we think we have escaped its clutches: it is only through the reaction of those who remain outside its sphere that we perceive that our speech, which we claim as universal, is ours and only ours. Better then to accept this cultural limit from the very beginning.

b) But in my case "inescapable" also means "irreplaceable": insofar as this is my religious mother tongue. My intention is to examine religious discourse and I do not believe this is possible *for me* outside the "Biblical paradigm". I am thinking here of the path trodden by R.W. Emerson. The remarks made at the end of his *Divinity School Address* quoted above are in a certain sense words of "farewell to theology" and the Bible. Yet, looked at more closely, the path he treads appears not so much one of a philosophical-religious eclecticism as the extending of a vocabulary, of a conceptual universe and of an interpretative stance that remain fundamentally Biblical and drawn above all from sapiential Biblical literature. Because of this extension it is possible to place the book of nature alongside the Bible, or rather to see them both as expressions of a single wisdom.

Emerson's way was to enlarge the Jewish-Christian tradition, to secularize and expand the Biblical text so that it could contain the totality of human scriptures and nature. Everything is created by the same wisdom. Everything must be read, as we have seen, "in the same spirit in which it was made".

c) This is how Ruskin expressed his recognition that the Bible was for him a paradigm of every other reading:

> I am no despiser of profane literature. So far from it, that I believe no interpretations of Greek religion have ever been so affectionate, none of Roman religion so reverent, as those which will be found at the base of my art teaching, and current through the entire body of my works. But it was from the Bible that I learned the symbols of Homer, and the faith of Horace: the duty enforced upon me in early youth of reading every word of the gospels and prophecies as if written by the hand of God gave me the habit of awed attention which afterwards made many passages of the profane writers, frivolous to an irreligious reader, deeply grave to me. How far my mind has been paralysed by the faults and sorrow of life, — how far short its language may be of what light I have known, had I more faithfully walked in the light I had, is beyond my conjecture or confession: but as I never wrote for my own pleasure or self-proclaiming, I have been guarded, as men who so write always will be, from errors dangerous to others; and the fragmentary expressions of feeling I have been able to give, will be found by an attentive reader to bind themselves together into a general system of interpretation of Sacred literature — both classic and Christian, which will enable him without injustice to sympathize in the faith of candid and generous souls, of every age and every clime.[1]

3. Linguistic-Cultural Plurality, Translatability and Historical Continuities

a) I am thinking of a page by Max Müller, all the more significant because the link between language and religious culture is spelled out by the

---

[1] *The Bible of Amiens*, III, §52 (*Works*, vol. 33, pp. 118 f.). Cf. the autobiography of R.M. Jones, historian of the Quaker movement: "The very fact that the spirit of God could impress his thought and will upon holy men of old and had done it made me feel confident that he could continue to do that, and consequently that more light and truth could break through men in our times and in those to come. I cannot be too thankful that the little group of believers who made the Bible my living book and who helped me to find and to love its treasures also had spiritual depth enough to give me the key to a larger freedom that enabled me in later years to keep the Bible still as my book, without at the same time preventing me from making use of all that science and history have revealed or can reveal of God's creative work and of his dealing with men", in *Finding the Trail of Life*, 1954, 65-6.

great linguist and historian of religions in extremely clear terms. At the same time the ineluctability, subjective uniqueness, "the absolute nature for me" of my language and the irreducible plurality of languages is recognized:

> To each individual his own religion, if he really believes in it, is something quite inseparable from himself, something unique, that cannot be compared to anything else or replaced by anything else. Our religions, in this respect, are something like our language. In its form it may be like other languages; in its essence and its relation to ourselves it stands alone and admits no peer or rival.[2]

b) The remarks made by Simone Weil in her *Notebooks* are for me an exemplary witness of thinking "in the plural":

> Each religion is alone true, that is to say, that at the moment we are thinking on it we must bring as much attention to bear on it as if there were nothing else; in the same way, each landscape, each picture, each poem etc. is alone beautiful. A "synthesis" of religions implies a lower quality of attention.
>
> When a thing is perfectly beautiful, as soon as we fix our attention upon it, it represents unique and single beauty. Two Greek statues: the one we are looking at is beatitiful. The same is true of the Catholic faith, Platonic thought, Hindu thought etc.

Reflecting on the identity of acting for the Good (Plato) and for the Atman in the Upanishad, she comments:

> We should conceive of the identity of various traditions, not by reconciling them through what they have in common, but by my grasping the essence of what is specific in each. For this essence is one and the same.[3]

c) I am also thinking of the essay by Walter Benjamin on the *Task of the Translator*. We do not use an explicit "pure language" nor a meta-language. Rather, the task of the translator is not to "preserve the state in which his own language happens to be but instead to allow his language to be powerfully affected by the foreign language", by the language of the other great normative texts. And yet these texts are "translatable by definition" because they have a deep and common linguistic reality underlying them.

---

2   *Selected Essays on the Language, Mythology and Religion*, I (London: Longmans, Green and Co., 1881) p. 20.
3   *The Notebooks of Simone Weil*, trans. A. Wills (New York: G.P. Putnam's Sons, 1976) I, pp. 228, 244 f.; II, p. 502.

All suprahistorical kinship of languages rests on the intention underlying each language as a whole — an intention, however, which no single language can attain by itself but which is realized only by the totality of their intentions supplementing each other: pure language.[4]

d) Schleiermacher's pages on *The different methods in translation* (1813) are also relevant here. According to him, the translator cannot think with full determination of anything that is beyond the confines of his language; the form of his concepts, including the type and limits of their translatability is fixed by the language into which he was born and was educated; his intellect and imagination are tied to this. On the other hand, however, each freely thinking and intellectually independent individual is able to mould language.[5] Benjamin's position mirrors in fact romantic hermeneutics and in particular Schleiermacher's and von Humboldt's historically and philologically rich cultural project: a universalizing project which is still aware of its cultural-linguistic, nationalistic limits, and therefore not "imperialistic" and suspicious of Hegelian speculation and its ethnocentric presumption.

e) In general, I think that the attitude of those who see history as a sensational irruption of absolute novelties, epoch-making ruptures and paradigmatic revolutions should be transformed into a more pondered (and cultured) attention to continuity and interconnections. In this sense, I am thinking of the important, confident contributions that come from the consideration of long periods and large areas. In my research I have learned a great deal from Russian culture: Michail Bachtin, for example, for whom attention to great cultural cycles is extremely important, invites us to think of complex cultural realities in terms of continuity and not in isolation, as is usually the case with the Byzantine or Western monastic tradition.[6]

---

4 "The Task of the Translator", in *Illuminations,* trans. H. Zohn (New York: Harcourt, Brace and World Inc., 1969) pp. 81 and 74.
5 Cf. F. Schleiermacher, *Ermeneutica ed etica*, G. Moretto ed. (Napoli: Bibliopolis, 1984) p. 90 f.
6 S.S. Averincev's *Poetika ronnevizantijskoj literatury* should be read in this sense, as I suggest in the preface to its Italian translation, *L'anima e lo specchio. Poetica della letteratura anticobizantina* , trans. G. Ghini (Bologna: Il Mulino, 1988). Averincev insists on the stability of a great cultural cycle, from Hellenism to the Enlightenment, rather than on rupture and discontinuity. I made the same suggestion in the introduction to the Italian public of the 2nd edition of another important book, J. Leclercq's *L'amour des lettres et le désir de Dieu* , It. trans. *Cultura umanistica e desiderio di Dio. Studio sulla letteratura monastica del Medio Evo* (Firenze: Sansoni, 1988).

f) Even the emergence of conceptions and techniques which are usually connected to the Enlightenment and the scientific revolution can be seriously considered over a long period. From this point of view, for example, I have asked myself if the birth of psychoanalysis is to be considered within a historiographic model dominated by the idea of rupture and absolute novelty, or if it is not possible to consider it in terms of continuity, of transformation and, more precisely, of the secularisation of ancient visions of the world. The view that psychoanalysis is a uniquely modern episode can be problematic and uncertain if, following Oskar Pfister (the first "lay" analyst and for decades one of Freud's interlocutors) and ignoring some of his more ingenuous apologetics, we think of Freud's work in a context of "If you raised to your consciousness and fully felt your place in the great design, which to me is as necessary as the synthesis of the notes is to a Beethoven symphony, I should say of you: 'A better Christian there never was'".[7]

---

[7]   Letter of O. Pfister to S. Freud, October 29th, 1918, in *Psycho-analysis and Faith, The Letters of S.Freud and O.Pfister*, H. Meng and E.L. Freud eds., trans. E. Mosbacher (London: The Hogarth Press, 1963) p. 63. See my introduction to P. Gay, *A Godless Jew*, in the Italian edition, *Un Ebreo senza Dio. Freud, l'ateismo e le origini della psicoanalisi* (Bologna: Il Mulino, 1988) pp. 9-27, where I concluded: "There is one final point to be made regarding Oskar Pfister's search for a synthesis. There was a risk in this, that Freud sometimes reminded him of: 'It seems to me that you want to make a synthesis before prior analysis'" (October 9th, 1918). The most import fact seems to me the stress he put on the necessity of the insertion (*Einbeziehung, Einfügung, Ergänzung* etc.) of psychoanalysis into a more complete historical and theoretical framework , in a *Weltanschauung* that psycho-analysis *per se* cannot create or, as he said once , in quite candid terms, into a "philosophy well-suited to the nature of man and cosmos" (November 24th, 1927). Was this simply the effect of his apologetic concern to reconcile science and faith and to subordinate psychoanalysis to theology or philosophy? Or was it rather, as I would suggest, an attempt to place psychoanalysis within the tradition, of psychotherapy , seeing *Seelsorge* as the prehistory of psychotherapy? The following proposal arises from Pfister's work: to see "the making of psychoanalysis" not from the point of view of the paradigm of discontinuity and absolute novelty, but rather from that of continuity (the *nihil sub sole novi*, "nothing new under the sun", that Freud applied in his *Moses and Monotheism*). Or, more exactly, to see it from the point of view of secularization as Pfister meant it, as the positive transformation and assumption into modernity of ancient *Weltanschauungen*. We could here recall Pfister's claim (dropping his naive apologism, "a better Christian never was…") that Freud's work should be seen in a greater context: "an insertion as necessary", he continued, as "the synthesis of single notes into the musical totality of Beethoven's symphonies". See also my essays on Oskar Pfister, and *Moses the Great Stranger*, below II, 6 and 7.

g) In more specific terms, despite the criticism generally reserved for this text, I find Freud's *Moses and Monotheism* to be of the utmost importance. Here, in this courageous and dramatic book, rather than an ultimate and definitive disaffection towards Judaism, I see an apologia for Judaism which has been "suppressed in the isolation of its historical genesis but saved in its universality, led back to the origins of ancient civilization and a solar classicism, grasped in its peculiarity and praised for the great spirituality (Geistigkeit) it owes to the ancient leader, master of 'truth and justice'".[8] Apart from the concrete verification of the daring historical proposal, what emerges from an unprejudiced reading of this singular text is the impression of an impulse toward "truth/justice" and the desire that this may be also our impulse in a secular reading of the Bible and the other scriptures.

4. Universality

a) In the area of the human sciences I have no difficulty in admitting the validity of Rousseau's comment in his *Essay on the Origin of Languages*: "When we want to study men we must look near to us, but when we want to study man we must learn to look elsewhere, we must first observe the differences in order to discover the properties".[9] Here our interest is in the description of differences, or rather, in the enunciation of the essential through difference. Of interest is the individual, understood however through causal sequences and through possible comparisons.

b) However, Weber's image of the human sciences as a construction of self-centered cultural models seems now to have been discarded in favour of a different approach that is emerging from various fields and disciplines. This is an approach that from within an individualized consideration of the object discovers universalizing indications and tensions. Carlo Ginzburg, faced with the morphological constants which come to the historian's eye, admits not only cases of homology which can be explained by their origins in a common genesis but also the existence of

---

8　This is the conclusion of my essay *Un pagina inedita di Freud. La premessa al romanzo storico su Mosè*, now in *L'estasi del profeta e altri saggi tra ebraismo e cristianesimo dalle origini sino al "Mosè" di Freud* (Bologna: Il Mulino, 1989).

9　"Quand on veut étudier les hommes il faut regarder près de soi; mais pour étudier l'homme il faut apprendere à porter sa vüe au loin; il faut d'abord observer les différences pour découvrir les propietés": J.J. Rousseau, *Essai sur l'origine des langues* (Paris: Gallimard, 1990) pp. 89 f.

analogies which, where this common origin cannot be traced are explainable — he suggests — by a fundamental corporeal symbolism: thus returning to the theme of "human nature". The analogy or persistence of certain forms comes about not because there are archetypes (Ginzburg argues against Jungian archetypes), but because there is a "formal external constraint", formed by "human nature, by the body".[10] In the act of producing metaphors, the cultural activity *par excellence*, culture draws continuously on and is limited by corporeal self-representation: in this way, for example, we can explain how a physical anomaly (walking crookedly) is always connected to special functions of mediation between worlds. The interest of this suggestion lies in its coming from within the field of historical studies and in its coherence with the languages of this discipline. Ginzburg is therefore right when he rejects the criticism that he ignores a biological approach to the theme of nature.[11]

c) It should be observed, however, that the constancy and universality of symbolic production depends not so much on the universal presence of ours and others' corporeal form (above all the mother's) but on the affective contents that are universally and constantly connected to it.[12] The analogies are possible because there are certain emotional constants, fundamental and universal feelings that form the link between biological and symbolic levels and which find in language and cultures different formulations which intercommunicate though their common emotional fabric (here I have in mind the notions of affective ontology and affective competence on which Franco Fornari has worked).[13] This level must be assumed if we are to explain the possibility of inter-linguistic and inter-cultural communication that takes place in the aesthetic fruition of culturally distant works,[14] above all if we are to admit the possibility of translation. We have seen in fact how for W. Benjamin the great texts are "translatable by definition" because they are subtended by a common meta-text, a "pure language" that, not existing per se, can have its concrete expression only in the different human

---

10 Cf. C. Ginzburg , *Storia notturna. Una decifrazione del sabba* (Torino: Einaudi , 1989) p. XXXVII.
11 For this criticism, cf. P. Rossi, "Gli storici e la natura umana", *Rivista di filosofia* 81 (1990) pp. 331-370.
12 Cf. F. Fortini, "Il corpo e la storia", *L'indice* VI:10 (1989) p.10
13 F. Fornari, *La riscoperta dell'anima* (Bari: Laterza, 1984) pp. 28 e 67.
14 According to L. Tolstoy's suggestion, art renders the feelings experienced by their predecessors accessible to men of all generations, especially the most simple and universal feelings, like happiness, compassion, moral strength. See *What is art?* ch. 16.

languages. I am not speaking, however, of a language of the angels. I am speaking of a low, common, material language of feelings in which everyone is competent if only we can reach or recuperate an awareness of it, as is the case with the original situation of the learning child and the teaching and narrating mother in a situation of mutual trust (see Thesis IV).

d) Relevant here is the notion of "trust" that George Steiner proposes at the beginning of his description of the "hermeneutic motion".[15] The poles of a work of intepretation are formed on the one hand by the plurality of languages, which is irreducible because the original speech is born of inner, domestic needs, but also by a universal communicability, which has both a realistic and an "idealistic" ground. The first consists in the experience that "no entirely undecipherable or entirely untranslatable body of speech has ever turned up. The idealistic premise is one of universal homology and rationality. It can take diverse forms: ecumenical, Cartesian, anthropological. But the conclusion is the same: "the similarities between men are finally much greater than the differences".[16]

e) We may recall here the pages of Albert Schweitzer's *Quest of the Historical Jesus* in which while denying the plausibility of the "liberal" image of Jesus and affirming the unbridgeable historical gap between ourselves and the "late-Judaic" apocalyptic conception of the world (in which Jesus lived), he also maintains the possibility of discovering the real "spirit" and "will" of Jesus despite the difficulties involved in reconstructing the historical figure.[17] Our thoughts are led back once again to German romantic hermeneutics and its notions of feeling (*Gesinnung*), interpretation, sychology, affinity,

---

[15] "The hermeneutic motion, the act of elicitation and appropriative transfer of meaning, is fourfold. There is initiative trust, an investment of belief, underwritten by previous experience, but epistemologically exposed and psychologically hazardous, in the meaningfulness, in the 'seriousness' of the facing or, strictly speaking, adverse text. We venture a leap: we grant *ab initio* that there is 'something there' to be understood, that the transfer will not be void. All understanding, and the demonstrative statement of understanding which is translation, starts with an act of trust": *After Babel. Aspects of Language and Translation* (Oxford University Press, 1975) p. 297. Cf. also p. 353: the "initiative trust" "is at once most hazardous and most pronounced where the translator aims to convey meaning between remote languages and cultures" (W.V.O. Quine speaks of "radical translation" in the case of the "language of an hitherto untouched people").

[16] *Ib.* , pp. 353 f.

[17] *The Quest of the Historical Jesus. A Critical study of its Progress from Reimarus to Wrede* (New York: Macmillan, 1956). But one should see directly the conclusions of the 2nd edition (1913) of the *Geschichte der Leben Jesu-Forschung*.

congeniality, sympathetic comprehension, vital relation and communion. These are notions, to which Bultman makes continual reference in drawing on the work of Dilthey, who in turn had drawn on Schleiermacher, Wilhelm von Humboldt, Boeckh and Droysen.[18]

f) Informing all these suggestions (with one or two exceptions) we can see the presence of Jean-Jacques Rousseau.[19] Above all I recall how Claude Lévi-Strauss reads him as the "founder of the sciences of man".

> It is possible to believe the demonstration of the *Discourse* [*on the Origin of Inequality*] that a threefold passage (from nature to culture, from feelings to knowledge, from animality to humanity) occurred with the appearance of society — it can only be by attributing to man, even in his primitive state, an essential faculty which moves him to get over these three obstacles. It is a faculty which possesses originally and immediately some contradictory attributes, although not precisely within itself; which is both natural and cultural, affective and rational, animal and human; and which (provided only that it become conscious) can tranform itself from one plane to the other. This faculty — Rousseau did not neglect to repeat — is compassion, deriving from the identification with another which is not only a parent, a relative, a compatriot , but any man whatsoever, seeing that he is a man, and much more: any living being, seeing that it is living. Thus man begins by experiencing himself as identical to all his fellows. [20]

Lévi-Strauss also refers to Rousseau in a more recent essay: "one must know what one does not know, *Durch Mitleid wissend* ("knowing through compassion") — not through an act of communication but through a surge of pity".[21]

---

18 Cf. H.-G. Gadamer, *Truth and Method*, trans. G. Barden and J. Cumming (New York: The Seabury Press, 1975) pp. 162 ff. and R. Bultmann, *Das problem der Hermeneutik, Glauben und Verstehen* (Tübingen: J.C.B. Mohr, 1952) II, pp. 217 f., with reference to the problem of translation.

19 Cf. Gadamer, *Truth and Method* , p. 56: J. J. Rousseau's *Confessions* lay at the prehistory of *Erlebnis* (a fundamental notion for Dilthey).

20 Jean-Jacques Rousseau, *Founder of the Sciences of Man, Structural Anthropology*, trans. M. Layton (New York: Basic Books, 1976) II, pp. 37 f.

21 The whole passage is worth quoting (it is the conclusion of the essay *From Chrétien de Troyes to Richard Wagner)*: "To this world of debauchery and unbridled communication [Klingsor's world] that of Amfortas opposes an image of frozen communication; this world is ruled by an impotent monarch, who is incapable of performing his office; here, plants, beasts and men perish, and an answer is offered in vain to a question that no one thinks of asking. Mediation between these two worlds is nullified because of excess in one and a lack in the other; and their poles are marked by the *laughter* of Herodias at Christ's sufferings and the *silence* of the Grail visitors at Amfortas' suffering. Thus, the problem, in mythological terms, would be to establish an equilibrium between the two opposite worlds.

g) Here are the famous and fundamental lines of the *Essay on the Origin of Languages*. I quote in French: "... Les passions arrachèrent les prémiers voix". "Comment nous laissons nous émouvoir à la piété? En nous transportant hors de nous-mêmes; en nous identifiant avec l'être souffrant. Nous ne souffrons qu'autant que nous jugeons qu'il souffre; ce n'est pas dans nous, c'est dans lui que nous souffrons"[22] (We suffer only insofar as we see that he suffers: it is not in ourselves, but in him that we are suffering). Equally important texts are in the *Discourse on the Origin and Fundamentals of the Inequality of Men.*[23]

To do so, one should probably, like Parsifal, go into and come out of the one world and be excluded from and re-enter the other world. Above all, however (and this is Wagner's contribution to universal mythology), one must know what one does not know, *Durch Mitleid wissend* ("knowing through compassion") – not through an act of communication but through a surge of pity, which provides mythical thinking with a way out of the dilemma in which its long unrecognized intellectualism has risked imprisoning it", *The View from Afar*, trans. J. Neugroschel and Ph. Hoss (New York: Basic Books, 1985).

[22] *Essai sur l'origine des langues* (Paris: Gallimard, 1990) pp. 66 e 92 (J. Starobinski's commentary supplies many parallel passages).

[23] "Whatever the moralists may say about it, human understanding owes much to the passions, which by common agreement also owe much to it. It is by their activity that our reason is perfected; we seek to know only because we desire to have pleasure; and it is impossible to conceive why one who has neither desires nor fears would go to the trouble of reasoning"; "Let us not conclude with Hobbes that because man has no idea of goodness he is naturally evil; that he is vicious because he does not know virtue; that he always refuses his fellow-men services he does not believe he owes them; nor that, by virtue of the right he reasonably claims to things he needs, he foolishly imagines himself to be the sole proprietor of the whole universe"; and finally: "One sees with pleasure the author of the *Fable of the Bees* [Mandeville] forced to recognize man as a compassionate and sensitive being, departing from his cold and subtle style in the example he gives in order to offer us the pathetic image of an imprisoned man who sees outside a wild beast tearing a child from his mother's breast [...] What horrible agitation must be felt by this witness of an event in which he takes no personal interest! What anguish must he suffer at this sight, unable to bring help to the fainting mother or to the dying child! Such is the pure movement of nature, prior to all reflection. Such is the force of natural piety, which the most depraved morals still have difficulty destroying": from *The First and Second Discourses*, trans. R.D. and J.R. Masters (New York: St Martins's Press, 1964) pp. 115 f., 128 f., 130 f.

III

Wisdom

The classical tradition (particularly Socratic teaching), the Biblical tradition, Oriental traditions and modern authors all distinguish between a divided and abstract knowledge and a wisdom that attempts to grasp the connection between part and whole, between thinking and acting, and agree that the latter is the only form of wisdom worth pursuing.

1. The Bible as a Text of Wisdom

a) Wisdom (didactic, gnomic) literature in the Bible (at least what has reached us, because a great deal has been lost) can be found in a range of writings: *Proverbs*, *Qohelet*, *Sirach* and the *Wisdom of Solomon* (the last two are deuterocanonic in the Catholic tradition, and do not belong to the Protestant or Hebrew Bible). Alongside these, there is *Job*, the *Song of Solomon*, a certain part of the *Psalms*. The temporal span of these texts is very wide, and an accurate dating is almost always impossible. The wisdom genre is present in Mesopotamia and in Egypt. On it depend, sometimes literally, Jewish texts. For example, Prov. 22:20 f. depends on and refers to the Egyptian *Instruction of Amenemopet* ("Have I not written for you thirty sayings of admonitions and knowledge, to show you what is right and true, so that you give a true answer to those who sent you?").[1] The model is formed from texts which have as their aim the instruction of the Sovereign: wisdom must be his basic quality. Solomon is the sovereign wise man par excellence, the prototype for all wise men in the tradition of Israel.[2] This kind of wisdom has practical

---

[1] The complete text of the *The Instruction of Amenemopet* can be found for instance in *The Ancient Near East. An Anthology of Texts and Pictures*, J.B. Pritchard ed., 1958. I generally use the *New Revised Standard Version* of the Bible.

[2] Cf. Solomon's prayer: "And Solomon said: 'You have shown great and steadfast love to your servant my father David, because he walked before you in faithfulness, in righteousness, and in uprightness of heart toward you; and you have kept for him this great and steadfast love and have given him a son to sit in his throne today. And now, o Lord, my God, you have made your servant king in place of

rather than metaphysical value: it is concerned with how to live, with the "understanding of one's own way" (Prov. 14:8), and not with the ultimate causes and ends of reality. Sofia, the divine *hokma* who is partner to God and who helps him in the Creation, according to the beautiful mythical representation in chapter 8 of the *Book of Proverbs* [3] cannot be reached by man. At the beginning of human wisdom we find the acceptance of the ultimate incomprehensibility of origins and causes, the refusal of metaphysical speculation and the recognition that we are not masters of our own lives: the "fear of God".[4] But there is also a desire for truth and justice in the things that depend on man in his and in others' lives.

b) In this sense wisdom like the law is accessible to all: it is "popular culture"(*grammatèia laou*, Sir. 44:4). In the *Book of Proverbs* there is another

---

my father David, although I am only a little child; I do not know how to go out or come in. And your servant is in the midst of the people whom you have chosen, a great people, so numerous they cannot be numbered or counted. Give your servant therefore an understanding mind (*leb shome'a*) to govern your people, able to discern between good and evil; for who can govern this your great people?'. It pleased to the Lord that Solomon had asked this. God said to him: 'Because you have asked this, and have not asked for yourself long life or riches, or for the life of your enemies, but have asked for yourself understanding to discern what is right, I now do according to your word. Indeed I give you a wise and discerning mind (*leb hakam wenabon*): no one like you has been before you, and no one like you shall rise after you'"(1 *Kings* 3:6-12).

3 "The Lord created me at the beginning of his work [...] When he established the heavens, I was there [...] when he marked out the foundations of the earth, then I was daily beside him, like a master worker; and I was daily his delight, rejoicing before him always, and delighting in the human race" (see the whole text in Prov. 8:22-31). The feminine image of Wisdom who collaborates with God in the work of creation appears here to be inspired by the Egyptian figure of the goddess of truth-justice, Maat, who stands at Ammon's side.

4 See *Job* 28:12-28: there is surely a technique to find in metals in the depth of the earth, "but where shall wisdom be found? And where is the place of understanding? Mortals do not know the way to it, and it is not found in the land of the living. The deep says, 'It is not with me', and the sea says, 'It is not with me' [...] Where then does wisdom come from? And where is the place of understanding? It is hidden from the eyes of all living, and concealed from the birds of the air [...] God understands the way to it, and he knows its place, for he looks to the ends of the earth, and sees everything under the heavens. When he gave to the wind its weight, and apportioned out the waters by measure; when he made a decree for the rain, and a way for the thunderbolt; then he saw it and declared it; he established it, and searched it out. And he said to mankind, 'Truly, the fear of the Lord, that is wisdom, and to depart from evils is understanding'". *Qohelet* also represents a moment of reflection of Wisdom about its own limits.

image, which also has "erotic" overtones, but of a different kind, of Sofia who offers herself as man's companion, opening to him her house and table: "Wisdom has built her house, she has hewn her seven pillars; she has prepared her food, she has mixed her wine; she has also set her table. She has sent out her servant-girls; she calls from the highest places of the town: 'You that are simple, turn in here!'. To those without sense she says: 'Come eat of my bread, and drink of the wine I have mixed'. Lay aside immaturity, and live; and walk in the way of insight" (Prov. 9:1-6, cf. Is. 55:1-3). In the later formulation in the *Wisdom of Solomon*, "Wisdom is radiant and unfading; and she is easily discerned by those who love her, and is found by those who seek her. She hastens to make herself known to those who desire her. He who raises early to seek her will have no difficulty, for he will find her sitting at his gates" (Wis. 6:12-14 RSV).

c) Of course Israel boasts of being the prime depository of wisdom. In the description of *Sirach* 24, Wisdom says:

> I came forth from the mouth of the Most High, and covered the earth like a mist [...] Alone I have made the circuit of the vault of heaven, and have walked in the depth of the abyss. In the waves of the seas, in the whole earth and over every people and nation I have gotten a possession. Among all these I sought a resting place; I sought in whose territory I might lodge. Then the Creator of all things gave me a commandment, and the one who created me assigned a place for my tent. And he said: 'Make your dwelling place in Jacob, and in Israel receive your inheritance' (Sir. 24:3-8 RSV).

It is true that here we are speaking of the law, of which Israel is the bearer. And yet according to Gerhard von Rad:

> Notice that it is wisdom who speaks here, not Torah, and this is where Sirach's heart beats. Primeval wisdom is here regarded as a fascinating, aesthetic phenomenon. Where Torah is concerned, Sirach does not rise to such enthusiastic statements [...] If one compares the rhetorical vitality which grips him whenever he can praise wisdom, the effect when he describes the content of the Torah is poor [...] No, the Torah is not a subject of particular interest to Sirach. He knows about it, it has a part to play, but basically for Sirach it is of relevance only in so far as it is to be understood on the basis of, or as it is otherwise connected with, the great complex of wisdom teachings.[5]

Wisdom is connected to the Torah and to historical narrations which basically tell the story of the gift of the Law, because Wisdom is Wisdom in applying the law. It is also connected to the prophecy whose prime task is

---

5   G. V. Rad, *Wisdom in Israel*, trans. J.D. Martin (London: SCM, 1972) pp. 246 f.

to preach the law to the often unfaithful nation, a nation which is often a victim because of its lack of faith. But wisdom is essentially broader than the positively determined space of the historical revelation and prophecy that renews it: it has something of an experimental quality (as well as being transmittable and traditional), it is also rational, worldly, secular, open therefore to "foreign wisdom".

d) This characteristic is pointed out by Gerhard von Rad when he speaks of the post-salomonic age:

> The intellectual curiosity of old wisdom, its cultural impetus and the zeal with which it studied the corresponding cultural achievements of other nations stands in considerable contrast to the spirituality of the pre-monarchical period, even of the period of Saul. Whether we speak of a process of secularization starting fairly suddenly, of the discovery of man, that is of a humanisation, or of the beginning of a rational search for knowledge, at any rate this strong intellectual movement must have been preceded by an inner decline, the disintegration of an understanding of reality which we can describe, in a felicitous expression of Martin Buber's: "pan-sacralism".[6]

And later:

> If we understand the word enlightenment, along the lines of a well known definition by Kant, as the coming-of-age of man, then one would have to think of the adulthood thus achieved in Israel, too, as, in the first instance, a critical encounter with the whole world of experience, and its inherent laws.[7]

e) Despite the complexity of the historical problem, I do not think that the thought and figure of Jesus are very far away from this image. We have to hypothesize that he shared the same general concern as the Pharisees' movement, that of going out to the people in order to bring them within the law. We seem to understand, however, that he did not think he could resolve the matter through the exegesis of the law, through, that is, schooling and doctrine. Rather, it was to be resolved through an interpretation of his own, which, moving from the constant, impelling perception of the divine presence and the imminence of judgment, consisted in a hard-hitting critique of the sacral conception of legal duty, and in a shift of attention and responsibility towards conscience, towards the "secret", the "heart" of man. This was an intransigent reference to the essential contents of the law which also had the

---

6 *Ib.*, pp. 58 f.
7 *Ib.*, p. 98.

effect of reclaiming those who could be excluded for purely formal reasons. This was not achieved through apodictic declarations of the formulas of sacred right, or through the authority of the word revealed to the prophet, but through a fundamentally argumentative attitude (even if they were accompanied by charismatic gestures). See for example his way of arguing: "You clean the outside of the cup and of the dish; but inside you are full of greed and wickedness. You fools! did not the one who made the outside make the inside also? So give for alms those things that are within; and see, everything will be clean for you" (Lk. 11:39-41).

f) It is interesting to notice the importance of a number of sapiential texts which define the position of Jesus. The wisdom that characterizes Jesus from his earliest years (Lk. 2:47) is different from that of the learned and the wise. His is a wisdom that is revealed to children, whom he invites to come to him to restore their strength, to the tired and to the weary: his is a light yoke (Mt. 11:28 f., cf. Sir. 51:25-30). The conviviality with which he welcomes the excluded is typical of Jesus: he states that in this way wisdom is finally recognized by all his sons (Lk. 7:35), because that is how one accepts and acts on the invitation contained in the book of *Proverbs* 9:1-6.[8] It is once more to *Proverbs* that we must go to understand the speech of the bread of life, as words that are "spirit and life" (Jn. 6:63). The very "logos-Christology" receives light, at least in part, from the image of pre-existent-wisdom (Prov. 8:22-31). When we focus on its "common" "low","secular" characteristics, as something accessible to all, we begin to understand how this wisdom, according to the beginning of *I Corinthians,* was crucified because it was not accepted either by the Jews, who demanded "miracles" or by the Greeks who demanded "sublimity of speech or of wisdom".

g) We believe we can trace out the lines of a possible general reading of the Jewish-Christian Bible in which the sapiential idea is put into the foreground as its central axis, as the most mature place in which legal,

---

8   "The earliest Jesus traditions perceive this God of gracious goodness in a woman's *Gestalt* as divine *Sophia* (wisdom). The very old saying, 'Sophia is justified [or vindicated] by all her children' (Lk. 7:35 [Q]) probably had its setting in Jesus' table community with tax collectors, prostitutes, and sinners, as well. The Sophia-God of Jesus recognizes all Israelites as her children and she is proven 'right' by all of them. The Q community qualifies these by stressing that the most eminent of the children of Sophia are John and Jesus", E. Schlüsser Fiorenza, *In Memory of Her. A Feminist Theological Reconstruction of Christian Origins* (New York: Crossroad, 1987) p. 158. Cf. also *Aspects of Wisdom in Judaism and Early Christianity,* L. Wilken ed. (Notre Dame: University Press, 1975); H. von Lips, *Weiheits-traditionen im Neuen Testament* (Neukirchen, 1990).

prophetic and historical traditions (before and after the deuteronomistic work), converge, are rethought and re-expressed, even sometimes re-translated (the Greek of *Sirach* and of the *Wisdom of Solomon*). The sapiential dialectic between absolute divine immanence and ethical dualism can be seen as decisive in Jesus' teachings, even considering the complexity of the motives that cross it, determined as it is by specific personal matters and the apocalyptic climate in which it takes place.

h) What I am here proposing is not, however, a sophianic turn, one which has already been attempted and taken to its limits in the history of Russian religious philosophy: divine wisdom, according to the biblical tradition we have just examined, no matter how romantically courted and poetically pursued,[9] is in truth unapproachable in its essence. And yet the indications we receive from it are clear and essential as guide-lines for our own praxis. I agree then with Spinoza when he states that "The Scripture does not show us but the simplest things and does not aim but at obedience" and that "it does not teach but what men can imitate by a certain way of living".[10]

i) As a consequence of this position, research should focus on doctrinal and ethical elements essential to Biblical teaching and to that of Jesus in particular. We may now perhaps return to the model proposed in the

---

[9] Cf. the poem *Tri svidanija* [*Three Appointments*], by Vladimir Solov'ëv, in which the poet tells of his meetings with godly Sophia. Solov'ëv was the founder of the Russian sophiology. I examined in particular one of its protagonists, S.N. Bulgakov, in my *Il prezzo del progresso* (Casale Monferrato: Marietti, 1984) (with an introduction reproduced in *La Madonna di S.Sisto di Raffaello. Saggi sulla cultura russa* [Bologna: Il Mulino, 1990]). P. Florenskij speaks of the Sophia in his *Stolp i utverzhdenie istiny* (*Column and fundament of the truth*, Moskva 1914), "Letter 10". G. Florosvkij, in his *Ways of Russian Theology*, severely criticizes Solov'ëv, S. Bulgakov and P. Florenskij.

[10] *Tractatus theologico-philosophicus*, XIII: "Ostenditur Scripturam non nisi simplicissima ostendere, nec aliud praeter obedientiam intendere; nec de divina Natura aliud docere, quam quod homines certa vivendi ratione imitari possunt". On Biblical wisdom in Spinoza, cf. ch. 4 at the end, where he supplies the key for a sapiential reading of the whole Bible, indicating the model of Solomon "of whom the Scripture exalts, rather than his prophetic gifts and piety, his prudence and wisdom. In his Proverbs Solomon calls human intellect the source of true life and makes unhappiness consist uniquely in foolishness". See also what he says about Christ: "I say that for salvation it is not at all necessary that we know Christ according to the flesh; the contrary must be said for what concerns that eternal son of God who is the eternal wisdom of God, who manifested herself in everything and most of all in the human mind and most particularly in Jesus Christ" (Ep. 73).

discussion over the "essence of Christianity" characteristic of a "liberal" theology whose high point is the important book of the same name published in 1900 by Adolf von Harnack.[11] In his book von Harnack, who had worked for a long time on the synoptic question, gives great importance in his definition of the "essence of Christianity" to the teaching of Jesus and to Jesus as teacher. Albert Schweitzer's *Quest of the Historical Jesus* (1906) showed how not only the message but also the life of Jesus is marked by the expectation of the coming of the Kingdom of God: the sign of eschatology marks in a decisive manner the figure and the work of Jesus, to the point of making it "extraneous and enigmatic". In one way dialectical theology accepted the inaccessibility of the historical Jesus: historical research cannot go beyond the Christ of faith and the *Formgeschichte* showed how the message of Jesus is tied to the experience and to the practice of Christian communities. Beginning with the 1950s, thanks to the positive exegetic and historical work carried out in the "history of traditions", new investigation was undertaken into the historical Jesus based on the conviction of the indivisibility of the two aspects: the historical Jesus and the Christ of faith. This task was carried out in several directions. One was decidedly theological and emphasized history as the place of salvation, or salvation as history, and opened up the possibility, in the 1970s, of valorizing patristic, historical-narrative theology, as a link with the romantic philosophy of history (Hegel, Schelling, even Marxism), and of merging with a certain positive political-religious climate. Others, to whom it seemed clear that the *heilsgeschichtlich* tone, the emphasis on the "history of salvation", the insistence on the unrepeatable and incomparable uniqueness of figures, facts and words was not enough to found its absolute quality, which is apologetically taken for granted,[12] moved toward a strong re-historicization of the figure of Jesus in the context of the Judaism of his time, and particularly that of normative rabbinic Judaism. All this was seen against the more general background of ancient history (thanks to the work of Jewish scholars). While from this point of view the admirable, monumental

---

[11] Cf. my introduction to a new Italian edition of A. v. Harnack's *The Essence of Christianity*, trans. G. Bonola (Brescia: Queriniana, 1980), now in *L'estasi del profeta e altri saggi tra ebraismo e cristianesimo dalle origini sino al «Mosè» di Freud* (Bologna: Il Mulino, 1989).

[12] According to Spinoza, faith in history, despite its certainty, cannot give the knowledge and consequently the love of God ("Nec fides historiarum, quamvis certa, Dei cognitionem et consequenter nec Dei amorem nobis dare potest"): *Tractatus theologico-politicus*, IV.

exegetic and historical works, above all those of Germanic origin, show a certain fragility on account of their lack of an adequate Judaistic basis. If interest in Jesus's teaching becomes once again crucial, the essential contribution of "liberal" historiography will take on a renewed importance.[13] (This will be possible, however, only together with a markedly different attention to the relation between Jewish and Christian writings, compared to what liberal historiography has been able to offer, at least as far as its Christian-Protestant exponents are concerned: the difficulties of A. von Harnack on the Old Testament, for example, are well known). Thus, research will be able once again to take into account other extra-biblical writings in a comparative framework, from an ethical-doctrinal point of view. I am thinking especially of the short work by Ernst Troeltsch on *The Absoluteness of Christianity and the History of Religions* (1902). Admirable for the strength of its synthesis[14] and the courage of its comparative analysis, despite its ethnocentrism its greatest moment comes when the author honestly describes Christianity as "the highest religious truth that has relevance for us".[15]

2. The Only Wisdom Worth Pursuing

a) In the background in particular here we have the pathetic image of

---

[13] It is interesting to remark from his *Letters and Papers from Prison* how Dietrich Bonhoeffer criticized K. Barth's "positivism of revelation" and turned his attention to liberal theology.

[14] In his definition of "the essence of Christianity", rejecting Harnack's position, Troeltsch maintains that this "essence" "combines Israelite prophecy, the preaching of Jesus, the mysticism of Paul, the idealism of Platonism and Stoicism, the integration of medieval European culture in terms of a religious conception, the Germanic individualism of Luther, and the consciousness and activism of Protestantism": *The Absoluteness of Christianity and the History of Religions*, trans. D. Reid (Richmond: John Knox Press) p. 108.

[15] "The historical way of thinking does not preclude our acknowledging Christianity as the highest truth that has relevance for us", *ib.*, p. 107. Cf. pp. 122 f.: "To wish to possess the absolute in an absolute way at a particular point of history is a delusion. Wherever this delusion has crystallized into serious theories, there has swept over religion a doctrinaire rigidity and a deathlike chill [...] Alternatively, this delusion may result in a harsh fanaticism that loses sight of every tenderness and magnanimity [...]. That is why living piety that speaks out of its relation with God has never put forward such theories; it has called for a simple decision pro or con, but has left the matter of absolute truth to the future, to the end of history".

many *maitres à penser* who remained oblivious of Fascism, Nazism and Stalinism. My concern is to avoid their example and above all elaborate a culture whose solid foundations grant it the necessary attention to concrete reality and adequate criteria to make judgments on the latter. I recall the observation made by Leo Strauss about "our social science": "What Machiavelli did apparently, our social science would actually do if it did not prefer — only God knows why — generous liberalism to consistency: namely, to give advice with equal competence and alacrity to tyrants as well as to free peoples".[16]

b) I also recall Leo Tolstoy's description of the intellectual classes in his *Confessions*. Tolstoy speaks of the Fifties:

> Now that I think of that time, of my mental state, and of the mental state of those men (however, there are thousands of such even nowadays), I feel pity, and terror, and amusement; there arises precisely the feeling that one experiences in a mad house. We were all convinced at that time that we must talk and talk, and write, and print, as fast as possible, and that that was necessary for the good of humanity. And thousands of us, denying and cursing one another, printed and wrote, teaching others. And without noticing that we knew nothing, that to the simplest question of life, — what is good, and what is bad, — we did not know what answer to give, we all spoke together, without listening to our neighbors, and now and then encouraged and praised each other, so that we, too, might be encouraged and praised, and now and then were irritated toward one another, precisely as in madhouse. Thousands of workmen day and night worked with all their strength, setting type and printing millions of words, and the post-

---

[16] L. Strauss, *Natural Right and History* (Chicago: The University of Chicago Press, 1953) p. 4. Cf. also his attack on Max Weber and his notion of a value-free or ethically neutral social science. He contends that Weber's thesis leads to nihilism, according to which "every preference has to be judged before the tribunal of reason to be as legitimate as any other preference". Strauss sees a sign of this nihilistic attitude in a statement of Weber about the future of Western civilization. Weber poses the alternative of "either a spiritual renewal ('wholly new prophets or a powerful renaissance of old thoughts and ideals'), or else 'mechanized petrifaction, varnished by a kind of convulsive sense of self-importance', i.e. the extinction of every human possibility except that of 'specialists without spirit or vision and voluptuaries without heart'. Confronted by this alternative — Strauss continues — Weber felt that the decision in favour of either possibility would be a judgment of value or of faith, and hence beyond the competence of reason. This amounts to an admission that the way of life of 'specialists without spirit or vision and voluptuaries without heart' is as defensible as the way of life recommended by Amos or Socrates", *ib.*, pp. 41 f. Strauss is referring to Weber's *Religionssoziologie*, I, p. 204 and *Wissenschaftslehre*, pp. 150 f. and 469 f.

office spread them all over Russia, and we proceeded to teach, and did not have time enough to teach everything, and kept growing angry because little attention was paid to us.[17]

c) And Henry David Thoreau:

There are nowadays professors of philosophy, but not philosophers. Yet it is admirable to profess because it was once admirable to live. To be a philosopher is not merely to have subtle thoughts, nor even to found a school, but so to love wisdom as to live according to its dictates, a life of simplicity, independence, magnanimity and trust. It is to solve some of the problems of life, not only theoretically, but practically (in *Walden*, "Economy").[18]

d) Kant, in his *Critique of Practical Reason*:

It would also do no harm to deter the self-conceit of whoever presumed to the title of philosopher, if one merely held before him the definition as the standard for his self-estimation, as this would lower his pretensions very much. For to be a teacher of wisdom would mean something more than to be a scholar, who has not yet progressed far enough to conduct himself, and even less anyone else, to so high an end; it would mean to be a master of knowledge of wisdom, which says more than a modest man would himself presume to claim. Philosophy as well as wisdom itself would always remain an ideal, which objectively is represented completely only in reason and which subjectivity is only the goal for the person's unceasing endeavors. No one would be justified in professing to be in possession of it, under the assumed name of philosopher, unless he could show its infallible effect (in self-mastery and the unquestioned interest which he pre-eminently takes in the general good) on his person as an example. This the ancients required as a condition for deserving that honorable title.[19]

e) These last words bring us back to the ancient conception of wisdom.[20] When I speak of a "classical tradition" I am thinking of the mark left by

---

17 *My Confession*, ch .1, trans. L. Wiener (Boston and Dana Estes & C. Publishers, 1904) p. 11.

18 *Walden*, ch. 1, "Economy". See my essay on Thoreau, below II, 4.

19 *Critique of Practical Reason* I, II, ch. 1, trans. L. White Beck (Chicago: The University of Chicago Press, 194) p. 213. For Kant, science represents the "narrow door" through which it will be possible to restore critically today the ancient "doctrine of wisdom". See further on, Thesis V, 3, a.

20 But also to my quotation from Thoreau. The attributes of the philosopher, in his words, are the ancient ones: simplicity, *aplotes*, deriving from inward unification, consistency, coherence, having found the center around to which to organize all the rest. Independence, *autarkeia*, which means to be sufficient to oneself, according to one's material and spiritual resources. Magnanimity or *megalopsychia*, rather

Socrates, and the circumstances surrounding his death, as reflected in the *Apologia*:

> Men of Athens, I respect and love you, but I shall obey the god rather than you, and while I live and am able to continue, I shall never give up philosophy or stop exhorting you and pointing out the truth to any one of you whom I may meet, saying in my accustomed way: "Most excellent man, are you who are a citizen of Athens, the greatest of cities and the most famous for wisdom and power, not ashamed to care for the acquisition of wealth and for reputation and honour, when you neither care nor take thought for wisdom and truth and the perfection of your soul? "And if any of you argues the point and says he does care, I shall not let him go at once, nor shall I go away, but I shall question and examine and cross-examine him, and if I find that he does not possess virtue, but says he does, I shall rebuke him from scorning the things that are of most importance and caring more for what is of less worth. This I shall do to whomever I meet, young and old, foreigner and citizen, but most to the citizen, inasmuch as you are more nearly related to me.[21]

Wisdom, then, is the only thing that is worth pursuing: it has its basis in divinity but consists in the ability to order human things correctly, beginning with oneself and continuing with political activity. The ethical, educational and political project of the *Republic*, above all Book VII, is to be seen as a continuation of the Socratic project:

> We shall require them to turn upwards the vision of their souls and fix their gaze on that which shed light on all, and when they have thus beheld the good itself they shall use it as a pattern for the right ordering of the state and the citizens and themselves throughout the remainder of their lives, each in his turn, devoting the greater part of their time to the study of philosophy, but when the turn comes for each, toiling in the service of the state and holding office for the city's sake, regarding the task not as a fine thing but as a necessity; and so, when each generation has educated others like themselves to take their place as guardians of the state, they shall depart to the Islands of the Blest and there dwell.[22]

This characteristic of wisdom, which is both knowledge of ultimate things and *ars vivendi* is continually proposed by Greek philosophy, including Philo, where, as in the *Wisdom of Solomon*, Biblical and classical traditions

---

than generosity, appears to be spiritual strength, or courage. Trust is *fides*, not faith in transcendence, but precisely faith in possible communion with others, not for what they are, but for what they might become.

[21] *Apol. Socr.* 29d-30a, trans. H. North Fowler (Loeb Classical Library).

[22] *Rep.* 540a-c, trans. P. Shorey (Loeb Classical Library). These words apply also "to all women who arise among them endowed with the requisite qualities".

flow together.[23] I could add here texts which can be found in Seneca, Epictetus, and Marcus Aurelius, restating what has already been outlined in Thesis I about philosophy as learning how to live, how to converse, how to read, how to die.

f) Aristotle, on the other hand, offers a definition of wisdom as knowledge of principles, as dianoetic virtue different from the practical virtue of *phronesis*. In doing so he transmits to the history of European culture that split between contemplation and action, between theory and practice that was to have such serious consequences.

g) On the subject of Eastern tradition, I am also thinking of Chinese culture, and in particular of the first and fundamental Confucian text, *Ta hsueh, The Great Study*, "The gate by which first learners enter into virtue". This text in particular summarizes the Confucian position very well, although there are many probably earlier texts, both from Confucius and from Mencius.[24] Here is the text attributed to Confucius:

> The way of learning to be great consists in shining with the illustrious power of moral personality, in making a new people, in abiding in the highest goodness. To know one's abiding place leads to fixity of purpose, fixity of purpose to calmness of mind, calmness of mind to serenity of life, serenity of life to careful consideration of means, careful consideration of means to the achievement of the end. Things have their roots and branches, human affairs their endings as well as beginnings. So to know what comes first and what comes afterwards heads one near to the Way. The men of old who wished to shine with the illustrious power of personality throughout the Great Society, first had to govern their own states efficiently. Wishing to do this, they first had to make an ordered harmony in their own families. Wishing to do this they first had to cultivate their individual selves. Wishing to do this, they first had to put their minds right. Wishing to do this, they first had to make their purposes genuine. Wishing to do this, they first had to extend their knowledge to the utmost. Such extension of knowledge consists in appreciating the nature of things. For with the appreciation of the nature of things knowledge reaches its height. With the completion of knowledge purposes become genuine. With purposes genuine the mind becomes right. With the mind right the individual self comes into flower. With the self in flower the family becomes an ordered harmony. With the families ordered harmonies the State is efficiently governed. With states efficiently governed the Great Society is at peace. Thus from the Son of Heaven down to the common people there is unity in this; that for everybody the bringing of the individual self to flower is to be taken as the root. Since that is so, for the root

---

[23] A useful synthesis by Wilckens, "Sophia", in *Theol. Wört. zum N. Testament*, VII, pp. 466-528.

[24] Cf. M. Scarpari, *La concezione della natura umana in Confucio e Mencio* (Venezia: Cafoscarina, 1991).

to be out of order and the branches to be in order is an impossibility. For a man to despise what he should respect and then be respected for having what he despises, is contrary to human experience. This is to be described as knowing the root.[25]

h) We must also mention Taoist writings, which represent an important correction to the ritualism into which Confucian tradition can fall. The "wise man" as he appears in the *Tao-te-ching*, in particularly important, often to be found in the formula "because of this the wise man...". Here is the first example in which it appears:

The whole world recognizes the beautiful as the beautiful, yet this is only the ugly:
The whole world recognizes the good as the good Yet this is only the bad.
Thus Something and Nothing produce each other;
The difficult and the easy complement each other;
The long and the short off-set each other;
The high and the low incline towards each other;
Note and sound harmonize each other;
Before and after follow each other.
Therefore the sage keeps to the deed that consists in taking no action and practices the teaching that uses no words.
The myriad creatures rise from it yet it claims no authority;
It gives them life yet claims no possession;
It benefits them yet exacts no gratitude;
It accomplishes its task yet lays claim to no merit.
It is because it lays claim to no merit
That its merit never deserts it (2).

Another example:

Heaven and earth are enduring. The reason why heaven and earth can be enduring is that they do not give themselves life. Hence they are able to be long-lived.
Therefore the sage puts his person last and it comes first.
Treats it as extraneous to himself and it is preserved.
It is not because he is without thought of self that he is able to accomplish his private ends? (7).

And here is yet another passage, in which the idea of knowing what is constant (*chih ch'ang*) appears:

---

25 *The Great Learning and the Mean-in-Action*, trans. E.R. Hughes (New York: E.P. Dutton and C., 1943 [repr. 1979]).

I do my utmost to attain emptiness;
I hold firmly to stillness.
The myriad creatures all rise together
And I watch their return.
The teeming creatures
All return to their separate roots.
Returning to one's roots is known as stillness.
This is what is meant by returning to one's destiny.
Returning to one's destiny is known as the constant.
Knowledge of the constant is known as discernment.
Woe to him that willfully innovates
While ignorant of the constant,
But should one act from knowledge of the constant
One's action will lead to impartiality,
Impartiality to kingliness,
Kingliness to heaven,
Heaven to the way,
The way to perpetuity,
And to the end of one's days will meet no danger (16).

To these and to many other texts we could add still more, in which the notion of wisdom (*sheng*) and prudence (*chih*) are often contested on account of their artificial quality. The result is an incomparable pairing of radicalism and spontaneity:

Exterminate the sage, discard the wise,
And the people will benefit a hundredfold;
Exterminate benevolence, discard rectitude,
And the people will again be filial;
Exterminate ingenuity, discard profit,
And there will be no more thieves and bandits.
These three, being false adornments, are not enough
And the people must have something
To which they can attach themselves:
Exhibit the unadorned and embrace the uncarved block,
Have little thought of self and as few desires as possible (19).[26]

i) For the Indian tradition I refer to the *Bhagavadgita* and to the relation between yoga of knowledge (*jnanayoga*) and yoga of action (*karmayoga*). The text states that there are two ways, the discipline of action, and the discipline of knowledge. But "a man cannot escape the force of action by abstaining from actions; he does not attain success just by renunciation. No one exists

---

[26] *Chinese Classics. Tao Te Ching*, trans. D.C. Lau (Hong Kong: The Chinese University Press, 1989).

for even an instant without performing action" (III, 3-5; even Divinity, III, 23). Thus, "renunciation and discipline in action both effect good beyond measure; but of the two, discipline in action surpasses renunciation in action" (V, 2). These are fundamental texts for the studies of the young Gandhi, who takes over the idea of a wisdom that is both contemplative and political. He finds, as we have seen, the core of the *Bhagavadgita* in II, 54-72 which contains the picture of the *sthitaprajna*, the "man of stable thought".[27]

l) Despite its sharper theological character, which brings it close to Christian theology, the works of al-Ghazali are also important. They convey the richness of his spiritual journey, leading him from scholastic Muslim theology to philosophy, to the esoteric interpretation of the Koran and to sufism. From him came, in fact, the development in the Islamic world (with the exception of the Shi'ite area) of a moderate, anti-philosophic and anti-esoteric sufic position. He gives us his intellectual biography in the short text *Salvation from Perdition*.[28] *The Letter to a Disciple*, written a few years before dying, contains many pertinent lessons, on those "who read one hundred thousand questions and learn them by heart and do not put them into practice". And a little later: "Knowledge without practice is foolishness, practice without knowledge, uselessness".[29]

k) None of the preceding examples would serve any purpose if the concept of "wisdom" around which they revolve were not clear. A great effort both to elaborate this notion and to document its universal promulgation has been made in Leo Tolstoy's philosophical-religious works. Of particular importance is his interpretation of *logos* in the prologue to the Gospel according to John as *razumenie*: a term generally translated as "understanding" (French "intendement") but which could also be "wisdom".[30] In a letter to A.A. Fet in mid-October 1880 he justifies his

---

27 See above, footnote 10.
28 *Al-munqid min adalal (Erreur et délivrance)*, with Arabic Text and French trans. F. Jabre (Beyrouth: Commission Libanaise pour la Traduction des Chefs-d'Oeuvre, 1969).
29 *Lettre au disciple (Ayyuha 'l walad)* with Arabic Text and French trans. T. Sabbagh (Beyrouth: Commission Libanaise pour la Traduction des Chefs-d'Oeuvre, 1969) pp. 8 f. and 16 f. In both passages Arabic rhetorically opposes the two roots, *'lm* e *'ml*, to learn and to practice.
30 See my *Lev Tolstoj. Oltre la letteratura (1875-1910)* (Firenze: Edizioni cultura della pace, 1990) ch. 2; for a more analytical treatment, see "Antico Testamento, Evangelo, Legge eterna in Lev Tolstoj esegeta", *Annali di storia dell'esegesi* 8:1 (1991) pp. 193-234. A synthesis can be found in Leo Tolstoy's *Cycle of Reading*, below II, 5.

version of the prologue.The starting point for this interpretation seems to stem from *John* 1:18, which Tolstoy reads thus: "God, nobody will be able to know him, *razumenie* manifested God". *Razumenie*-wisdom is here proposed against Spinoza, Hegel and Schopenhauer as a principle of knowledge that is non-metaphysical, tied to praxis; as a wisdom that correctly directs man's desire and aims at happiness, which in its essence consists in not resisting evil, in forgiveness and in love for one's neighbour. This is a non-rationalistic reason, neither gnostic nor esoteric, a wisdom drawn from life supported and confirmed by the individual and the collective experience of all humankind.[31]

---

[31] In his exegesis of the Prologue of the *Gospel according to John*, contained in his "Unification and translation of the Four Gospels", Tolstoy justifies his translation more analytically. It must be recalled that Tolstoy had just read with admiration the wisdom literature of the Bible (see his letter to Fet on August 30/31, 1879, and the marks in the margin of his personal Bible of 1862). It must be noticed that razume*t'*, *razumenie* is the Russian translation of Biblical terms: see the translation of Mt. 22:37: "Love God... with all your *razumenie*". Tolstoyan *razum* and *razumenie* belong to gnomic Biblical and popular culture and do not convey either rationalism or intellectualism. On the contrary they can be linked with Rousseau's antirationalistic Enlightenment.

IV

Wisdom, Scripture and the Mother

> The relation between mother and child represents the prototype which illuminates the sapiential situation, where the discipline and liberation of the generating power of desire constitute the task of wisdom and the yearning of desire, understood as a unique and undivided force.

1. The Mother-Child Relationship as Prototype

a) This hypothesis has already emerged in some sections of the present work. I have already spoken of the "original situation of the learning child and the teaching and narrating mother in a situation of mutual trust" (II, 4,c). At this point we need to draw on a number of suggestions principally but not exclusively from the field of psychoanalysis. The first object with the gift of cognitive permanence, and therefore the first object of conceptual or symbolic representation, is a person, and not an inanimate object. Admitted in general terms even by J. Piaget this is a fundamental position for psychoanalytic research.[1] This object is the mother's body. Her breast is seen as an infinite reserve of power and is invested with love, but also envy and destructive feelings. Important, then, is the function of objects that symbolically replace the mother's absent body, toward which are directed destructive fantasies and reparative needs, and toward which the "epistemophilic" need (M. Klein)[2] can be directed. The mother gathers the sensorial elements projected

---

[1] Cf. *I percorsi del simbolo. Teoria e clinica psicoanalitica*, G. Giaconia and A. Racalbuto eds. (Milano: Cortina editore, 1990) p. 8.

[2] I develop here M. Klein's suggestion: "...her [Erna's, a neurotic child] extraordinary sadism, which was fused with Erna's intense desire for knowledge, led – as a defense against it – to a complete inhibition of a number of activities which were based upon her desire for knowledge. Arithmetic and writing symbolized violent sadistic attacks upon her mother's body and her father's penis. In her unconscious, these activities were equated with tearing, cutting up

onto her by the child and returns them to him/her in a processed form: her thought apparatus has effects which structure that of the child's. In the absence of the breasts, thought comes forward, which is fundamentally the idea of a breast that is no longer there (W. Bion), of a lost fusional object, but with which the rapport is maintained. At the moment of separation from the mother, the function of the "transitional object" is essential: the symbol (unlike the fetish, which forms a stable defence against the illusion of integration into the maternal body) is a bridge between self and other, a mental construct that is formed at the transitional stage between mother and child, where play, thought, the distinction between self and other, and creativity (D.W. Winnicott) are born. The mother feeds the child and at the same time directs and form s his/her desire (J. Lacan): she gives sense to what the child can feel only with anxiety, carrying out an affective-linguistic operation which is expressed by nursing, by nourishment, by exchange: through these operations the mother gives to the child a gestural and linguistic code not made up of signs alone, but also of affection.

b) Elsewhere I have indicated a number of elements that point towards the connection between Scripture and the mother-figure of the Catholic tradition: "the Scripture has also a body, animated by the Spirit, by which it generates the divine word. Its bosom offers a spiritual nourishment infinitely

---

or burning her mother's body, together with the children it contained, and castrating her father. Reading, too, in consequence of the symbolic equation of their mother's body with books, had come to mean a violent removal of substances, children, etc. from the inside of her mother": *The Psycho-analysis of Children*, trans. A. Strachey (Seymour Lawrence: Delacorte Press, 1975). The feminine symbolism of paper and book are remarked by S. Freud, *Introduction to Psycho-analysis*, ch. 10, cf. J. Strachey, "Some unconscious factors in reading", *International Journal of Psychoanalysis* 11 (1930) pp. 322-331. Strachey uses also a suggestion by E. Jones about the association between books and excrement. Strachey was already aware of Klein's work at this time. His hypothesis is that "if the book symbolizes the mother, its author must be the father; and the printed words, the author's thoughts, fertilizing and precious, yet defiling the virgin page, must be the father's penis or faeces within the mother. And now comes the reader, the son, hungry, voracious, destructive and defiling in his turn, eager to force his way into his mother, to find out what is inside her, to tear his father's traces out of her, to devour them, to make them his own, and to be fertilized by them himself", p. 22 (Strachey resorts also Ezek. 2:9-3:4, the prophet eating a book). See also P. Schneider, "Illusion und Grunstörung. Psychoanalytische Überlegungen zum Lesen", *Psyche* 36 (1982) pp. 327-342, who sees the acts of reading in the context of primary love according to M. e E. Balint (see in their *Thrills and Regressions*, 1959, their criticism of Freud's attitude to "oceanic feeling").

rich and fit for everybody. [3] In the *Bhagavadgita* Gandhi saw the figure of Kamadhuk, and there are many other examples to be found elsewhere.[4] The analogy between the sacred scripture and the mother, and between reader and child can be further elaborated. We can think of an initial hermeneutic moment in which the attitude toward scripture can be explained as a prolonging of the archaic use of maternal communicative acts by the child, in which use language, whatever its content, simply means the perfect union between mother and child, standing for the breasts or the maternal body. Writing contains an infinite power and wealth that can be infinitely adapted to the reader. It is the "author" (from Latin *augeo*, the same root as "augment") of the reader's growth, thanks to the unique vital-spiritual sphere to which both belong. Reading is an act of fusion between text and reader, who from any of the text's fragments draws the meanings which are most useful to his/ her affective (more than cognitive) needs, according to a paradigmatic and symbolic interpretive modality.[5] Such an approach is all the more necessary if we want to avoid aggressive feelings when in its materiality, in its literalness, the text-body does not feed us sufficiently or not at all, absenting

---

3 *L'interpretazione infinita*, cit., p. 161.

4 It is interesting to notice the presence of a maternal nucleus in a passage of the Coran: "He is the one who has sent down to you the Book; in it there are firmly established verses [*ayyat muhkamât*], which are the mother of the Book [*umm 'l kitab*], and others that are allegorical [*mutashabihât*]. Those in whose hearts is perversity pursue what is allegoric, seeking to create schism and looking for their interpretation, and no one knows their interpretation, except God; and those who are firmly grounded in knowledge ['*ilm*] say: 'We believe in it; all of it comes from our Lord'" (3:7). This passage is fundamental for Muslim hermeneutics. What immediately precedes prepares perhaps the maternal metaphor: "He is the one who fashions you in the wombs ['*arham*], as he wills; there is no one worthy of worship beside him, the mighty, the wise [*hâkim*]".

5 I am here thinking of Ju.M. Lotman, with his model of a medieval universe as ruled by a paradigmatic or symbolic organization of meaning, in which the part is omeomorphic to ("stands for") the whole, and is not a fraction of it. As a consequence "'reading' in the medieval sense is not a quantitative accumulation of texts, but consists in pursuing an always deeper knowledge of one text with a continual and repeated effort to penetrate into its structure". I read Lotman's essay on "the problem of sign and sign system in the typology of Russian culture before XX century" in *Ricerche semiotiche*, Ju.M. Lotman and B.A. Uspenskij eds. (It. trans., Torino: Einaudi, 1973) p. 45 (*Semioticheskie issledovaniya*, a collection of essays especially prepared for the Italian edition).

itself and betraying the pact of trust which ties it to its reader.[6]

c) But the absence of that body, together with the inadequacy of the purely affective-figural use of authoritative words, is what gradually generates the abstraction and the awareness of their greater truth, a more abstract and content-based second-degree truth. This becomes apparent and then predominant when the words of the mother-figure become stronger and are taken on as wise teaching which directs desire, giving it limits and realistic objectives. Even when depressed and nostalgic, this teaching will, however, maintain the affective sign, the erotic tie which characterizes the original situation: this latter receives new vigour when it is evoked at the time of falling in love, and the beloved is welcomed in the luminous halo of memory. The original split can also, more or less successfully, precede and prepare other splits. Vice-versa, divine wisdom will be loved and pursued like a beloved, a spouse, a queen, who, as with the poet Solov'ëv, will eventually come forward and let herself be discovered by those who look for her.[7]

d) I think that these reflections have already indicated the anthropological background against which we must place ancient (but always present) allegorical interpretation as well as both the distinction and the link between this and sapiential interpretation. This latter is characterized by an increase in its conceptual character, by an insistence on its ethical and pragmatic aspects[8] and also by its secularity, according to which the observation,

---

[6] This aggressivity manifests itself not only in the rejection of literal meaning, but also in allegorical excess: then the bosom does not give milk but blood: "Who presses with strength the breast brings forth butter and who milks vehemently produces blood" ("Qui autem fortiter premit ubera ad eliciendum lac exprimit butyrum, et qui vehementer emungit elicit sanguinem", Prov. 30:33, but only according to the Vulgate). Many medieval authors applied this text to eccessive allogorism, cf. H. De Lubac, *Exégèses médiévale, Le quatres senses de l'Ecriture* (Paris: Aubier, 1959 ff.) pp. 537 ff., in the section devoted to Hugh of St.-Victor ("The too much pressed breast").

[7] Cf. G. von Rad, *Wisdom in Israel*, in the paragraph devoted to "spiritual love (eros)". See also footnote 9, p. 31, on V. Solov'ëv.

[8] Unlike speculative theology, and especially its sophiologic version. In the same years in which Solov'ëv pursued his personified Sophia, Tolstoy read the Wisdom literature and elaborated his notion of *razumenie* (see footnote 30, p. 40). In my essay on "La Madonna di S. Sisto di Raffaello nella cultura russa," in *La Madonna di S.Sisto*, cit., I reconstruct the conflict between L. Tolstoy and S. Bulgakov precisely over the image of Raffaello's Madonna. This conflict is particularly meaningful. For Bulgakov this Madonna was transfigured by a mystic light that Tolstoy was incapable of seeing.

elaboration and assimilation of other meanings and other necessary figures do not exclude the original maternal text, towards which a spiritual rapport, a link of adult trust founded on the child's affection, is maintained.

2. The Discipline and Liberation of Desire

a) Desire, as a unique and indivisible force. There is here a certain idea of love, of an eros capable of the greatest accomplishments because it is a force rooted in the depths of human corporeality. A unique and indivisible force, eros (unlike in the analysis of P. Florensky [9] and A. Nygren[10]) must be seen as containing no dualistic opposition[11] between carnal and spiritual love, or between a possessive eros and an agape that is compassionate and willing to sacrifice itself. Difficult as it is to think without dualistic oppositions, it is precisely the task of wisdom to think of love as a unitary force in its distinct expressions and transformations: maternal, paternal, filial, brotherly love; love between men and women; friendship; compassion; dedication to tasks as in service; love of the beautiful and the good... This anti-dualistic claim, which makes up one of modern anthropology's most basic conquests (even though its implications can be questioned)[12] harks back to Socrates. Or rather to a woman, Diotima,

---

[9] Cf. the already mentioned *Stolp' i utverzhdenie istiny* (*Column and foundation of the truth*) "Letter 10", in which he insists upon the antinomy *agàpe-filìa*, which, according to him, was perhaps confusedly perceived already before Christ, by the Greek, but in the New Testament appeared with extreme clarity.

[10] *Agape and eros*, trans. Ph.S. Watson (New York and Evanston: Harper Torchbooks, 1969) conclusion: "In attacking the Catholic doctrine of love, Luther has no thought of putting an end to love. What he seeks to destroy is that interpretation of Christian love which finds expression in the idea of Caritas, which fundamentally contains more Hellenistic Eros-love than primitive Christian Agape-love. Here, as elsewhere, Catholicism is a *complexio oppositorum*, a synthesis of opposed fundamental motifs. In Luther, on the other hand, a clear distinction is made. His view of love is throughout determined by the Christian Agape motif. We look in vain here for any single feature of Eros. And we try in vain to think of any possible expression of the idea of Agape, which Luther has not found and used"(p. 739).

[11] My *The Golden Calf and the Origins of the anti-Jewish Controversy*, trans D. Ward (Atlanta, Georgia: Scholars Press, 1990) examines the ancient anti-Jewish polemical use of the opposition flesh-spirit, as an ideological premise to anti-semitism: the Jewish people, in this polemic, is a carnal people, subject to every worldly passion, therefore justly destined to a servile condition.

[12] G. Santas, *Plato and Freud, Two Theories of Love* (New York: Basil Blackwell, 1988). The discussion between Freud and Pfister is of great interest. Around 1920, while he is definitively elaborating his idea of the essence of Christianity, Pfister reads

in the *Symposium*. Against the rhetoric which exalts the nobility and antiquity of Love (Faedrus), the duality between celestial and vulgar love (Pausanias), love as a cosmic principal (Eriximachus), love as an attempt to reach one's partner (Aristophanes), love as the sum of all virtues (Agatho), against all these Socrates proposes an examination of what love really is: it is not a "great god", but it is desire, a sense of something lacking; it has low, common origins, it is the son, according to the myth, of Poros and Penia, that is, "sagacity" and "poverty" (203b-d).

b) Eros does not possess but aspires to wisdom and beauty: "they are of the intermediate sort, and amongst these also is love. For wisdom has to do with the fairest things, and love is a love directed to what is fair; so that love must be a friend of wisdom and, as such, must be between wisdom and

---

Nachmansohn's essay, which compares Freud's theory of love with Plato's ("Freuds Libidotheorie verglichen mit der Lehre Platos", *Internationale Zeitschrift für artzliche Psychoanalyse* 3 [1915] pp. 65-83). Pfister appreciates this essay, and completes it with a discovery of his own: reading Plato's *Symposium*, he emphasizes Eriximachus' speech, in which the task of medicine is seen as "the restoration of love" (O. Pfister, "Plato als Vorläufer der Psychoanalyse", *Zentralblatt für Psychotherapie*, 7 [1921] pp. 264-269). He announces his discovery to Freud with great enthusiasm: "I have made a wonderful discovery in Plato which will give you pleasure. Nachmansohn in his paper missed the most important thing of all. Plato wrote the following: 'For the art of healing... is knowledge of the body's loves... and he who is able to distinguish between the good and bad acquires one kind of love instead of the other, and is able to impart love to those in whom there is none... is the best physician'. Plato traces back all art, religion, morality, to love, and he also has an admirable knowledge of the unconscious, the conflicting aspirations of the mind" (*Psycho-analysis and Faith, The Letters of S.Freud and O.Pfister*, cit., October 10, 1918, p.80). Pfister refers to *Symp.* 186c-d. Freud replied censuring Pfister's instinctual monism, which seemed to him aprioristic. Pfister in his turn declared: "I regard the 'death instinct', not as a real instinct, but only as a slackening of the 'life force', and even the death of the individual cannot hold up the advance of the universal will, but only help it forward" (*Psycho-analysis and Faith*, February 4, 1930, p. 131). Freud remained steadfast in declaring that the death instinct "is not a requirement of my heart: it seems to me to be only an inevitable assumption on both biological and psychological grounds" (*ib.*, February 7, 1930, p. 133). These are also the assumptions on which Freud's *Civilisation and its Discontents* (1929) is based, with its severe objections to Christianity. It is hard to think that, in writing it, Freud did not have in mind Pfister (cf. my *Oskar Pfister*, below II, 6). In my introduction to P. Gay's *A Godless Jew*, in the Italian edition, *Un Ebreo senza Dio*, cit., I pointed out that behind Pfister's somewhat naive identification of Platonic love, Christian agape and Freudian eros, there is the problem of the precedents and precursors of psycho-analysis.

ignorance" (204b).[13] Eros/love submits itself to its discipline, which consists (for man, but with analogies in the infra-human world) in educating oneself to contemplate ever higher and more refined forms and manifestations of beauty.

c) This process does not have its end simply in the contemplation of higher beauty. Rather, it culminates in the generation of beauty "in the presence of beauty" (as Penia from Poros generates Eros in Aphrodite's garden): "For you are wrong, Socrates, in supposing that love is of the beautiful... It is of engendering and begetting upon the beautiful" (206e). The liberation of generative power is the final result of discipline and the educative process: "But tell me, what would happen if one of you had the fortune to look upon essential beauty entire, pure and unalloyed; not infected with the flesh and colour of humanity, and ever so much more of mortal trash? What if he could behold the divine beauty itself, in its unique form? Do you call it a pitiful life for a man to lead — looking that way, observing that vision by the proper means, and having it ever with him? Do not consider... that there only will it befall, as he sees the beautiful through that which makes it visible, to breed not illusions but true examples of virtue, since the contact is not with illusion but with truth. So when he has begotten a true virtue and has reared it up he is destined to win the friendship of heaven; he, above all men , is immortal" (211e-212b).

d) Obedience and creativity are the elements whose fusion is most difficult, even in the freest, most spiritual readings of the biblical text. Platonism's emphasis on beauty, on eros, on the generative, productive, creative character of the meeting of the two — eros and beauty — at various levels of being, represents perhaps one of its most basic tenets, at least historically when compared to the Jewish-Christian tradition. But the sapiential tradition and approach, including its beginnings in the primary situation, could constitute the space in which to effect the transition between the two terms. To read the biblical text no longer as an encyclopedic reserve for every kind of knowledge, but as a body of vital teachings, of appropriate words of wisdom to which we must desire to submit ourselves ("I opened my mouth wide and panted, for I longed for Thy commandment", Ps. 119:31) in order to become able to speak, to generate, to work, to create. In other words: "power through submission":[14] this could be the formula

---

[13] Trans. W.R.M. Lamb (Loeb Classical Library).

[14] See my *Emerson and Wisdom*, quoted: "Thus, there is a human power over Nature, which consists in calling living creatures according to their own names... Nature has the power to interpret our thoughts and the will and the desire to communicate", below II, 3.

which reconciles the two terms. Even the gift of wisdom to the simple (Ps. 119:130) can be understood better: "The unfolding to Thy words gives light; it gives understanding to the simple" (Ps. 119:130; cf. Mt. 11:27-31; Sir. 51).

3. Augustine

a) The study of St. Augustine may be a good illustration of what I have hitherto said concerning the connection between the sapiential hermeneutic and maternal model, with special regard to ancient, allegoric interpretation (see above 1.d). One could in fact show that Augustine's relation to Scripture is that of a conflict which develops alongside that with his mother and both conflicts are resolved by means of the transformation which touches on both relationships, his mother and the Book. Augustine's departure from Carthage (a. 383), when Augustine deceives his mother, who "clings wildly" to him (*Conf.* V, 8, 15), is certainly the apex of a conflict of which the *Confessions* contain several hints. Augustine sees in his experience at that time a re-enactment of the original sin. In Monica's "carnal desire" for her son, says Augustine, "Eve's heritage" reveals itself. In Augustine's desire for self-affirmation, which leads him away to Rome, where he falls severely sick, the "original sin" discloses itself in all its strength (this is one of the first occurrences of this expression, around the year 397).

b) Eve-Monica's groans will save Adam-Augustine from a double death, spiritual and corporal. She shall give birth to Augustine again. Her feelings towards her son, change from being seductive and possessive and become generative. In the perspective of analytical psychology this critical moment could be seen as the passage from the "elementary" maternal character (who wildly clings to him) to the "transforming" maternal character.[15] The story which follows shows how the figure of Wisdom (with which Augustine had fallen in love reading Cicero's *Hortensius*) will progressively converge with the image of Monica: up to Augustine's conversion, up to Monica's participation in the philosophical dialogues at Cassiciacum, as a wise old woman, up to the ecstasy at Ostia and Monica's edifying death, soon afterwards.

c) Augustine's conversion consists also, and above all, in his final acceptance of the Biblical scriptures. At the beginning of his pursuit of wisdom, after his reading of *Hortensius*, these scriptures seemed to reject him: in fact, he refused to become a child in front of them:

---

[15] Cf. E. Neumann, *Die Grosse Mutter* (Zürich: Rhein-Verlag, 1956).

I therefore decided to pay attention to the holy scriptures and to find out what they were like. And this is what met me: something neither open to the proud nor laid bare to mere children; a text lowly to the beginner but, on further reading, of mountainous difficulty and enveloped in mysteries. I was not in any state to be able to enter into that, or to bow my head to climb its steps. What I am now saying did not then enter my mind when I gave my attention to the scripture. It seemed to me unworthy in comparison with the dignity of Cicero. My inflated conceit shunned the Bible's restraint, and my gaze never penetrated to its inwardness. Yet the Bible was composed in such a way that as children mature, its meaning grows with them. I disdained to be a little child. Puffed up with pride, I considered myself a mature adult (III, 5, 9).[16]

This first impression of narrowness, of suffocating constriction, of mortal danger, as in front of a sepulchre, finds confirmation in Manichaean arguments against the Christian Scriptures (*Conf.* III, 7, 12). From this moment, and for some considerable time, the Jewish-Christian Scriptures would be for Augustine only the letter that kills. As the motherly bosom gives rise to feelings of ferocious frustration when it does not nourish, or does not nourish enough, or even offers itself to a rival in love and in need (Augustine's direct observation, *Conf.* I, 7, 11), so the sacred text can become "mortal" when in its materiality it proposes a rough, unintelligible or impossible meaning. The text then can lead its hungry and impatient reader to desperation. Such was Augustine's condition, for a long time. Only when listening to Ambrose preaching in Milan would he find the solution, in the allegorical reading of the Scriptures. The more Augustine reduced his arrogance and became a "little child", the more the "huge tomes" containing Manichaean scriptures became a series of absurd phantasies: it was like eating in a dream, and waking up hungry, he says (*Conf.* III, 6, 10). Neo-platonic writings contain elements of wisdom, but are full of presumption and do not possess that healing and beatifying power which is the quality of Christian scriptures (*Conf.* VII, 20, 26), and especially of the apostle Paul's letters (*Conf.* VII, 20, 26 - 21, 27). The more he stoops down to pass through its narrow entrance, the more the Christian scripture appears to Augustine a living reality, a body animated by the spirit, by which the divine word is generated in the reader. In Milan the impression of absurdity the Scriptures had given is replaced by his respect for such a high, venerable, but nevertheless accessible authority. The Scripture is a

---

16 In my *L'intepretazione infinita*, cit., pp. 29 ff. I examine the Augustinian formula, according to which the Scripture *crescit cum parvulis.*

bosom of infinite power and richness, and is at the same time a womb capable of receiving every kind of reader, whatever his condition and spiritual age: she is the *popularis sinus*, literally the "popular bosom", the "womb of holy humility", "open to everyone to read", "in very accessible words and the most humble style", being meanwhile exacting with those who are more exacting, and who are at the same time disposed to pass through its "narrow openings".

d) It must be here emphasized how the argument and the metaphors apply both to the Scripture and to the Catholic Church. The Church is also a "popular bosom", a universal womb that receives with maternal "authority" whoever wants to enter, nourishing everyone with the fittest food. Church and Scripture are like a container and its contents, in a relationship that again finds concrete expression in a maternal image: the food of the Scripture can be tasted only in the womb of the Church. It was the experience of Augustine himself, that the catholicity of the Scripture, of "the ecclesiastical books", which can nourish everybody, and grows with little children, could be learnt by only in the catholic Church, in his case through the bishop Ambrose, by means of a spiritual reading.

e) The case of Augustine is a splendid, moving example, of what has been said both about the prototypical sapiential relationship, and about the dialectic of desire. On the other hand, I do not believe his case can be normative, that is, that it represents the most mature or even less the only possible relationship with Scripture. It is possible, I think, in a modern individualistic social context, on the basis of a different anthropology and of a critical exegesis, to maintain a bond with Augustine's way of reading the Scripture, with its maternal affective characteristics, but reject his negative anthropology, his mystic-juridic anthropology and his allegorical hermeneutics. Augustine himself in some pages, in which he affirms the primacy of the *caritas* over the "ludic" nature of historical reality, including the institutions and the sacraments of the Church, seems to hint in this direction, although he did not follow it through, nor perhaps was he able to do so.

V

Wisdom and Law

The law is at the center of Jewish and Christian Biblical wisdom. We cannot suspend the practice of the law while waiting to know the existence of God, but faithful submission to the evidently and immediately binding commandments, including those implicit in the beatitudes, is already a beginning of knowledge, as well as of happiness and communion.

1. The Law, the Center of Wisdom.

a) It is important, when reading Scriptures, not to construct progressive sequences between different texts within the same scripture, or in relation to other scriptures. However, there are Biblical texts which on account of their special clarity can be used to organize a greater meaning of the whole of Scripture.[1] These texts are at the basis of the comparison with other scriptures. Clarity is the *claritas Scripturae*, a Lutheran notion (as the idea of "center", *Mitte*) which opens up the possibility of individual interpretation of Scripture.

b) In the Jewish and Christian Bible, according to the point of view I am proposing, the center is a segment, the axis that joins the two fires of an ellipsis, *Deuteronomy* and the "Sermon on the Mount" (the speeches made by Moses and Jesus), joined by the notion of law, which has been revealed through election and alliance. All Judaism sees the Torah at the center of Scripture. *Deuteronomy* indicates that it is in the possession of the Law that the wisdom of Israel is contained:

Behold, I have taught you statutes and ordinances as the Lord my God commanded to me, that you should do them in the land which you are

---

[1] In the same way, as we have seen, Gandhi saw in *Bhagavadgita*, II, pp. 54-72, the portrait of the *sthitaprajna*, the kernel and the criterion of interpretation of the whole book, see above n. 9, p. 9.

entering to take possession of. Keep and do them, for that will be your wisdom and your understanding in the sight of the peoples, who, when they hear all these statutes, will say: "Surely this great nation is a wise and understanding people". For what great nation is there that has a god so near to it as is the Lord our God is to us, whenever we call upon him? And what great nation is there that has statutes and ordinances so righteous as all this law which I set before you this day? (Deut. 4:5-8).

c) Jesus is usually placed in the general area of rabbinical Judaism ("I did not come to abolish but to fulfil"). However, I see his preaching more as an extension of the prophetic and above all sapiential line: intimacy, accessibility, practicality, and a tendential universality of divine law, along with a request for conversion and a guarantee of forgiveness that the eschatological certainty and personal authority of Jesus make possible. In following Jesus as teacher and in obedience to his universalistic and secular interpretation of the law (cf. Thesis VI), which we find in Mt. 5-7 (and parallels), I see the link with the Jewish tradition and the essential vantage point from which to observe and organize the meaning of the New Testament.

d) I would also like to consider in this light the writings referring to Paul in the New Testament. Today it seems far too simplistic to set up an oppositon, as Paul does, between Christianity and Judaism in terms of justice through works or justice through faith. Judaism and Christianity share not only the idea of law, election and alliance, but also salvation through grace and justice according to works.[2] From the point of view I am taking here (a "non-theological" interpretation), Paul's position can well be seen and explained as an improvement on the law, understood as "spiritual law", as an extension and coherent translation of the universalizing and secular instance already present in Jesus. In consequence of the weakening of eschatological expectations and of the grave decisions imposed by the mission in the Hellenic-Roman world (the *Acts of the Apostles*) and by the fall of Jerusalem, it is understandable how Christological confession and mystique took on an essential role, beginning with communion with Christ, through faith, baptism, and supper in his Spirit.[3] Similarly, we can explain how in

---

[2] "Covenantal nomism" is fundamental for E.P. Sanders, *Paul and Palestinian Judaism. A Comparison of Patterns of Religion* (London: SCM Press, 1977). His conclusion is that Paul's religion is a pattern different from Palestinian Judaism not because of the different role attributed to grace and works, but because for Paul the "immanence" "in Christ" substitutes the immanence "in Israel". Therefore Paul's Christianity is not a covenantal nomism, for Sanders, as W.D. Davies argues.

[3] I examined this theme in *KOINONIA. L'idea della comunione nell'ecclesiologia recente e nel Nuovo Testamento* (Brescia: Paideia, 1972).

this context the following oppositions dominated: justice through the works of the law/justice through faith in the redeeming work of Christ; law/ gospel; Hellenistic and Jewish wisdom/Christian wisdom; and finally, Jewish priesthood/Christian priesthood (*Letter to the Hebrews*).

e) Similar considerations can be made on the literature which refers to John. Here, Jesus' interpretation is in terms of the *logos* which, no matter how complicated the historical-exegetic decision, is fundamental. Without excluding the possibility of more complex explanations, I would read it as a summary against the background of *Proverbs* 8 (and *Wisdom*) The strict opposition to Judaism, the realization of eschatology, the emphasis of the "in Christ"with its cognitive, "gnostic" meaning do not stop the notion of "commandment" in John's 1st Letter from taking on a central and even a cognitive role. What follows aims precisely to affirm the possibility of knowledge through obedience without theoretical clarifications, mystical experiences or either preliminary or founding ascetic choices.

2. The Evidently and Immediately Binding Commandments

a) Fundamental here is the idea of the commandments' accessibility, understood as the intelligibility and practicality of the law (this does not mean it is easy to follow): "For this commandment which I command you this day is not too hard for you, neither is it far off" (Deut. 30:11). In the Bible we can speak of "evidently and immediately binding commandments including the more radical ones implicit in the beatitudes" because the commandment is rooted in the very heart of creation through logos-wisdom: obedience is its constitutive need and the source of its joy: "For ever, Lord, Thy word is firmly fixed in the heavens. Thy faithfulness endures to all generations; Thou hast established the earth, and it stands fast. By Thy appointment they stand this day; for all things are Thy servants" (Ps. 119:89-91).

b) The commandment is at the same time a need (see IV, 2), rooted in the "ontology of feelings" in the unique and undivided strength of desire ("naturalness" in the sense it has in the Chinese tradition).[4] But above all I

---

4   "The Master said: The path (*tao*) is not far from man. When men try to pursue a course, which is far from the common indications of consciousness, this course cannot be considered the path. In the book of Poetry it is said, 'In hewing an axe handle, the pattern is not far off', *The Doctrine of the Mean*, p. xiii. The first paragraph of this short book runs as follows: "What heaven has conferred is called the nature; an accordance with this nature is called the path (of duty); the regulation of this

am thinking of Tolstoy's comment on the Gospels, and of his perspective, which tends to collapse radicality and "rational" ("sapiential") evidence. Rather than its content (which should not, however, be overlooked) what is of interest here is the methodological approach.[5]

3. Faithful Submission as the Beginning of Knowledge

a) The pages that Kant dedicates to the premises of practical reason must be appreciated to the full. Their major claim is cognitive, not consolatory. Kant himself, presenting his dialectic as a confirmation and completion of ancient wisdom, indicates the background against which his demonstration is to be seen: that it is possible to broach the unconditioned through a praxis

---

path is called instruction". Confucian sincerity lies in harmonizing internal and external, desire and norm, so that one could spontaneously succeed in standing "in the middle". This sincerity can be a gift of nature, or the fruit of study: "When we have intelligence resulting from sincerity, this condition is to be ascribed to nature; when we have sincerity resulting from intelligence, this condition can be ascribed to instruction. But given the sincerity, and there shall be the intelligence; given the intelligence, and there shall be the sincerity" (p. xxi, trans. J. Legge).

5   This is how Tolstoy illustrates Jesus' commandments in his *Brief Exposition of the Gospel*: "Jesus was unhappy that people did not know what was really good, and so he taught them. He said: blessed are those who have nothing and have no reason to boast and to worry about their possessions. Unhappy are those who look for riches and glory because the poor and the persecuted embody the will of the Father, but the rich and the famous look for recognition only from others in this world. To follow the will of the Father, you must not fear being poor and despised, but instead be happy in order to show men what real good is. In order to carry out the will of the Father, who gives life and food to all men, it is necessary to follow five commandments:

First commandment: Do not offend anyone and do not act in any way that might give rise to evil feelings, because evil comes from evil.

Second commandment: Do not make love to this or that women, abandoning the woman you have been with, because abandoning and changing women leads to the worst deviations.

Third commandment: Do not swear on any occasion, for nobody can make promises. All are in the power of the Father, and oaths are made for evil things.

Fourth commandment: Do not resist evil, endure insults and do even more than is asked you. Do not judge or be judged by others, because men are full of errors and cannot teach others. Vendettas only teach others to do likewise.

Fifth commandment: Make no difference between your country and others, because all men are sons of the same Father.

These five commandments must be obeyed not in order to gain appreciation on the part of others but for oneself, for one's own happiness. It is not necessary to

exempt from eudamonistic motivations. "Pure practical faith" is offered as a critical scientific translation of ancient "wisdom" (*Weisheit*).[6]

b) In Ps. 119, an essential text for Jewish religious feeling, the desire for God is the desire to know his law, to discover, that is, how God wants humankind to live: "Open my eyes, that I may behold wondrous things out of thy law. I am a sojourner in the earth; hide not thy commandments from me" (v. 18 f.). But the fulfilment of the law and the knowledge of God are reciprocally implied: "Blessed are those who keep his testimonies, who seek him with their whole heart" (v.2): the search for God presupposes the practice of the commandments. But also, vice versa, "Give me understanding, that I may keep thy law, and observe it with my whole heart" (v. 34); "Teach me good judgement and knowledge, for I believe in thy commandments" (v. 66): the root `mn (an idea of stability, certainty) indicates faith or trust, a belief

---

pray because the Father knows all that is necessary to know. There is no reason to pray to him; it is only necessary to strive to follow his will. The will of the Father can be found in not harboring evil thoughts about others. It is not necessary to fast: men fast only in order to be praised by other men, but the praise of other men does not give happiness. It is only necessary to strive to follow the will of the Father, the rest comes on its own. If one is concerned about material matters, it is impossible to be concerned about the reign of heaven. Without worry for food or clothes, man will be free. The Father gives life. It is only necessary to strive to be part of the will of the Father. The Father gives all that is necessary. Only that strength of spirit that the Father gives can be desired. The five commandments define the way to heaven. Only this narrow path leads to eternal life. False teachers, wolves in sheep's clothing, are always trying to make men stray from this path. Beware. It is always possible to recognize false teachers because they teach evil in place of good. If they teach violence and punishment, they are false teachers. They can be recognized by what they teach. The will of the Father is carried out not by those who invoke the name of God but by those who do good works. Thus whoever follows these five commandments will be certain to lead a life that no one can take away from him. Whoever does not follow them will have a life that will be taken away from him quickly, and will remain with nothing. The teaching of Jesus enthrals and captivates everyone, for it gives liberty to all. The teaching of Jesus was the fulfilment of the prophecy of Isaiah when he said that God's chosen one would bring light to all men, would conquer evil and establish truth and justice with mildness, humility and goodness, not with violence. Cf. *Antico testamento, Evangelo, legge eterna* in L.Tolstoj *esegeta*, quoted., § 5, devoted to the relation between the law of Moses and eternal law.

6 *Critique of Practical Reason*, II, II, 7, at the end: "... the path to wisdom, if it is assured and not made impassable or misleading, must for us men unavoidably pass through science" (ed. cit., p. 243). The famous comparison between the starred sky and moral law has a sapiential flavour.

in the basic goodness of the precepts, even before one has full knowledge of them (or in a reciprocal manner: this is why one says "All thy commandments are *'emuna"* (v. 86). Again: "I have more understanding than all my teachers, for thy testimonies are my meditation. I understand more than the aged, because I keep thy precepts" (v. 99: note the parallelism between "meditate" and "observe"). In a shorter form: "Through thy precepts I get understanding" (v. 104).

c) In Isaiah's protest, God's revelation is tied to the practice of the commandments: "Is it not the fast which I choose, to loose the bonds of the wickedness, to undo the thongs of the yoke, and to let the oppressed go free and break every yoke? Is it not to share your bread with the hungry and bring the homeless poor into your house; when you see the naked, to cover him; and not to hide yourself from your own flesh? Then your light will break out forth like the dawn, and your healing shall spring up speedily" (Is. 58:6-8: "flesh" is the common condition of all creatures). And in the Christian Scriptures, there is the great scene in Chapter 25 of the Gospel according to Matthew.[7] Also the *First Letter of John*: "No man has ever seen God; if we love one another, God abides in us" (4:12).

d) Here is Tolstoy (for whom *1 John* was fundamental): "Life in the universe is there because of somebody's will; and somebody in the universe is using this life for some purpose of his. In order to be able to hope to find what this means, it is necessary first of all to submit, to do what is being asked. And if I do not do what is being asked, then I shall understand neither what is asked of me, nor, much less, what is asked of all me and of all the universe".[8] In a letter to his friend Strachov Tolstoy explains that "Christ teaches and explains the meaning of our life. But at the same time he always says that one must fulfil what he says, and then one will see that what he says

---

[7] "So if you want to find God and the poor, you must stop somewhere, stop reading and studying and dedicate all your time to teaching schoolchildren or adults. Not another word about equality. Equality at this moment will be about passing school exams, everything else is privilege. When you have completely lost yourself, like I did, trying to look after twenty or thirty kids, you will find God like a prize. You will have to find him because you can't teach without a stable faith. This is a promise of the Lord found in the parable of the sheep, in the marvel of those who find themselves, after death, to be friends and benefactors of the Lord without even having known him. What you have done for these little ones etc. It is no good beating yourself on the head in the search for God and not-God". *Lettere di Don Lorenzo Milani, priore di Barbiana* (Milano: Mondadori) pp. 277 f.

[8] *My Confessions*, p. xi. A preparatory note to *Ispoved'*, contains these words: "works are the faith".

is true. This is to say, whoever believes in the Son of Man does the works of God. There is here a metaphysical knot, which cannot be solved by reason, but only by one's whole life".[9]

e) It is also interesting to read Marx's first and second Theses on Feuerbach against the background of his Jewish origins: it is in praxis that man must show the truth. This is the reality and the power, the worldly character, the *Diesseitigkeit* of his thought.[10]

f) "He commands. And to those who obey him, whether they be wise or simple, he will reveal himself in the toils, the conflicts, the sufferings in which they shall pass through in his fellowship, and, as an ineffable mystery, they shall learn in their own experience, who he is". These are the concluding words of Albert Schweitzer's *Quest of the Historical Jesus*.

g) Circularity between the discipline of knowledge and discipline of action is a characteristic of the *Bhagavadgita*, but its most original aspect is its affirmation, on the one hand, of the inevitability of action and, on the other, of the cognitive fertility of action, carried out with regret, as a sacrifice: "Perform necessary action; it is more powerful than inaction; without action you even fail to sustain your own body. Action imprisons the world, unless it is done as sacrifice; freed from attachment, Arjuna, perform action as sacrifice" (III, 8 f.). In this way, Arjuna's fight is a fight against desire: "Great warrior, kill the enemy menacing you in the form of desire!" (III, 43). And, more specifically, desire for "the fruits of action":

> A man who sees inaction in action and action in inaction has understanding among men; and is disciplined in all the action he performs. The wise say a man is learned when his plans lack constructs of desire, when his actions are burned by the fire of knowledge. Abandoning attachment to fruits of action, always content, independent, he does nothing at all, even when he engages in action... When a man is unattached and free, his reason deep in knowledge, his action is wholly dissolved... Many forms of sacrifice

---

[9]   November 19-22, 1879 (PSS 6, p. 502). The famous passage in Pascal's *Pensées*, in which he suggests external practice, in order to obtain the internal attitude of faith, was very important for Tolstoy. In general he had great admiration for Pascal.

[10] "I. [...] Hence, his *Essence of Christianity*, he regards the theoretical attitude as the only genuinely human attitude, while practice is conceived and fixed only in its dirty-juridical form of appearance. Hence he does not grasp the significance of 'revolutionary', of 'practical-critical', activity. II. The question whether objective truth can be attributed to human thinking is not a question of theory but a practical question. In practice man must prove the truth, that is, the reality and power, the this-sidedness of his thinking".

expand toward the infinite spirit; know that the source of them all is action, and you will be free (V, 17-20.23.32).[11]

h) This is an opportune moment to recall what Gandhi considers the first rule for the interpretation of the *Bhagavadgita*: only those who practice the Shastra, the religious laws, can interpret them and explain their real meaning.[12]

i) Against a number of objections (the Pelagian position? works against faith?) it should be remembered that I cannot go back on the methodological approach I have adopted: the refusal to use theological support — salvation, grace, election or predestination. Let me say, however, that I do not want here to support works against faith. To operate according to the law is a gift and an (always problematical) sign of faith and grace, and election. But this already means penetrating a theological space. I will limit myself to saying, with Ralph Waldo Emerson in *The Over-Soul* : "Insight proceeds from obedience".

j) Corresponding to this "working by faith", to this "professing with facts",[13] is the immediate perception of freedom, peace, the "blessedness". Thus the fundamental first Psalm: "Blessed is the man, who does not walk in the counsel of the wicked, nor stand in the path of the sinners, but whose delight is in the law of the Lord". So too the crucial Ps. 119: "Blessed are those who keep his testimonies, who seek him with their whole heart... In the way of thy testimonies I delight, as much as in all riches" (1 and 14 and several other times). Against this background of present happiness, of joy for the gift of the law, I believe we should also read the beginning of the Sermon on the Mount.[14] Only by intuition can we understand how, in this tradition, a promise of life ("do this and you shall live") corresponds to the fulfilment of the commandments; how the commandment is defined as a "way of life"

---

[11] About the Kantian character of ethics according to *Bhagavadgita*, cf. G.R. Franci, "La crisi morale di Arjuna nella Bhagavadgita e la soluzione kamayogica: alcune difficoltà. Superabili?", *Studi orientali e linguistici* III (1986) pp. 131-158, 145.

[12] See footnote 9, p. 9.

[13] Cf. Tolstoy's preface to his *Unification and Translation of the Four Gospels*.

[14] This happiness is not the purpose, but a concomitant effect of the fulfilment of the commandments. See Kant, "On the Common Saying: 'This may be true in theory, but it does not apply in practice'", i, where the study of morals is defined as "the introduction to a discipline which would teach us not how to be happy, but how we should become worthy of happiness" (Kant, *Political writings*, trans. N.B. Nisbet, Cambridge: Cambridge University Press, 1992, p. 64).

and a principle of joy and of life without end; and how those who put themselves on this road, even if alone, declare that they feel in the presence and company of the just and the witnesses about whom the Scriptures speak, and which themselves speak through Scripture. And yet from the standpoint I have chosen there is no place for "christology" (for which, however, the warning given to those who say "Lord, Lord" and do not practice remains valid), nor for "ecclesiology". For this is a secular reading .

VI

A Secular Reading of the Bible

Ancient Christian Biblical exegesis is characterized by the ascetic/ mystical context in which the interpreter is located; the exegesis of the Evangelical and Reform movements is marked by a new but also original secular instance. This secularity is taken over as a method and developed by historical-critical exegesis, but in academic and confessional literature it is not brought to completion.

1. Ancient Christian Biblical Exegesis

a) According to the ancient hermeneutic notion,[1] held by authors like Origen and Augustine, up to Gregory the Great, the sacred book is full of prophetic and figurative meanings even in its minor and apparently irrelevant parts. The reader's application of the meaning to himself/herself is not external to the act of interpretation but forms its final necessary moment: the text "grows" as Gregory the Great says, until it reaches the reader, wherever he/she is, involving the reader in its prophecies, its advice, and its figures. Everything in the Scriptures speaks of Christ. Through the identification of the Church with Christ and the believer with the Church, the entire text speaks mysteriously of the believer, that is, of the reader, who through Christ and the Church is gradually able to identify with every word and event of the history of salvation. Technically this is achieved through a theological/rhetorical procedure which multiplies the intertextual links internal to the biblical totality through which infinite, ever new meanings can be generated within the same Scripture. In this way, each unit of Scripture potentially contains and can represent paradigmatically not only Scripture's totality but also the reader/believer's inner world, any possible new situation and experience that may arise. The vital situation in which exegesis is carried out is mainly one of mystical meditation, which through

---

[1] I refer to my *L'interpretazione infinita*, cit.

Christ aims to immerse the reader in the text with the words and the figures it contains and, lastly, with the divine author of Scripture.

b) According to Christian hermeneutics the events of sacred history, its protagonists and the words pronounced, while never entirely losing their proper meaning, are resignified mystically to represent something else (allegory) and ultimately all other things. This tendency seems to be already in decline by the beginning of scholastic theology in the 14th century. The mystical instance is replaced by a theoretical and often controversial one which emphasizes literal meaning as the "meaning intended by the author". Despite this change, from the historical/critical point of view the new hermeneutic rule produces few fruitful results. In fact, the elaboration of the biblical text by scholasticism often brings about a further lowering of vital needs, which are now satisfied in a different way, through devotion.

2. Evangelical Movements and the New and Original Secular Instance

a) Jesus' preaching is itself an act of secular, "intraworldly" interpretation of the Jewish legal tradition, both on the part of the teacher and his method, and on the part of those for whom the teaching was intended. Its very general terms lead back to the Jewish context and to previous prophetic preaching, but secularity forms the basic standpoint from which Jesus approaches the law, a point of view that the interpreter has to assume. Jesus' preaching bears on an essential element of the Law itself, its proximity, its accessibility, its intimacy ("For this commandment which I command you today is not too difficult for you, nor is it out of reach, it is not in heaven, that you say 'Who will go up to heaven for us to get it for us and make us hear it, that we may observe it?' Nor is it beyond the sea, that you should say 'Who will cross the sea for us to get it for us and make us hear it, that we may observe it?' But the word is very near to you, in your mouth and in your heart, that you may observe it" Deut. 30:11-14). The secular concern, as it emerges, for example, in the fundamental discussion on ritual purity (Mk. 7)[2] is indispensable if we are to to understand the divergence which would soon split the Judaism of that time and primitive Christianity. The invitation is not to annul but vigorously repropose the commandment in its essence so that it is once more accessible, understandable and feasible in any situation and for anyone who accepts the invitation to change their life. This, in all its

---

[2] Cf. R.P. Booth, "Jesus and the laws of purity. Tradition history and legal history in Marc 7", *Journal for the Study of the N.T.*, Suppl.13, Sheffield 1986. Cf. also Thesis III, 2, e.

eschatological urgency and despite its apocalyptic concerns, seems to be the core of Jesus' teaching. To affirm the essential, radical nature, the urgency but also the accessibility and universality of the commandment also forms Paul's and John's major concern, whatever their specific soteriological orientations.

b) In those Reformation and medieval evangelical movements which were not tied to groups of ascetes, the same instance and secular viewpoint reappears. In the Reformation, the theological/conceptual core identified as center, substance and essence of the message contained in Scripture — the law/gospel opposition (or rather: sin/grace, faith/works, letter/spirit) — is taken on as a dualism immanent in the entire biblical history and in the situation of each believer. Each believer lives in the world, in flesh and blood, with the necessity of the law, of the letter, of the works which still imply and invoke (but cannot produce) their opposite: grace, faith and spirit.[3] Basic to the Protestant reading is not a mystical immersion, but the acute perception of the split between the demands of the Law and the secular context in which the believer lives. The secular context allows the historicity[4] and legal-normative dimension of the biblical text, above all (but not only) that of the Old Testament, to be reappropriated. This is a dialectical valorization in the sense that, as I have said, the law points toward, demands but does not express, its necessary completion/overcoming, which lies in grace. With the Reformation, Scripture is intended as the letter which kills and at the same time as the spirit which gives life, and interpretation means rediscovering oneself in this conflict, at the center of the secular situation.

c) If this is true, the secular instance is vital if we are to understand Christian origins. First of all, it must be taken on by the interpreter, even before making exegetical choices in single cases, as a general *Sitz im Leben*, as a concern which must be mentally and vitally renewed each time in order

---

[3] The difference concerns the way the opposition spirit/letter is understood. Patristic interpretation (partly renewed by the Humanists) looks for the explanation of the "mystery" contained in the Biblical text, using allegorical interpretation, which allows sense of be made to every detail of the Scripture. The Reformation, in its exegesis, pursues in the text the pure, self-evident light of the Gospel, which illuminates and judges the Scripture. It is interesting to examine the way in which Luther reads Augustine's *De spiritu et littera*. Cf. my *L'interpretazione infinita*, cit., pp. 120-5.

[4] See for instance what Luther says in his *Tischreden*: "When I was a monk I was an expert in allegory. I made allegories out of everything. Then by means of the Epistle to the Romans I came to know Christ a little. Then I realised that there was no allegory, not what Christ meant but what Christ was" (WA 1, p. 136, n. 335).

to allow our understanding of the biblical text to be reactivated. While immediately recognizing and supporting the objective nature of the exegetical proceedings and their historical progress, it is also necessary to be aware that the life-position of the exegete and the praxis from which he/she comes and to which he/she tends, in qualifying the questions put to the text, also qualify greatly the objective results of knowledge. These results will be greater the more homogeneous to the text is the position of the interpreter and the questions he/she asks of the text. For this reason, from the epistemological point of view, the testing-out and correction of the life-situation of the interpreter is also an inevitable stage.[5]

d) The secular instance derives from the Jewish interpreters' equal zeal for the law, even if this turns into a concern that no-one be exempted from its observance, for reasons which may be basically irrelevant and may even contradict the spirit of the law. On the other hand, the mystical reading, despite the importance it had and in a certain sense still has in stressing the unavoidable *pro me* in the spiritual meeting with the text, takes our attention away from the point of view of the Jewish reader's approach to Scripture. The Jewish reader regards the law as something given to him to regulate all aspects of his daily, worldly existence: the Law does not deny corporeality, and spirituality is not understood as its opposite, but as its discipline and transformation.[6] The secular reading restores this point of view.

---

[5]   I have in mind here R. Bultmann, "Das Problem der Hermeneutik", in *Glauben und Verstehen*, II, 1952. I share Bultmann's conviction (derived from Dilthey and early romantic hermeneutics) that the text must be addressed (*Fragestellung*), moving from a vital communion with it (*Lebensgemeinschaft*) (but I would prefer to speak of an "ethical", rather of a the "existential" question: "what should I do?", or better: "what should I desire?").

[6]   See the conclusions of my *The Golden Calf and the Origins of the anti-Jewish Controversy*: "An even more serious consequence derives from a certain literal reading where the 'growth of Scripture with he who reads', of which Gregory the Great speaks (in other words, a creative hermeneutics), is no longer at issue. In its place stands the loss of contact, under the profile of religious anthropology, with the meaning of the doctrinal contents and the Jewish religious experience" (p. 81). Let me also quote the last words of this book: "The main phenomenon with which this work has been concerned is not, however, the historic or mystical distance between the two religions, Jewish and Christian. Rather, my concern has been with the more precise phenomenon of the early construction of the abstract image of Judaism as an exponent of carnality, an image which met the needs of Christianity and furnished a guarantee and reassurance of Christianity's superior spiritual extraction to such a point that any affinity or common ground between the two

3. Critical-Historical Exegesis

a) Secularity means interrogation starting from the concrete worldly situation in which the text and its interpreter operate. This situation is made up of numerous elements (during the Reformation these were work, family, political responsibility, all seen as religious "vocation"). Among these, from the cognitive point of view, we also find the use of reason, a critical approach in terms of autonomy of judgment, even vis-a-vis theology and dominant ideologies, and of the development and use of adequate analytical tools. The historical-critical approach, guaranteed by the relative independence of the university context, can be seen as a continuation of the secular instance. Thanks to this, biblical hermeneutics ceased to be "sacred hermeneutics" and became hermeneutics *tout court*[7] and from a scientific viewpoint the "sacred" text ceased to be sacred. The results gathered as a consequence of this methodological turn are an extraordinary achievement that cannot be ignored.[8]

b) We must emphasize, however, the unfinished nature of this process, which is the object of my critique: the claims of neutrality, which determine the isolation of the discipline, turn it into the victim of confessional demands. The exegete, one could say, is both too far from and too close to his object. To the most radical and simple questions ("What happened?" "What does it mean?" "How does it connect to all the rest?"), he is not able to give or fears giving answers. I believe that the preceding proposals concerning reading and wisdom will make the meaning of these critiques clear.

---

peoples is denied. We see no relation between father and son, still less between brothers, rather a polar opposition, like that of flesh and spirit, begotten and unbegotten. Luther, when the fracture (*confractio*) occurs, opposes these things with all his weight and all the materiality of his language (alongside which only Rabelais can stand comparison). Although we can also charge him with incoherence (his mode of dealing with the Jews is a prime example), his insight remains crucial. He writes: 'their most spiritual moments, as they dream, are not only of the flesh, but also mightily impious' (WA 40, 2, 111 Dr). Impiety is not in the 'flesh', still less in the 'spirit' but in the travesty of carnal thoughts in the garb of spiritual thoughts" (p. 83).

7 Cf. Gadamer, *Truth and Method*, pp. 153 ff.
8 Cf. H.-J. Kraus, *Geschichte der historisch-kritischen Erforschung des Alten Testaments* (Neukirchen-Vluyn: Neukirchener Verlag, 1969); W.G. Kümmel, *Das Neue Testament. Geschichte der Erforschung seiner Probleme* (Freiburg-München: Karl Alber, 1970).

VII

Human Rights and Nature

The idea of a universality of human rights does not presuppose a definite and constant conception of human nature, but rather an idea of nature as a tendentially universal capacity to share the other's need and suffering (in different traditions: "humanity", "tender mercies", in the Declaration of Human Rights, 1948: "reason and conscience"

1. Human Nature and the Declaration of Human Rights.

a) I must now return to my reflections on universality (Thesis II, d), where I maintained a position which has also been of great ethical and juridical importance. The question here is about the possibility of pursuing ideas, hypotheses, hopes and universal practices while at the same time remaining aware of the extraordinary complexity of the theoretical and historical contradictions. The first step towards a culture of human rights, which could provide a solid basis for current practice, is the critique of one's own culture and the awareness of cultures different from one's own. It is difficult, perhaps impossible, to step outside one's own culture. But in our contacts with other cultures we should give the highest priority to those elements in our culture which lend themselves to an interpretation which goes in a universalizing direction. This interpretive process is based on the premiss that particularity and universality are not in conflict, but rather that they suggest a tendential, unexpressed and never fully expressible universality.

b) It is true that the concept of nature is not formally indispensable to the idea of human rights. The term itself was expunged from the final version of the Universal Declaration of Human Rights. The history of this declaration is interesting[1] because it allows us to reject the idea of the

---

[1] The debate can be recontructed through A. Verdoodt , *Naissance et signification de la déclaration universelle des droit de l'homme*, pref. by R. Cassin (Louvain-Paris: Naunelaerts). See my "Idea di 'natura umana' e sentimento dell'altro. Una lettura

ethnocentric character of the document. The first version stated:"All men are brothers. As human beings with the gift of reason and members of a single family, they are free and equal in dignity and rights". Alongside the idea of rationality, the Chinese delegate, P. Chang, attempted to add the "feeling that exist other men". This was translated as "who by nature are endowed with reason and conscience". Chang first opposed the entire formulation (which was defended by the Lebanese delegate Malik), then (with Cart de Wiart from Belgium, who wanted to avoid metaphysical discussions) he also opposed the attempt to introduce the term "nature". Finally, he accepted everything except the term "nature", saying that this article could be accepted by everyone, as long as it was understood in the light of eighteenth century philosophy, which was the basis of the different declarations of human rights, with its idea of the basic perfectibilty of man. Bogomolov, the delegate from the Soviet Union, opposed the whole of Article 1. He drew attention to the useless rhetoric of sentences taken both from "materialistic philosophies of the eighteenth century and the Gospel". Article 1 was approved with 26 in favour and 8 abstentions, all from socialist countries. The final version of the text reads thus: "All human beings are born free and equal in dignity and rights. They are endowed with reason and conscience and should act towards one another in a spirit of brotherhood".

c) Many voices, cultures and countries took part in the elaboration of this text. "The Universal Declaration – writes Cassese – is the result of several ideologies; the meeting point into which different conceptions of man and society converge... It is not simply the world-wide 'magnification' of national texts, but the 'adaptation' of those texts to a multi-cultural, deeply heterogeneous, divided world". Secondly, it must be remarked that the term "nature" no longer appears in the final version. To quote Cassese again, "the Declaration must speak to billions of people belonging to different religions, cultures, social traditions and political institutions. Only a very simple language, devoid of religious and philosophical echoes, could address to so different, often dissonant peoples".[2]

---

interculturale dell'art. 1 della 'Dichiarazione dei diritti dell'uomo' (1948)", *Democrazia e diritto*, 1 (1993). This paper was presented at the seminar on "Fondéments universels ou fondéments culturels des droits de l'homme?", Bologna, May 1991, with the Department of Politics of the Universities of Bologna and Tunis.

2 A. Cassese, *I diritti umani nel mondo contemporaneo* (Bari: Laterza, 1988) p. 41. While understanding his human reason, I do not agree with some of the positions expressed by Sami A. Aldeeb Abu-Sahlieh, "Dialogue conflictuel sur les droits de l'homme entre Occident et Islam", *Islamochristiana* 17 (1991) pp. 43-82, especially pp. 58 f.: "La Déclaration universalle de l'ONU comme expression de la conception occidentale des droits de l'homme".

d) From this point of view, the disappearance of "nature" in the final version after such a wide discussion is extremely significant. This final version simply reflects the success in the West of a strong critical attitude towards the concept of nature, the product of several factors: of the crisis (Machiavelli, Hobbes) of the stoic-christian conception of natural law; of cultural relativism, from M. de Montaigne up to cultural anthropology;[3] and of historicism, from its romantic origins up to Max Weber, with its conception of non-repeatable and non-comparable individualities by which history is made. Gramsci's reflections are very clear and characteristic:

> The fundamental novelty introduced by the philosophy of praxis into the science of politics and of history is the demonstration that an abstract, fixed, immutable "human nature" does not exist (as a concept coming from religious and transcendental thought), and that human nature is the complex of social, historically determined relations, that is a historical fact that can be ascertained, within certain limits, by philological and critical methods.[4]

Finally, in this suspicious attitude towards "nature" one can see concern over its more or less recent history: racism. But nevertheless the problem of nature continues to pose itself in connection with the urgent question about the fundamental and the universal character of human rights.[5]

e) Norberto Bobbio, in his 1964 essay, summarizes very well all the arguments against an absolute foundation of human rights, and concludes: "the basic problem about human rights is not that of *justifying them*, but of *protecting* them. It is not a philosophical, but a political problem".[6] I reject here the temptation to apply to this sentence the irony of Leo Strauss about the neutrality of science according to Max Weber. I would suggest rather that the influence of Giacomo Leopardi, and in a more general way that of Kant, can be see in Norberto Bobbio's comments. Thus the notion of nature, as the foundation of human rights, would be a sort of postulate of practical reason: something that cannot be justified, but finds however in praxis and in life its truth and evidence. This attitude is at the same time both noble and tragic, in its voluntaristic deontologism.

---

3. T. Todorov, *Nous et les autres. La réflexion française sur la diversité humaine* (Paris: Ed. du Seuil, 1989).
4. *Note sul Machiavelli*, pp. 8 f.; cf. *Il materialismo storico e la filosofia di B. Croce*, pp. 31 f.; 34 f.; *Passato e presente*, pp. 200-204.
5. In support of this idea, cf. P. Rossi, "Gli storici e la natura umana", cit.
6. *Sul fondamento dei diritti dell'uomo*, *L'età dei diritti* (Torino: Einaudi, 1990) p. 16.

2. Human Nature and the Suffering of Others

a) My comments on universality and the idea of nature (Thesis II, d) can help to root this idea in the objectivity of human emotions and needs. These comments moved from C. Ginzburg and through Lévi-Strauss and others before arriving at Rousseau, with his idea of "pity" as the most primary human instinct: "Nous ne souffrons qu'autant que nous jugeons qu'il souffre; ce n'est pas dans nous, c'est dans lui que nous souffrons". We could summarize this perspective by saying that human nature, rather than being an objective entity which derives from a complete and definitive anthropological inventory, appears as the tendentially universal attitude to share other men's suffering and needs.

b) When Professor Chang, rejecting the word "nature" and any reference to God the creator, explained at length to the U.N. assembly that Article 1 could be accepted by everybody when understood in the light of the philosophy of the 18th century, based on "man's fundamental goodness",[7] he probably did not have in mind a specific human model expressed by this philosophy, but rather its positive anthropological inspiration. He had in mind Rousseau's pity, what Montesquieu called "bienveillance générale", saying of it that "rien n'est plus près de la Providence" (nothing is nearer to Providence).[8] All this is very close to Confucianism. And it was precisely Confucianism that inspired one of Prof. Chang's first interventions. Commenting on the text of Article 1 (which was at that time: "all men are brothers, being endowed with reason and members of one family...") he proposed to add – I am quoting from the proceedings of July 17th, 1948 – "to the idea of 'reason', the idea which in a literal translation from the Chinese would be 'two-men-mindedness'. The English equivalent might be 'sympathy' or 'consciousness of his fellow men'. This new idea... might well be included as an essential human attribute". The chairman, Eleanor Roosevelt, proposed "Being endowed with reason, they must have the additional sense of understanding their fellow men about them". But she herself was not convinced ("she felt that the wording of this would need revision"),[9] and the final version expressed this idea simply by adding "conscience" to "reason".

---

[7] Verdoodt, *Naissance*, pp. 83 f.
[8] *Oeuvres complètes* (Paris: Pléiade, 1949) I, p. 1285.
[9] *United Nations Documents*, Part 6 D, n.1, E/CN4/AC 4/S. 8.

3. "Humanity"

a) Thus the Chinese notion underlying "conscience" is certainly *ren*, "benevolence", or "humanity". Certainly Prof. Chang was thinking of a famous passage by Mencius:

> No man is devoid of a heart sensitive to the suffering of others. [10] Such a sensitive heart was possessed by the Former Kings and this manifested itself in a compassionate government. With such a sensitive heart behind compassionate government, it was as easy to rule the Empire as rolling it on your palm. My reason for saying that no man is devoid of a heart sensitive to the suffering of others is this. Suppose a man were, all of a sudden, to see a young child on the verge of falling into a well. He would certainly be moved to compassion, not because he wished to win the praise of his fellow villagers or friends, nor yet because he disliked the cry of the child. From this it can be seen that whoever is devoid of the heart of shame is not human, whoever is devoid of the heart of courtesy and modesty is not human, and whoever is devoid of the heart of right and wrong is not human. The heart of compassion is the germ of benevolence;[11] the heart of shame, of dutyfulness; the heart of courtesy and modesty, of observance of the rites; the heart of right and wrong, of wisdom. [12] For a man possessing these four germs to deny his own potentialities is for him to cripple himself; for him to deny the potentialities of his prince is for him to cripple his prince.

Thus, in the context of the Declaration, conscience, rather than Paul's and Seneca's *sydeidesis* (as the voice of the internal court)[13] is the perception of others, a feeling which is not opposed to rational virtue, but on the contrary forms its emotional basis, a "germ" objectively present in every man as a man; a germ which reason must cultivate.

b) Mencius and Rousseau. In 1943, the sinologist Ernest Richard Hughes published an interesting little book, devoted to two Confucian Classics, *The Great Learning and The Mean-in-Action*. Its introduction is rich, lively and emotional: the author is conscious of the terrible split European culture has to face, between the German spirit and the European Enlightenment, and emphasizes the links between the latter and Chinese thought. He writes:

---

[10] The feeling of humanity *ren zhi xin* expresses itself in *bu ren* "not to bear the suffering of the other". I must here thank Maurizio Scarpari, for his useful suggestion concerning the translation of Chinese classical texts.

[11] Prof. Chang translates here *ren* (feeling of humanity) with "two-men-mindedness" because in current etymology this character is explained as formed by the character "man" with the numerical sign of "two".

[12] Benvolence, *ren*; duty, *yi*; the observance of the rites, *li* and wisdom, *zhi*, are the four Confucian virtues.

[13] Cf. M. Pohlenz, *Stoicism* (New York, 1987) on Seneca.

There is a striking coincidence between Mencius' view and Rousseau's. Not only is man credited with this instinct and aptitude for goodness apart from reason, but Rousseau's main argument is the one which Mencius has used as his main argument. It is that man cannot bear to see his fellowmen suffering or in danger. Reason may, on reflection, reveal incentives of self-interest for helping, but the impulse comes first.[14]

There is also a surprising coincidence between Hughes' book and Chang's intervention, especially when the latter, against the Soviet delegate's pretended realism, defends the realism of his own attitude: it is this positive aspect that makes up what is most real in man.[15] Had Chang read Hughes' book? I leave the question open. But one of the results of my reading is that we can now see better   not   only   the original meaning of the word "conscience" in Article 1, but also the possible link with "reason", as the faculty that develops the germs, the emotional positive elements which are present in everybody.

c) Here one must recall John Locke of course, who, at the beginning of the first of his *Letters concerning Toleration* (1689, 1690 and 1692), indicates the essence of Christianity as "charity", "meekness", "good will" (in the Latin version, *Epistula de tolerantia, charitas, mansuetudo, benevolentia*) and not in its dogmatic content (he quotes Paul, 1 Cor. 13: "but without love, I am nothing"). It is not an exaggeration to maintain that this represents a third interpretation of Christianity, after medieval Catholicism and after the Reformation, an interpretation that opened the way precisely to tolerance.

d) I would like to quote, in the same direction, a passage from a lesser known author, the American Quaker John Woolman (1720-1772). In his *Journal* he tells of his slaughter of some robin nestlings, after having killed the mother which tried to defend them "in a sportive way". He becomes aware of how cruel he has been, remembering the Bible: "The tender mercies of the wicked are cruel" (Prov. 12:10), and meditates:

---

14 *The Great Learning and The Mean-in-Action* (New York, 1943, repr. 1979), pp. 25 f. Hughes did not accept J. Maritain, *Trois réformateurs: Luther, Descartes et Rousseau*. J. Maritain, the neo-thomist philosopher,who played an important role in the elaboration of human rights in the nineteen forties, spoke in favour of natural law in his *Les droits de l'homme et la loi naturelle* (New York, 1942).

15 "Le réalisme – P.C. Chang declared – s'applique à ce qui est vraiment réel, à ce qu'on peut affirmer avec toute la force de son âme", Verdoodt, *La naissance*, p. 83.

> Thus he whose tender mercies are over all his works hath placed a
> principle in the human mind which incites to exercise goodness toward
> every living creature; and this being singly attended to, people become
> tender-hearted and sympathising, but being frequently and totally rejected,
> the mind shuts itself up in contrary disposition.[16]

4. "Mercy"

a) This is the same attitude and the same way of arguing that we have
found, in prof. Chang, Mencius and Locke, but a new word appears here,
alongside the ancient "sympathising" (stoic in origin): the archaic, very fine
"tender mercies". This term comes from *rahame hesed* (or vice-versa *hasde
rahamim*), which becomes in the New Testament Greek *splanchna oiktirmoi*,
or *splanchna eleous*, with the corresponding verb *splanchnizein* (adj.
eusplanchnos),[17] and in Latin *viscera misericordiae*, "misericordieuse tendresse"
(Bible de Jérusalem) and precisely in English *tender mercies* and *tenderness*.
The root RHM – the kind of love which moves "from above downwards"[18]
– is common to Semitic languages. It is easy to see here the context in which
we must place *ar-rahmân ar-rahîm*, "the Compassionate, the Merciful", in
the *basmala* opening the Suras of the Coran. "Mercy" is, alongside science,
the most essential attribute of God: with them both, he "embraces
everything" (S. 40:7). One prays "to enter into His mercies, the most merciful
among merciful ones" (S. 7:150).

b) The origin of all these words lies in the root which indicates the
womb (*rihm, raham*, in the Coran we find the plural *arhâm*). All these terms
evoke the powerful stream of emotions which constantly ties the generating
to the generated, a stream which expresses itself in continual donation: from
generation to the transmission of an even more necessary wisdom, to
forgiveness after transgression, to pity for suffering and death, and after
death.

I am thinking of Mohammed's own experience, according to S. 93, *Ad-
duha*: he who was an orphan, poor, and guideless, has received shelter, a
guide, and abundance of good (and is therefore asked to act likewise: *wa 'amma
bini'mati rabbika fahaddith*). One could even look at the "tender mercies" as

---

[16] *The Journal and Major Essays of John Woolman*, ed. by Ph. P. Moulton (New York: Oxford University Press) pp. 24 f.

[17] Cf. *Theol. Wört.z.N.Test.* 7, p. 522 (H. Köster).

[18] Studied by G. Schuttermayr, *Biblica* 51 (1970) pp. 499-525: in the O.T. this root indicates love "from above downwards" *(von oben nach unten)*. Cf. also *rehem* in *Theol. Wört.z. A. Test.* 7 (190) (Kronholm).

the drive which corresponds, from the parental point of view, to the child's desire (Thesis IV), in a sort of circularity between desire and compassion.

c) However, I would also like to emphasize how all this may be useful in understanding the link Article 1 of the Declaration establishes between the fact that human beings are endowed with "reason and conscience" and its consequence: that "they should act towards one another in a spirit of brotherhood". If in "conscience" we see the internal court, where reason verifies the application of norms to concrete situations, then it will be difficult to see the correspondence between this conscience and "brotherhood". This is much easier if we understand by "conscience" the feeling that other men exist, and a fundamental emotion that "reason" corroborates and amplifies: an emotion which has its roots in the sense of a common origin from the same bosom, and in the aptitude to share and reproduce in oneself the maternal (parental) feeling, before the other ("he must have a mother, too"). I would like to evoke two images, both crucial to the Western tradition. The first one is Antigone, who in Sophocles' tragedy claims to bury her brother, because she wants "to honour those who come from the same womb" (*homosplanchnous*) (v. 511). The second is the *Stabat mater*, the medieval sequence (maybe with G.B. Pergolesi's fascinating music), which is a contemplation-appropriation of the mother's suffering "Quis est homo qui non fleret / matrem Christi si videret / in tanto supplicio?" ("Who is the man who would not cry, seeing Christ's mother, in such an affliction?").

d) Art. 10 of the "Declaration of Human Rights in Islam" maintains that "Islam is the natural religion of mankind". The Coran S. 30:30 is certainly behind this affirmation: "Turn to religion (*dîn*), as a *hanîf*, the *fitra*, in which He created (*fatara*) mankind. No change in God's creation (*khalq*). It is the unchangeable (*qayyim*) religion (*dîn*), but most of men do not know it". The famous hadith: "every child is born in the *fitra* ('*ala-l-fitra*), his parents make of him a Jew or a Christian or a Pagan (*majusiyyun*)" must be linked to this *Sura* 30:30.[19] The notion of nature (*fitra*) is here evidently a theological one: man is dealt with here in connection with God's plan ("on God's plan", "selon le plan de Dieu" is D.B. Macdonald's translation of '*ala-l-fitra*, in

---

[19] Cf. M. Talbi, "Liberté religieuse et transmission de la foi", *Islamochristiana* 12 (1986), the long footnote n. 19, pp. 39-41. M. Talbi, on the basis of the root *ftr*, proposes to see in human *fitra* "sa specificité, sa nature singulière et originelle qui, en vertu de l'acte créateur, par une sorte de clivage et de rupture, le fit émerger du flot du vivant et rendit apte à porter l'*amana*" (p. 40). I thank Mohammad Kerrou for some important suggestions on this.

Encycl. de l'Islam).

Thus, as a creature and according to God's plan every man is appointed to Islam. This idea could be compared to the idea of "nature" in Christian theology: it is the condition of man who needs God's grace in order to be saved or even to reach full natural perfection. (I simplify here a very complicated history, full of unresolved controversies, parallel to the problems posed to Islam by the famous *hadith*). One can easily see how the notion of "nature" in the Islamic Declaration is vulnerable, being liable to a criticism corresponding to the one which led to the expulsion of the idea of nature in the Western declaration of human rights. This is the reason why I emphasized that such a term is a novelty in such a literary genre.

e) I would like now to pose two naive questions with regard to the definition of Islam as the religion of human nature. The first question, a very simple one, concerns the possibility of reading Article 10 of the Islamic Declaration (and the corresponding *hadith*) with this limitation: "in a context of Islamic culture". The second question refers to the possibility of reading the Coran, S. 30:30 seeing in the *fitra*, the religion of the creature, something that is more profound and simpler than all historical realities: something that is carried out each time *rahmata 'llah* is drawn into practice by women and men of good will.

5. "Reason and Conscience"

a) In conclusion, the 1948 Declaration is not based on an Aristotelian (man as a "rational animal") or Cartesian (the *cogito*) view of human nature. The formula "endowed with reason and conscience" must not be understood in this sense, but rather as the effective and affective foundation of the duty of "acting in the spirit of brotherhood", a duty which in turn is founded on the perception of our common origin.[20] One should understand this part of Art. 1 as a sort of reference, in a secularised and somewhat coded way, to the great ethical-religious traditions, through the mediation of Enlightened philosophical universalism.

b) The first part of this article – "All human beings are born free and equal in dignity and rights" – should be seen as the modern affirmation of the subject as a separate, autonomous individual, with a sort of tension between the evocation of ancient solidarity and the affirmation of modern

---

[20] *Physis,* one could say, not in the sense of "substance", but in the sense of Heraclytus, of "Nature who loves to hide herself" (*kryptesthai filei,* fr.123).

individuality. This tension must be resolved through interpretation, placing this affirmation in the context of that evocation, but also remembering that precisely the fact of having re-interpreted the ancient ethical-religious conception in terms of "benevolence" (Locke) allowed the 18th century to recognise equality and the rights to life, freedom, and the pursuit of happiness as self-evident truth (as in the American Declaration), and that allows us now to affirm (according to the model of the French Declaration) that "all human beings are born free and equal in dignity and rights".

VIII

Ethical Consensus

In the difficult present circumstances our task is not theological. Rather, it is to overcome the separation between ethics and politics and to contribute to the elaboration of an ethics that offers a consensual and tendentially universalistic base to the irrevocable modern culture of rights, and is the meeting point at which the plurality of traditions, taken over critically, converge in a group of fundamental convictions.

1. The Task not Theological

a) The difficult historical moment – the widespread ethical-cultural sense of non-belonging and the often extreme clash between cultural and religious blocks – makes it essential and urgent to work in the direction of a common ethical construct. My standpoint is "secular", and in its foreground is placed not ecumenism, or the reform of the churches, or a theological approach, but ethical consensus, in which Jewish-Christian culture must necessarily take on an essential role. This position is not the result, however, of any indifference toward ecclesiological and theological traditions. It comes rather from the need to turn away from the evolution of theology in the twentieth century. It is true that this theological period is one characterized by great authors and great works to which we of course owe much: K. Barth and his *History of Protestant Theology in the Nineteenth Century*, the thomism of E. Gilson, the patristic Catholic rebirth with H. de Lubac and H. von Balthasar, and G. Florovskij and his *Ways of Russian Theology*. It is also the period, if we want to pursue the parallel with the elaboration of Jewish thought, of F. Rosenzweig and G. Scholem. However, this period is also characterized by violent polemics, the derision and even the condemnation of the previous generation and its attempts at rational, "progressive", "liberal", "modernist" interpretations of Christianity, and by an insistence on the values of religious affiliation and on the recovery of this affiliation as the enabling condition for every possible discourse or presence in the world. This age began with the First World War and has lasted right up the present. The crisis in ex-Communist Europe and the arrival of the North/South conflict on the geopolitical stage have resulted and will increasingly result in the rejection of any attempt at "theological modernization".

b) The first step is to take up once again the threads of the great historical-religious culture of the eighteenth and nineteenth centuries. These are discourses which have been so severely condemned that even today it is difficult to go back to speaking of them with any real attention to their content. Dietrich Bonhoeffer[1] had already deplored this breakdown when he correlated the critique of "the positivism of revelation" to the search for and expectation of a new non-religious language for an "adult world": "Karl Barth and the Confessing Church have encouraged us to entrench ourselves persistently behind the 'faith of the Church', and evade the honest question as to what we ourselves really believe".[2] Bonhoeffer thought it necessary to reconsider the role of liberal theology, whose strength (he had in mind here especially Ernst Troeltsch) had been not to try to roll back history, but to have actually accepted the challenge of modernity, even if this ended in its defeat.

c) In other words, "he who begins loving Christianity more than truth, will love his sect or church more than Christianity and will end by loving himself more than any other": these lines from Coleridge, re-used by Tolstoy as an epigraph and repeated in his conclusion to his *Reply to the Synod* in 1901, form a text which expresses, I believe, the basic attitude that we need to take, beginning with the examples of courage that come from the past.

2. Beyond the Separation of Ethics and Politics

The purity of heart, as well as wisdom, law, justice and the love of which the Scripture speaks, concern whole and undivided man.[3] All of the above

---

[1] "I have been very impressed by Harnack's history of the Prussian Academy; it has made me feel both happy and unhappy. There are so few people now who want to have any intimate spiritual association with the eighteenth and nineteenth centuries [...] I believe that people will one day be quite amazed by what was achieved in that period, which is now so disregarded and so little known", D. Bonhoeffer, *Letters and Papers from Prison*, ed. by E. Bethge (New York: Macmillan, 1972) p. 300.

[2] *Ib.*, p. 210.

[3] Martin Buber considers that "the final scene in the tragedy of Moses, like those which had preceded it, derives from the resistance of the human material. Moses wished for an entire, undivided human life, as the right answer to the Divine revelation. But splitting up is the historical way of mankind, and the unsplit

concerns the totality of his relationships, including political ones. The separation of politics, ethics and religion constituted and still constitutes a necessary demand, where ethics is of a confessional and heteronomous kind. In this case the affirmation of the autonomy of politics from ethics was and still is necessary. Such a demand has also been taken over – in the form of the split between the "temporal" and "spiritual" – by the political projects of a moderate religious origin. But the negative results of this separation are clear to all. The result has been a pessimistic and resigned attitude that has admitted and admits that hypocrisy, non-truth, corruption, coercion and violence, in all forms can cohabit with politics. On the other hand, the first victories of modern democracy in Protestant England and North America (as well as France), freedom of conscience, political equality, the right to happiness, the ideal of brotherhood, are secular in their original and fundamental expressions – and therefore also interiorize and universalize – ethical-religious contents. Our task, however, is to bring into politics an ethics that maintains the essential and radical kernel of the religious tradition, but which drastically reduces the heteronomous ways in which traditional ethics, with its deference to authorities external to conscience, has presented itself. From this point of view, the absence of the Protestant experience in Catholic countries is very serious and still today not easily remedied.

3. The Basis of the Modern Culture of Rights

a) The modern culture of rights, which is basically what democracy is about, is made up of inalienable formal and substantive elements. It is this very complexity which constitutes a fixed and irremovable part of modern culture, of praxis and of political struggle and represents a definitive contribution coming from the culture of the socialist movement. Marxist culture, in fact, is characterized by the polemical demand for the necessity of a substantial economic and social emancipation against the formal proclamation of the rights of man and citizens. The constitutional elaboration of the post-World War Two period, as in the case of Italy, or the Universal Declaration of Human Rights (1948), brought together civil and political rights (rights of the "first generation": American and French revolutions), economic and social rights ("second generation": the socialist movement), while other rights, connected to peace, the environment, and animals ("third generation") have also appeared on the scene.

b) Nevertheless, to refer to the irrevocable values of the culture of rights, although an obligatory first step, is not enough to ensure they are protected. A culture of rights cannot on its own support all aspects of action and human and political cohabitation, and cannot take the place of public or private ethics. Here I put forward the hypothesis of a collective ethical project in which the plurality of traditions, including Jewish and Jewish-Christian traditions, are taken over critically and form the basis of a pool of fundamental convictions, on which agreement has been reached (even if inevitable contrasts and conflicts remain). The idea I am proposing, then, is a consensus based not only on a number of essential juridical propositions, as in the 1948 Universal Declaration of Human Rights, but on an open and pluralistic set of propositions, or rather of essential ethical perceptions, which are the expression of a new "intellectual-moral block". My reference to this kind of terminology suggests a certain analogy with Gramsci. My task must be faced in a different manner: on non-historicist presuppositions, in a multi-cultural context and with a universalistic tension that takes on consensus as its foundation and which aims to increase and elaborate this consensus, I repeat, around the fundamental ethical convictions that so much of humanity has posited and continues to posit as the basis of social life. What are these fundamental ethical convictions?

4. Ethics of Fundamental Convictions

a) The certainty that rights cannot be guaranteed unless we feel an obligation toward every human being;[4] the recognition of privilege and

---

person cannot do anything more than raise man to a higher level on which he may thereafter follow his course, as long as he is bound by the law of history": *Moses. The Revelation and the Covenant* (New York: Harper and Row, 1958) p. 199.

4 See the first page of S. Weil's *The Need for Roots*, trans. by A. Wills (New York: G.P. Putnam's Sons, 1952). About the necessity of a Declaration of Human Rights, Gandhi declared: "I learned from my illiterate, but wise, mother that all rights to be deserved and preserved came from a duty to be done. The very right to live accrues to us only when we do the duty of the citizenship of the world. From this one fundamental statement perhaps it is easy enough to define the duties of man and woman and correlate every right to some corresponding duty to be performed. Every other right can be shown to be a usurpation hardly worth fighting for": "Letter to Julian Huxley" (October 1947), in *The Collected Works of Mahatma Gandhi*, lxxxxix (The Publications Division, Ministry of Information and Broadcasting, Government of India, 1983), pp. 346 f. Some reflection should be devoted to the fact of the disappearance in Italy of the Mazzinian tradition, for which Gandhi felt much sympathy, and which precisely emphasized the role of the "duties of man".

honor to the weak;[5] the superiority of those who do not respond to evil with evil,[6] but with the persuasive force of the undefended word;[7] the value of acting according to conscience[8] regardless of the results;[9] the idea that one must be able to govern oneself and one's home before being able to govern others;[10] respect and pity toward every living being;[11] life gained by losing it;[12] the idea that the greatest war is against ourselves;[13] existence understood

---

5　Besides the "Sermon of the mount", see Mt. 11:25-27: "I thank thee, Father, Lord of heaven and earth, that thou hast hidden these things from the wise and understanding and revealed them to babes". But see also some more "naturalistic" affirmations of the *Tao Te Ching*: the wise man is like a baby, is muddled, puts his person last: that is the reason why he comes first.

6　One must remember here the servant of God in Is. 53: "He was oppressed, and he was afflicted, yet he opened not his mouth..." etc. The non resistance to evil by doing evil (Mt. 5:39) is the starting point of the tolstoyan rediscovery of Christianity. See my already quoted *Tolstoj, oltre la letteratura*. Tolstoy, in his *The Kingdom of God is Within You*, recalls the preceding traditions of Christian non resistance, starting from Quakerism.

7　Especially Socrates, see for example the *Apology*. "Persuasion" is Aldo Capitini's key word in his *Elementi di un'esperienza religiosa*, 1937 and in many other works. But see again the servant of God in Is. 42:1-4: "Behold my servant, whom I uphold, my chosen, in whom my soul delights; I have put my spirit upon him, he will bring forth justice to the nations. He will not cry or lift up his voice, or make it heard in the street; a bruised reed he will not break, and a dimly burning wick he will not quench; he will faithfully bring forth justice. He will not fail or be discouraged till he has established justice in the earth; and the coastlands wait for his law". The songs of the servant of God indicate the methodology of the affirmation of the Law. S. Weil often insists on the fact that "Eros does not use or undergo violence" (*Simp.* 196c). An undefended attitude is at the center of Gandhi's personality, see E. Erikson, *Gandhi's truth. On the Origins of Militant Non-Violence* (New York, 1969).

8　This is a theme of hellenistic philosophy, and essential to Jesus' preaching (do not act in order to be seen by men: the Father sees "in the secret", Mt. 5).

9　This is a Gandhian theme, connected with *Bhagavadgita* and with *karmayoga*, "the discipline of action" which consists in acting by renouncing the criterion of consensus and success (which does not mean action without purpose).

10　An ancient and – it may really be said – universal idea: see the Confucian (*The Great Learning*), Greco-Roman (Marcus Aurelius) and Biblical tradition .

11　Buddhist theme, reproposed by Albert Schweitzer (the "reverence for life"). See also C. Lévi-Strauss, recently in his *The View from Afar*, quoted.

12　"He shall see his offspring, he shall prolong his days; the will of the Lord shall prosper in his hand; he shall see the fruit of the travail of his soul and be satisfied" (Is. 53:10 f.). See also Gandhi's teaching on sacrifice, commenting on *Bhagavadgita* III.

13　To be found in Islamic spiritual interpretation of the *jihad*.

as a sum of benefits which must be paid back;[14] the life one gains when life is lost; the tranquillity and peace which come from the certainty of a justice that is not tied to history.[15] These and many others are some of the ancient, deep convictions that a great part, the best part of humanity has laid at the basis of their living in society, has expressed in an extraordinary variety of inter-connected popular cultures, and has transmitted, above all through the wisdom of woman, into the present. Recently reproposed by masters such as Weil, Schweitzer, Gandhi, Tolstoy and others, these convictions stand before us as an instruction necessary for human life, for human survival.

b) With these last few remarks, which serve purely as examples and suggestions of a perceptible but yet to be created moral atmosphere, I conclude my own journey towards a secular reading of the Bible. It will be clear by now that it began by following some of Bonhoeffer's general indications and by emphasizing the more specific ones concerning the necessity to recover a culture that has been abandoned by the theological turn that accompanied the First World War. This means that many opinions on "liberal theology", "rationalism", "ethical reduction", and also "religion" have to be turned upside down. What has already been achieved in this direction is due above all to L. Tolstoy (but thanks also to an impulse which paradoxically was not absent from the theological humanism of Barth's last years). A synthesis, directed toward and by praxis, beginning with the biblical tradition and expanding to join with other traditions, has gradually begun to take shape. At its center is the idea of wisdom, as an intercultural connective tissue and fundamental anthropological category. All this remains, however, for the moment, an aim and a project. To have put forward such positions would have been presumptuous had it not been for the need to verify with others the validity of the results and to call for collaboration in the elaboration of concrete tasks, which may emerge from these pages.

c) A passage from the beginning of *The Need for Roots* by Simon Weil puts it best. Suffering, dying one could say, of the serious deprivations to which she subjected herself, she writes of the problem of how to "root a people": what culture, what ethics could France have when it finally emerged from the ruins, above all the moral ruin, of the Second World War. A declaration

---

[14] See *Sura* 93:9-11 of the Coran "Did he [God] not find you an orphan and give you shelter? and find you going astray and give you guidance? and find you poor and bestowed richness on you? Then oppress not the orphan and chide not him who asks, and keep proclaiming the bounty of the Lord".

[15] This is the essence of S. Weil's criticism of Marxism, in the last period of her life.

of rights, Weil pointed out, would not be sufficient. The opening sentence of *The Need for Roots* is as follows: "The notion of obligations comes before that of rights, which is subordinate and relative to the former". She goes on: "An obligation which goes unrecognised by anybody loses none of the full force of its existence. A right which goes unrecognised by anybody is not worth very much... Rights are always to be related to certain conditions. Obligations alone remain independent of conditions. They belong to a realm situated above all conditions, because it is situated above this world".[16] There is a need to recover the idea of obligation toward human beings as such, beginning with concrete needs, first and foremost food. Weil points out that thousands of years ago the Egyptians thought that the soul could not be justified if he/she could not say: "I never starved anyone", which she compares with what... every Christian knows he shall one day hear from Christ: "I was hungry, and you gave me nothing to eat". This text helps us to sum up what has been said in the course of this work. Distinctions are here made between foundation, confirmation and the object of moral obligation. The unconditional absolute character of moral obligation corresponds to the concreteness of its object (in fact it is inversely proportional to it). The concreteness of the object emerges from the specificity and the anthropological, historical, and political determination of human needs, which form the content of all rights. And if a demonstration of this foundation is impossible, in its unconditioned purity and universality (because its truth can only be grasped in practical obedience) it is possible, nevertheless, to seek its confirmation in people's conscience.

d) It is in this direction that we must work, and it is on these grounds that we will be judged. Very effectively Simon Weil describes the scene of the final judgment according to Mt. 25 together with the psychostasis according to the Egyptian Book of the Dead. I take my leave of the reader with this scene. The dead man enters in to the presence of Osiris, accompanied by Anubi. His heart is placed on a scale. On the other scale lies truth, in the presence of Thot, the scribe. Pleading with his heart ("O heart of my mother! Do not bear witness against myself, do not accuse me in the court...") the dead man makes the confession, on which he is to be judged: "Here I am coming to you, and there is no fault in me, there is no ill, there is no accusation against me, there is no-one to whom I have done this. I live by truth, I know the truth... I gave bread to the hungry, water to the thirsty, clothes to the naked, a boat to him who was without it. Save me, protect me". Thot notes it all down.

---

[16] Trans. A. Wills, 1952, cf. D. McLellan, *Simone Weil. Utopian Pessimist* (London: Macmillan, 1991) p. 246.

II

AN IDEA OF READING

Maternal Images and Scripture
in Augustine's *Confessions*

1. In what was probably the summer of 383, disappointed by Faustus, the Manichaean bishop, and spurred on by his ambition to improve his professional position, and in particular to find a more qualified and disciplined audience for his teaching of rhetoric, the 29-year-old Augustine leaves Carthage. Deceiving his widowed mother, Monica, who "wildly clings" to him, he abandons her on the African shore. This is the apex of a conflict between the son and his mother that emerges in the *Confessions* in a large number of more or less overt charges: his parent's smile when he reported home on his teacher's blows during his childhood (I, 9, 15), his postponed baptism (I, 11, 18; V, 9 16) and even, perhaps rather hypocritically coming from Augustine, the fact of having deferred a marriage which could have prevented so much disorderliness in his life, all of this being due to his parents' ambition (II, 3, 6 f.). But Augustine's flight from Carthage is certainly the culminating point of this conflict. Let us read how he relates the facts, in the fifth book of his *Confessions*:

> But you knew, God, why I left Carthage and went to Rome, and of that you gave no hint either to me or to my mother, who was fearfully upset at my going and followed me, down to the sea. But as she vehemently held on to me calling me back or saying she would come with me, I deceived her. I pretended I had a friend I did not want to leave until the wind was right for him to sail. I lied to my mother – to such a mother – and I gave her the slip. Even this you forgave me, mercifully saving me from the waters of the sea, when I was full of abominable filth, so as to bring me to the water of your grace. This water was to wash me clean, and to dry the rivers flowing from my mother's eyes which daily before you irrigated the soil beneath her face.
> Nevertheless since she refused to return without me, with difficulty I persuaded her to stay that night in a place close to our ship, the memorial

At the basis of this essay is my "Figure materne e Scrittura in Agostino", *Annali di storia dell'esegesi* 9:2 (1992) pp. 387-420.

shrine to blessed Cyprian. But that night I secretly set out; she did not come, but remained praying and weeping. By her floods of tears what was she begging of you, my God, but that you would not allow me to sail? Yet in your deep counsel you heard the central point of her longing, though not granting her what she then asked, namely that you would make me what she continually prayed for. The wind blew and filled our sails and the shore was lost to our sight. There, when morning came, she was crazy with grief, and with recriminations and groans she filled your ears. But you paid no heed to her cries (V, 8, 14).[1]

Since Dodds'original suggestion,[2] increasing evidence has been presented to demonstrate that Augustine's narration contains many elements of the dramatic description in Virgil's Aeneid, of Aeneas abandoning Dido at Carthage. We are dealing here, evidently, with an interesting phenomenon of involuntary memory: Augustine, as is well known, repudiates the Virgilian model in the first book of his *Confessions*, where he reproaches his parents with the fact that the Bible was absent in his education whereas Virgil was given a very important role. This exercise was not only "smoke and wind" but also a sort of sacrifice to the fallen angel (I, 17, 27). But the emotions of the time in which Augustine was "forced to learn about the wandering of some Aeneas... and to weep over the death of a Dido who took her own life from love" (I, 13, 20-22) could not be completely cancelled and unmistakably reappear. The secret preparations for departure,[3] Dido's sufferings[4] and

---

[1] I use as a basis H. Chadwick's translation, Saint Augustine, *Confessions* (Oxford U.P., 1991) although in one or two cases I have left out some of the elaborations with which the translator explains or comments Augustine's thought.

[2] E.R. Dodds, "Augustine's ' Confessions': a Study of Spiritual Maladjustment", *The Hibbert Journal* in 1926-1927, pp. 459-473, now in *The Hunger of the Heart*, D. Capps and J. Dittes eds. (Purdue University, 1990) p. 46; Ch. Kligerman, "A Psychoanalytic Study of the Confessions of St. Augustine", *ib.*, pp. 95-108; M. Melchior, "The Teacher's Scrapbook. Two Loves that Built Two Cities", *The Classical Journal* 48 (1952) pp. 237-240; M. More O'Ferrall, "Monica, the Mother of Augustine. A Reconsideration", *Rech.aug.* 10 (1975) pp. 23-43; U. Mattioli, "Macrina e Monica. Temi del *bios* cristiano in due 'vite' di donna nel IV secolo", in *In verbis verum amare*, P. Serra Zanetti ed. (Firenze, 1980) pp. 165-203; C. Bennett, "The Conversion of Vergil", *Rev.et.aug.* 34 (1988) pp. 47-69, and especially A. Hunsaker Hawkins, "Archetypes of Conversion: The Autobiographies of Augustine, Bunyan, and Merton", in *The Hunger of the Heart* (Lewisburg, 1985) pp. 239-254. See my recent "Figure materne e Scrittura in Agostino", cit.

[3] "Arma parent, et quae rebus sit causa novandis, / dissimulent" (IV, pp. 289-291); "At regina dolos / quis fallere possit amantem?" (IV, p. 296); "Dissimulare etiam sperasti, perfide, tantum posse nefas tacitusque me decedere terra?" (pp. 305 f.).

[4] "Nox erat et placidum carpebant fessa soporem / corpora per terra" (pp. 322 f.); "At non infelix animi Phoenissa neque unquam / solvitur in somnos oculisve aut

Aeneas' flight with his fellows during the night,[5] the disappearing of the African shores and the fugitive's uninjured crossing of perilous waters,[6] Dido's mad desperation in the morning, when looking at the port from a high place she realized that Aeneas has gone,[7] her accusations of cruelty, weeping, lamentations and agonies,[8] Aeneas' inflexible firmness, notwithstanding his sorrow,[9] in holding on to a fate he had not chosen,[10] love as the fundamental motive of the whole incident, both Aeneas' (love for future homeland: "hic amor, hic patria est")[11] and Dido's ("ye wicked love, who compell mortals to such things", *improbe amor, quod non mortalia cogis Aen.* IV, 422), the prophecy that in some way the woman will follow her beloved:[12] all this, apart from clear literal parallels, forms the affective and symbolic texture that, coming from the Aeneid, underlies Augustine's *Confessions* as a subtext, at the moment in which he recalls his violent separation from his mother.

2. At this point Augustine inserts a meditation about his ambition (he is writing around the year 397), the reason for his separation from his mother, and, on the other hand, his mother's passionate clinging to him. Here Virgil's *Aeneid* disappears, and a new scene is evoked, from the third chapter of *Genesis*.

---

pectore noctem / accipit: ingeminant curae rursusque resurgens / saevit amor" (pp. 329-332).

5   "Solvite vela citi. Deus aethere missus ab alto / festinare fugam tortosque incidere funis / ecce iterum instimulat" (pp. 574-6).

6   "Litora deseruere" (p. 581) and *Aen.* V at the beginning.

7   "Et iam prima novo spargebat lumine terras [...] Regina e speculis ut primum albescere lucem / vidit et aequatis classem procedere velis / litoraque et vacuos sensit sine remige portus, / terque quaterque manu pectus percussa [...] Quid loquor aut ubi sum? quae mentem insania mutat? (pp. 584- 595).

8   "Lamentis gemituque et femineo ululatu / tecta fremunt, resonat magnis plangoribus aether" (pp. 667 f.).

9   We may recall "mens immota manet; lacrimae volvuntur inanes", well known to Augustine (p. 449). Cf. H. Hagendahl, *Augustin and Latin Classics*, I, (Goteborg, 1967) p. 423.

10   "Ille Iovis monitis immota tenebat / lumina et obnixus curam sub corde premebat" (pp. 331 f.).

11   "Se nunc Italiam magnam Gryneus Apollo, / Italiam Lyciae iussere sortes; / hic amor, haec patria est" (pp. 345-347).

12   "I, sequere Italiam ventis, pete regna per undas [...] Sequar [...] Omnibus umbra locis ero" (pp. 380 -386).

You were using my desires as a means towards putting an end to those desires, and the longing she felt for her own flesh and blood was justly chastised by the whip of sorrows. As mothers do, she loved to have me with her, but much more than most mothers; and she did not understand that you were to use my absence as a means of bringing her joy. She did not know that. So she wept and lamented, and these agonies proved that there survived in her the remnants of Eve, seeking with groaning for the child she had brought forth in sorrow. And yet after accusing me of deception and cruelty, she turned again to pray for me and to go back to her usual home. Meanwhile I came to Rome (V, 8, 15).

Augustine reflects on his own desires, *cupiditates* (Chadwick explains here: "ambitious" desires), which appear to drive him away from his mother, but in fact are the means by which God is freeing him from those passions. To these desires corresponds Monica's "carnal desire" (literally), her affection for her son, which according to Augustine exceeds most mothers' normal feelings towards their own sons.[13] Eve's image takes here the place of Dido's. "I will greatly multiply your sorrows and your wailing and in sorrows you shall bring forth your children; and your *desire shall be towards your man*, and he shall rule over you", this is the translation of the old Latin version of Gen. 3:6.[14] "Desire", lost by Jerome in his *Vulgate*, is, in the Latin version Augustine used, *conversio*, which corresponds to LXX *apostrophé*, hebr. *teshuqah*, which appear also in Gen. 4:17 and *Song* 7:11. Thus the roles of the mother and of the wife and, correspondingly, the roles of the son and of the husband appear here in some way considered under the same perspective. In Monica's affection for her son, says Augustine, "the remnants of Eve", reveal themselves. Eve's sin transmits itself to every woman, under the form of the sorrow in "bringing forth", and of an attraction towards the man (the husband, but also the son, according to Augustine) an attraction which has as its last, sad result the submission of the woman to the man. This "desire towards man", *conversio ad virum* (together with painful delivery) is for the women the specific form of that concupiscence which is, for Augustine, the general effect and manifestation of original guilt.

3. Monica returns quickly to everyday life, while Augustine, as soon as he arrives at Rome, where he stays as the guest of a Manichaean brother, is taken with a dangerous sickness, which brings him to the threshold of the underworld.

---

[13] *Carnale desiderium*, in 3 of the 4 occurrences of this expression according to the CETEDOC Library of Christian Texts, concerns precisely love towards sons.

[14] Cf. *De gen c. Manich.* II, 1, 2 with the complete text of the Latin version Augustine will continue to use up to the *City of God* (XV, 7).

At Rome my arrival was marked by the scourge of physical sickness, and I was on the way to the underworld, bearing all the evils I had committed against you, against myself, and against others – sins both numerous and serious, in addition to the chain of original sin by which "in Adam we all die" (V, 9, 16).

Recalling those moments, Aeneas' image vanishes (although a descent *ad inferos* belongs to *Aeneid* and Aeneas, too)[15] and Job appears for a moment (Augustine makes explicit reference to *Job* 7:9, and all its context is pertinent). But Adam's image prevails and the sickness is the "scourge" which, in perfect parallel with the "just scourge" which chastises Monica, hits Augustine-Adam.[16]

The appearance of the phrase "original sin" in Augustine's text, at this moment, is, I believe extremely significant. We are in about 397 and this is one of the earliest occurrences of this expression (if not the earliest, as Chadwick maintains, although I do not know on what basis). This passage must be compared with *De diversis quaestionibus ad Simplicianum*, which precedes the *Confessions* according to the *Retractationes*, and where "original sin" appears three times.[17] The first of these references, in particular, in *Ad Simplicianum* can be compared with our passage because of the presence not only of "original sin", but also of *cupiditas* and of the idea of personal sin as an "addition" to the original one. While *Ad Simplicianum* has been given an enormous deal of attention, our passage has not been given any importance

---

[15] "Sed pauci nostis in libris, multi in theatris, quia Aeneas descendit ad inferos, et ostendit illi pater suas animas romanorum magnorum venturas in corpora", *Serm.* 241, PL 38, 1135.

[16] L.C. Ferrari, "The boyhood beatings of Augustine", in *The Hunger of the heart*, rightly insists on the relevance of this aspect in Augustine's own education (but there is also here a well known Biblical theme).

[17] Saint Augustine, *Confessions*, cit., p. 82 ("This is the first occurence of this phrase..."). According to A. Sage, "Le peché originel. Naissance d'un dogme", *Rev.et.aug* 13 (1967) pp. 211-248, in *Ad Simplicianus* 10 f.: "pour la première fois apparait sous la plume d'Augustine l'expression de péché originel" (*ib.*, p. 219). I follow the chronology of, M.Pellegrino, *Le "Confessioni" di San t'Agostino*, Roma 1956, pp. 156 ff.

[18] This passage is not mentioned either by J. Gross, *Entstehungsgeschichte der Erbsündendogmas*, I (München-Basel, 1960), nor by Sage, "Le peché originel", cit., nor by P.F. Beatrice, *Tradux peccati. Alle fonti della dottrina origeniana del peccato originale* (Milano: Vita e Pensiero, 1978). But A. Mutzenbecher in his edition of *Ad Simplicianum* (CChr. 44) has correctly indicated the parallelism between *Conf.* V, 9,16 and *Ad Simpl.* 1, 1, 10.

at all by interpreters of Augustine and by historians of dogma.[18] It deserves much greater attention, as it offers some insight into the autobiographical substratum of Augustine's parallel theoretical formulations.

The expression, as it is used in Ad *Simplicianum*, turns on Rom. 7, and leads Augustine, as he explain in *Retractationes* (I, 23, 1) to the conclusion that the "I" of Rom. 7 may be the Apostle himself: such is the power of "concupiscence, most strong and unvanquished". In the *Confessions*, on the other hand, he looks at his own story: the passions, *cupiditates*, which brought his separation from his mother, Monica's immoderate affection and suffering, his own illness and the danger of death. He sees in all this the fullest, most explicit revelation, in his own past experience, and in his mother's closely related experience, of what he had just called "original sin" in his *Ad Simplicianum*. Thus behind his personal transgressions, "both numerous and serious", as well as Monica's carnal desire, there is, he thinks, the "chain of the original sin", which ties each man to Adam. This is why "we all die in Adam".[19]

4. It must be remarked that Augustine's major concern, at the time he is writing the *Confessions*, is not yet pelagianism, but still manichaeism. The text in fact continues, referring to Augustine's certain destination, the underworld:

> You had not yet forgiven me from the hostile disposition towards you which I had contracted by my sins. How could he deliver me from them if his cross was, as I had believed, a phantom? Insofar as the death of his flesh was in my opinion unreal, the death of my soul was real. And insofar as the death of his flesh was authentic, to that extent the life of my soul, which disbelieved that, was authentic. The fevers became worse, and I was on my way out and dying. If at that time I had died, where was I going but into the fire and to the torments which, by your true order of justice, my deeds deserved? (V, 9, 16).

At the time of his arrival at Rome Augustine was fully immersed in a dualistic way of thinking. He conceived of sin as the product of an alien power, as he himself explains a few lines further on: "I liked to excuse myself and to accuse some unidentifiable power which was with me and yet not I",

---

[19] 1 Cor. 15:22 is very frequently quoted by Augustine, and in this text "quo" may be an echo of Rom. 5:12, less frequent in Augustine, especially in this period. The first quotation of 1 Cor. 15:22 in Augustine seems to be in *De mor. eccl. cath.* 1, 19, 35, of the year 388, cf. A. Trapé, in *Patrologia*, A. Di Berardino ed., III (Casale M.: Marietti, 1978) pp. 411 f.

whilst he comments that "the whole was myself and what divided me against myself was my impiety" (V, 10, 18). At this point he conceives of the Saviour as an emanation from the dazzling body of light of God, and he thinks that a nature such as his could neither be born of the Virgin Mary without being mingled and defiled by the flesh (V, 10, 20), nor really die on a cross, reconciling humanity by one body (Eph. 2:16, echoed by the *Confessions* in our passage). In short, he cannot accept a symmetry between "in Adam" and "in Christ" or the possibility of separating oneself from the body of death of the first to adhere to the body of resurrection of the second, through baptism. Thus he is destined to certain death, according to God's true and just disposition, *veritas ordinis* (an expression which can be found in Ambrosiaster's commentary on *Romans*, and may be a hint that Augustine had this text in mind at this time, something which has been the issue of lively debate).[20]

The last part of Augustine's narration allows us to foresee the way out. While Augustine appears to be at "the threshold of the underworld", his mother does not abandon him.

> My mother did not know I was ill, but she was praying for me, though not beside me. But you are present everywhere. Where she was, you heard her, and where I was, you had mercy on me so that I recovered the health of my body. I still remained sick in my sacrilegious heart, for though in such great danger, I had no desire for your baptism. I did better as a boy when I begged for it from my devout mother, as I have recalled and confessed. But I had grown in shame and in my folly used to laugh at the counsels of your medicine. Yet you did not allow me to die in this sad condition of both body and soul. If my mother's heart had suffered that wound, she would never have recovered. I cannot speak enough of the love she had for me. She suffered greater pains in my spiritual pregnancy than when she bore me in the flesh.

Eve-Monica's groans will save Adam-Augustine from a double death, spiritual and corporal (*bis*). She shall give birth to Augustine again. Her feelings towards her son change from being seductive and possessive and become generative. In the perspective of analytic psychology this critical moment could be seen as the passage from the "elementary" maternal character (who "wildly clings" to him) to the "transforming" maternal character.[21] An anticipation of this transition might also be seen in the

---

[20] "Quoniam superius dei gratiam per Christum datam ostendit secundum ordinem veritatis, nunc ipsum ordinem unius dei patris... declarat" (CSEL 81, 1, 163). This passage may be useful in explaining Augustine's idea of a double death a few lines further on in the *Confessions*.

[21] Cf. E. Neumann, *Die Grosse Mutter* (Zürich: Rhein -Velag, 1956).

complex, dynamic metaphor which passed, in the first part of the narration, from the menacing waves to the mother's tears, and from these to the waters of grace: "Even this you forgave me, mercifully saving me from the waters of the sea, when I was full of abominable filth, so as to bring me to the water of your grace. This water was to wash me clean, and to dry the rivers flowing from my mother's eyes which daily before you irrigated the soil beneath her face".

But before this, Augustine, who "had grown in shame", must become as a little child. This time has not yet come: in these serious circumstances he does not seek baptism: "I did better as a boy when I begged for it from my devout mother". While Monica has already begun to bring him forth again, Augustine seems to be still very far from that moment: he "disdains to be a little child" (cf. III, 5, 9).

5. Augustine's journey was long and complex. The principal features of this journey of transformation and conversion are well known through his own narration. He passed through a sceptical phasis, which freed him from the pseudo-scientific manichaean cosmology. Neo-platonism, within a theological framework (VII, 7, 11) offered him the theoretical basis for his solution to the problem of evil. In Augustine's fully-developed cultural-theological perspective, elaborated in several phases, evil is no longer considered by him to be ontological, but rather an ethical and philogenetic substance: evil is no longer for him an autonomous entity, opposed to God, but is a moral entity, at the beginning of which there is Adam's sin, transmitted to all mankind. "Cultural" and at the same time "theological", because the Augustinian *theological* perspective, as well as the biblical one, finds its credibility in a *cultural* context ruled by an organic or "holistic" conception: in this conception the individual has meaning only as a part of a greater whole.

I shall return later to this last aspect, although it is not the central point of my presentation. Here I would like to emphasize how Augustine's transformation consists also (may be, consists principally) in the transformation of some feminine figures, essential to him.

First of all, we may note the progressive convergence of two images originally divided and contradictory, that of wisdom, and that of the mother. At Carthage many things had happened. He had been in love with love, and hated safety and a path free of snares (*Conf.* I, 1, 1), like Eros in the *Symposion*: "a famous hunter, always waving some stratagem, desiderous and competent of wisdom» (*Symp.* 203d). This search had brought him to Cicero's *Hortensius*, by which he had met Wisdom, *sophia*. He had fallen in love with her:

> The book changed my feelings... Suddenly every vain hope became
> empty to me, and I longed for the immortality of wisdom with an incredible
> ardour in my heart... My God, how I burned, how I burned with longing to
> leave earthly things and fly back to you. I did not know what you were doing
> with me. For "with you is wisdom". "Love of wisdom" is the meaning of the
> Greek word *philosophia*. This book kindled my love for it... At that time... the
> one thing that delighted me in Cicero's exhortation was the advice "not to
> study one particular sect but to love and seek and pursue and hold fast and
> strongly embrace wisdom itself, wherever found (III, 4, 7-8).

But that book could not fully satisfy Augustine's eager desire for truth,
because of the absence of the name of Christ, a name, as he says, essentially
connected with his childhood.

> One thing alone put a brake on my intense enthusiasm – that the name
> of Christ was not contained in the book. This name, by your mercy Lord, this
> name of my Saviour your son, my infant heart had piously drunk in with
> my mother's milk, and at a deep level I retained the memory. Any book
> which lacked this name, however well written or polished or true, could not
> entirely grip me (II, 4, 8).

For some ten years he thought he had found that wisdom in Manichaean
doctrine. He would afterwards affirm:

> I had stumbled on that bold-faced woman, lacking of prudence, who in
> Solomon's allegory sits on a chair outside her door and says "Enjoy a meal
> of secret brand and drink sweet stolen water" (III, 6, 11; Prov. 9:17).

In Italy, he became disillusioned with Manichaeism, in which he had
believed that he could find that Wisdom, rather than in the Christian Bible;
then he began to accept the authority of the "ecclesiastical books" and that
first apparition of the Wisdom presented itself again to his mind (VI, 11, 18).

Later, his searches led him to discover Neo-platonic writings. He
discovered there the Word, the Wisdom, but not the incarnate Word, not the
Wisdom revealed to little children (Mt 11:25 frequent in the *Confessions*). In
the final moment, immediately before the *tolle, lege* ("pick up and read"), he
recalled again the *Hortensius*, and his search for Wisdom, which is in these
pages connected with the image of "dignified and chaste Continence" (the
Wisdom of Solomon, 8:31, suggests this connection). "Serene and cheerful", in
a maternal way she speaks to him (VIII, 11, 27).

6. Monica meanwhile had changed very much, through the sufferings
of her spiritual delivery. She had followed him to Carthage, clinging to him

vehemently, and weeping desperately at his treacherous departure. She returned for a moment to peaceful ordinary occupations, the time necessary to gather her strength, and then decided to join her son in Italy. Meanwhile, Augustine had lost all sense of who he was. He was no longer a Manichee, and not yet Christian. He was in the deepest depression. "I was walking through darkness and in a slippery place. I was seeking for you outside myself, and I failed to find the God of my heart. I had come into the depth of the sea. I had no confidence, and had lost hope that truth could be found".[22] In the spring of 385 Monica undertook a dangerous voyage, during which, helped by a vision, she even encouraged the sailors. Thus, "strong in her devotion, in all dangers confident" in God, she joined her son whom she had "followed by land and sea". The memory of Eurialus' mother[23] transforms itself here into that of the widow who presents to Jesus the dead son waiting for him to say: "Young man, arise" (Lk. 7:12). It is interesting to remark the symmetry between this beginning of Book VI of the *Confessions* and the narration of Augustine's departure in the preceding book. Themes, images, and underlying Virgilian elements appear here too: once more a voyage through dangerous waters, once more a mortal illness and the tears, and the perception of a still distant salvation. A distance that nevertheless is lessening, because of Monica's courageous presence.

Monica followed Augustine in his further vicissitudes and was the first, with Alipius, to receive the news of his full conversion. She recognized in it the fulfilment of her prophetic vision: Augustine was now adhering to that "ruler" of the faith that the dream had shown her (end of book VIII). Monica remained close to him at Cassiciacum: "my mother, close by us, a woman as for clothing, but virile in the faith, calm as befitted her age, motherly in love, Christian in piety" (IX, 4, 8). She took part in philosophical discussions, shared her son's and his friends' enthusiasm for the *Ortensius* and received praises: "Mother, you have conquered the stronghold of philosophy" (thus *De beata vita* 2, 10).

Wisdom's last apparition was at Ostia. Monica was with Augustine. This "ecstasy in two" ended precisely by the contemplation of Wisdom:

> We moved beyond them so as to attain to the region of inexhaustible abundance where you feed Israel eternally with truth for food. There life is the wisdom by which all creatures come into being, both things which were and which will be (XI, 10, 24).

---

[22] See Ps. 34:6; 72:26; 67:23.

[23] "Iam venerat ad me mater pietate fortis, terra marique sequens et in periculis omnibus de te secura", VI, 1 (1), cf. *Aen.* IX, 492.

Monica's death occurred not long after the words by which she took her leave of her son: "My son, as for myself, I now find no pleasure in this life..." (IX, 10, 26). Her way of dying fully demonstrated how far she had spiritually progressed. Her image, in Augustine's eyes and memory, finally became as one with that wisdom which, when he was younger, he had sought far from home. Monica was absent, from now on, but Augustine definitively possessed (or was possessed by) "mother Wisdom herself, who, being a solid food for the angels, condescended to become milk for the little children, when the Word became flesh and dwelt among us". [24]

7. Augustine's conversion consisted also, and above all, in his final acceptance of the Biblical scriptures. At the beginning of his pursuit of wisdom, after his reading of the *Hortensius*, these scriptures seemed to reject him: in fact, he refused to become a child before them.

> I therefore decided to give attention to the holy scriptures and to find out what they were like. And this is what met me: something neither open to the proud nor laid bare to mere children; a text lowly to the beginner but, on further reading, of mountainous difficulty and enveloped in mysteries. I was not in any state to be able to enter into that, or to bow my head to climb its steps. What I am now saying did not then enter my mind when I gave my attention to the scripture. It seemed to me unworthy in comparison with the dignity of Cicero. My inflated conceit shunned the Bible's restraint, and my gaze never penetrated to its inwardness. Yet the Bible was composed in such a way that as children mature, its meaning grows with them. I disdained to be a little child. Puffed up with pride, I considered myself a mature adult (III, 5, 9).[25]

This first impression of narrowness, of suffocating straitness, of mortal danger, as in front of a sepulchre, was confirmed for Augustine by Manichaean arguments against the Christian scriptures (III, 7, 12). From now on, and for a rather long time, the Jewish-Christian scriptures would be for Augustine only the letter that kills. As the motherly bosom gives rise to feelings of ferocious frustration when it does not nourish, or does not nourish enough, or even offers itself to a rival in love and in need (Augustine's direct observation, I, 7, 11), so the sacred text can become "mortal" when in its materiality it proposes rough, unintelligible or impossible

---

[24] This comes from a later text (*In Io.* 98,6) in which are brought together meaningfully the metaphor of wisdom-milk with that of word-flesh.

[25] In my *L'intepretazione infinita* (Bologna: Il Mulino, 1987) pp. 29 ff. (French trans., *L'interprétation infinie*, Paris 1991, pp. 25 ff.) I study this Augustinian formula, according to which the Scripture *crescit cum parvulis*.

contents. The text, then, can lead its hungry and impatient reader to desperation. Such was Augustine's condition, for a long time. Only by listening to Ambrose preaching in Milan , would he find the solution.

> Above all I heard first one, then another, then many difficult passages in the Old Testament scriptures figuratively interpreted, where I, by taking them literally, had found them to kill. So after several passages in the Old Testament had been expounded spiritually, I now found fault with that despair of mine, caused by my belief that the law and the prophets could not be defended at all against the mockery of hostile critics (V, 14, 24). And I was delighted to hear Ambrose in his sermons to the people saying, as if he were most carefully enunciating a principle of exegesis: "The letter kills, the spirit gives life". Those texts which, taken literally, seemed to contain perverse teaching he would expound spiritually, removing the mystical veil. He did not say any thing that I felt to be a difficulty; but whether what he said was true I still did not know (VI, 4, 6, cf. 2 Cor. 3:6) .

The more Augustine reduced his arrogance and became a "little child", the more the "huge tomes" containing Manichaean scriptures became a series of absurd phantasies: it was like eating in a dream, and waking up hungry, he says (III, 6, 10). Neo-platonic writings contained elements of wisdom, but were full of presumption and did not possess that healing and beatifying power which is the quality of Christian scriptures (VII, 20, 26), and especially of the apostle Paul's letters (VII, 20, 26 - 21, 27). The more he stooped down to pass through its narrow entrance, the more the Christian scripture appeared to Augustine a living reality, a body animated by the spirit, by which the divine word is generated in the reader. In Milan the impression of absurdity the Scriptures had given him was replaced by respect towards such a high, venerable, but nevertheless accessible authority.

The Scripture was a bosom of infinite power and richness, and at the same time a womb capable of receiving every kind of reader, whatever his condition and spiritual age. She was the *popularis sinus*, literally the "popular bosom", the "womb of holy humility", "open to everyone to read", "in very accessible words and the most humble style", being at the same time exacting with those who are more exacting, and are disposed to pass through its "narrow openings". It was worth bowing one's head to get into its "low entrance", as Augustine was finally able to do. Let us read the complete text, paying attention to maternal metaphors.

> I now began to believe that you would never have conferred such .
> preeminent authority on the scripture, now diffused through all lands,
> unless you had willed that it would be a means of coming to faith in you and
> a means of seeking to know you. Already the absurdity that used to offend
> me in those books, after I had heard many passages being given persuasive

expositions, I understood to be significant of the profundity of their mysteries. The authority of the Bible seemed the more to be venerated and more worthy of a holy faith on the ground that it was open to everyone to read, while keeping the dignity of its secret meaning for a profounder interpretation. The Bible offered itself to all in very accessible words and the most humble style of diction, while also exercising the concentration of those who are not "light of heart" [Ecclus. 19:4]. It welcomes all people to its generous embrace, and also brings a few to you through narrow openings [cf. Mt. 7:13-14]. Though the latter are few, they are much more numerous than would be the case if the Bible did not stand out by its high authority and if had not drawn crowds to the bosom of its holy humility (VI, 5, 8).

8. It must be emphasized here how the argument and the metaphors apply at the same time to the scripture and to the Catholic church. The church too is a "popular bosom", a universal womb that receives with maternal "authority" whoever wants to enter, nourishing everyone with the fittest food. This passage can be compared with *On the True Religion*, ch. 51 (written in 389-390 at Tagaste), where Augustine speaks of the "great and spiritual men in the church", who give to the wise little solid food, while nursing the majority with milk (cf. 1Cor. 2:6 and 3:3), sometimes concealing something from them, but never lying to them.

Notwithstanding the importance of the scriptural theme and of spiritual hermeneutics, confirmed also by quantitative evidence (in the *Confessions* the passages devoted to the Scripture are much more numerous than those devoted to the Church), it cannot be said that the ecclesiological theme is subordinated to the Scriptural one, still less that there is a conflict between the two "authorities". Rather, they relate to each other as the container and its contents, in a relationship that, again, is concretely expressed in a maternal image: the food of the Scripture can be tasted only in the womb of the Church. This was Augustine's own experience: he had learnt from Ambrose the catholicity of the Scripture, of "the ecclesiastical books",[26] which can nourish everybody, and grow with little children. From this moment onwards, there has hardly been a more vivid demonstration of the theorem of Catholicism. With that theorem Augustine was ready to face Donatism.

9. Finally, the transformation of the maternal image into a sapiential figure and the recovery of the Scripture in the Church can be seen as coherent manifestations of a more radical, anthropological change in Augustine's self

---

[26] Cf. VII, 7, 11: "... in Christ your Son our Lord, and by your scripture commended by the authority of the Church".

representation, and in his representation of the human condition. This transformation took place in the period between the violent separation and the subsequent reconciliation, in different terms, with his mother. Reflecting about fifteen years later on those moments, Augustine found a perfectly suitable interpretation according to which these events were a repetition, in his life, of the story of the first chapters of *Genesis*. Having lost with Africa the paradise of his youth, he had been driven downwards, towards the underworld, tied by the chain of the original sin, by which we all die in Adam, overwhelmed by the burden of his personal sins, and tormented by the thought of his mother. Monica too, on her part, carried the burden of the sin of Eve, with the frustration of her affection and with the pains of bringing forth again her son. This must have been, for Augustine, the most acute experience of radical and universal evil. And the formula "original sin" emerged in the *Confessions* at precisely this point in close contact with the more theoretical elaboration of the *Questions to Simplicianus*.

What follows in the *Confessions* describes the way out Augustine found. From a theological point of view (developing the suggestions of the apostle Paul), this way consisted in interpreting the human condition, from birth and for the very fact of birth, as the condition of a being tied to and driven by Adam's body towards sin and death. The way consisted in finding salvation by substituting this chain with an analogous and contrary solidarity with Christ's body, through sacramental signs. The cultural-anthropological presuppositions of this solidaristic conception, with its hermeneutic and ecclesiological consequences, appear now to be far from our individualistic and critical sensibility. Objections worthy of close consideration were raised against them already at the time of Augustine. But, notwithstanding all these just reservations, the exploration of the processes through which Augustine arrived at his theological formulation, and in particular the transformation of his relationship with his mother, leads us into deep and ancient emotions, which are perhaps the most solid basis for historical reconstruction and full understanding.

From an inner psychological point of view the way out Augustine followed can be recognized and shared. It consisted of renouncing pride, and no longer attributing his own frail and feeble characteristics to someone else, to an anonymous negative power. It consisted of becoming a little child. It consisted of admitting being simply a son of Monica.

2

The Vision of Paradise
in the *Journal* of George Fox

What follows is an attempt to re-read some of the most significant pages of Fox's diary, concerning the earliest years of his mission.[1] I am aware there is a great deal of work still to be done, an awareness that grows the more I learn about the man and his age, and the more I think about Emerson's telling observation: "But his true biography must be found in those revelations which in orchards, in lonesome places, and by the wayside, were made to him, and which are characterized by these two traits, 1. That they are of liberal and philosophical tendency so as to agree well with the maxims of the schools of philosophy; 2. That they have a direct bearing on practical morals".[2]

1. In 1643 at the age of 19 George Fox left his home and his job[3] and began a wandering existence through the countryside, the towns and villages of the Midlands, clothed in a suit of skins he had made himself. A voice had led him to set out: "Thou seest how young people go together into vanity and old people into the earth; and thou must forsake all, both young and old, and keep out of all, and be a stranger unto all" (J 3). This is how he

---

[1] This article appeared in *Annali di storia dell'esegesi* 10:1 (1993) pp. 45-59, and was also used in a slightly shorter version as a preface for a short selection of Quaker texts edited by myself and Massimo Lollini: *La società degli amici* (Milano: Linea d'ombra, 1992).

[2] "George Fox", in *Early Lectures*, I, pp. 165-182, p. 170. Emerson's discovery of Fox was very important. Cf. F.B. Tolles, "Emerson and Quakerism", *American Literature* 10 (1938) pp. 142-165, and below my "Emerson and Wisdom".

[3] "I was put to a man, a shoemaker by trade, and that dealt in wool, and used grazing, and sold cattle", J 2. I quote from *The Journal of George Fox. A revised Edition by John L.Nickalls* (Cambrige U.P., 1952) abbreviated as "J". The diary was dictated by Fox thirty years after the events we are examining, probably from about 1674.

described himself in his diary in those years of seeking and suffering:

> I fasted much, and walked abroad in solitary places many days, and often took my Bible and went and sat in hollow trees and lonesome places till night came on; and frequently in the night walked mournfully about by myself, for I was a man of sorrows in the times of the first workings of the Lord in me (J 9-10). I was about twenty years of age when these exercises came upon me, and some years I continued in that condition, in great trouble; and fain I would have put it from me. And I went to many a priest to look for comfort but found no comfort from them (J 4).

In fact he got precious little help from the clergy. One priest told him "to take tobacco and sing psalms" and he replied that he didn't smoke and was not in any condition to sing. As soon as he was out of ear-shot this same priest recounted all his secrets to the lads milking the cows. Another one put him off by attacking him for accidentally treading on a flowerbed. Another suggested he should get himself bled ("but they could not get one drop of blood from me"). "I thought them miserable comforters, and I saw they were all as nothing to me, for they could not reach my condition" (J 6).

In the meantime however he found himself accompanied and gradually guided by signs and "openings". At the beginning of 1646 he was led to an understanding of the sufferings of Christ; and how those who called themselves Christians, whether Papists or Protestants, weren't really any such thing; and that having studied at Oxford or Cambridge and having many "notions" was not enough to be a true minister of Christ. To his family, who disapproved of his not going to church, choosing rather the fields and orchards, he replied that the Apostle taught that believers don't need teachers, because their anointed spirit teaches them (J 7). On another occasion he was shown that the All-High does not dwell in temples made by human hands (J 8). Fox's most profound formative experience takes place in 1647:

> But as I had forsaken all the priests, so I left the separate preachers also, and those called the most experienced people; for I saw there was none among them that could speak to my condition. And when all my hopes in them and in all men were gone, so that I had nothing outwardly to help me, nor could tell what to do, then, Oh then, I heard a voice which said: "There is one, even Jesus Christ, that can speak to thy condition", and when I heard it my heart did leap for joy. Then the Lord did let me see why there was none upon the earth that could speak to my condition, namely, that I might give him all the glory; for all are concluded under sin, and shut up in unbelief as I had been, that Jesus Christ might have the pre-eminence, who enlightens, and gives grace, and faith, and power (J 11).

A desire for the pure knowledge of God and Christ thereby grows up in him "without the help of any man, book or writing. For though the Scriptures that spoke of Christ and of God, yet I knew him not but by revelation, and he who hath the key did open, and as the Father of life drew me to his son by his spirit" (J 11).

The visions continue:

> And one day when I had been walking solitarily abroad and was come home, I was taken up in the love of God, so that I could not but admire the greatness of his love. And while I was in that condition it was opened unto me by the eternal Light and power, and therein saw clearly that all was done and to be done in and by Christ (J 14).

A pure fire appears to him, the fire of the discerning of spirits (J 14 f.). He learns he must nourish himself with the food others trample on, that is true life, the life of Christ (J 19 f.). He sees the mountains come down, so that the glory of the Lord may come to pass (J 16). He sees Babylon, Sodom and Gomorra, and his own tomb:

> Then could I say I had been in spiritual Babylon, Sodom, Egypt, and the grave; but by the eternal power of God I was come out of it, and was brought over it and the power of it, into the power of Christ. And I saw the harvest white, and the seed of God lying thick in the ground, as ever did wheat that was sown outwardly, and none to gather it; and for this I mourned with tears (J 21).

In 1648 he sees the earth crack open, so that the divine seed may be planted therein (J 22). He sees the blood of Christ, the blood of the new covenant (J 23). His preaching strengthened by extraordinary signs, shows an ample correspondence between words and deeds.

2. But again we have a momentary return of darkness:

> And one morning, as I was sitting by the fire, a great cloud came over me, and a temptation beset me; but I sat still. And it was said: "All things come by nature"; and the elements and stars came over me so that I was in a manner quite clouded with it. But inasmuch as I sat, still and silent, the people of the house perceived nothing. And as I sat still under it, and let it alone, a living hope arose in me, and a true voice, which said: "There is a living God who made all things". And immediately the cloud and temptation vanished away, and life rose over it all, and my heart was glad, and I praised the living God. And after some time, I met with some people who had such a notion that there was no God but that all things came by nature. And I had a great dispute with them and overturned them and made some of them confess that there was a living God. Then I saw that it was good that I had gone through that exercise (J 25).

3. The *Journal* relates various other episodes, all of them related to those first great preaching successes, but a little further along he has another vision, which is apparently connected to the previous one: one which represents the culminating point of this period of initiation, in which Fox's basic formative experiences take place. This vision defines the essential contents of his preaching:

> Now was I come up in spirit through the flaming sword into the paradise of God. All things were new, and all the creation gave another smell unto me than before, beyond what words can utter. I knew nothing but pureness, and innocency, and righteousness, being renewed up into the image of God by Christ Jesus, so that I say I was come up to the state of Adam which he was in before he fell. The creation was opened to me, and it was showed me how all things had their names according to their nature and virtue. And I was in a stand of mind whether I should practise physic for the good of mankind, seeing the nature and virtues of the creatures were so opened to me by the Lord. But I was immediately taken up in spirit, to see into another or more steadfast state than Adam's innocency, even into a state in Christ Jesus, that should never fall. And the Lord showed me that such as were faithful to him in the power and light of Christ, should come up into that state in which Adam was before he fell, in which the admirable works of the creation, and the virtues thereof, may be known, through the openings of that divine Word of wisdom and power by which they were made. Great things did the Lord lead me into, and wonderful depths were opened unto me, beyond what can by words be declared; but as people come into subjection to the spirit of God, and grow up in the image and power of the Almighty, they may receive the Word of wisdom, that opens all things, and come to know the hidden unity in the Eternal Being (J 27-8).

The story of Fox's preaching is still at its very beginnings, but we have to stop at this page and the others immediately following, for the decisive character of the statements they contain. Fox continues to wander about. Arriving at the Vale of Belvoir, he receives another "opening" connected to the one above:

> While I was there, the Lord opened to me three things relating to those three great professions in the world, physic, divinity (so called), and law. And he showed me that the physicians were out of the wisdom of God by which the creatures were made, and so knew not the virtues of the creatures, because they were out of the Word of wisdom by which they were made. And he showed me that the priests were out of the true faith which Christ is the author of, the faith which purifies and gives victory and brings people to have access to God, by which they please God, which mystery of faith is held in a pure conscience. He showed me also, that lawyers were out of the equity and out of the true justice, and out of the law of God, which went over the first transgression and over all sin, and answered the spirit of God that was grieved and transgressed in man. And that these three, the physicians, the priests, and the lawyers, ruled the world out of the wisdom, out of the

faith and out of the equity and law of God, the one pretending the cure of the body, the other the cure of the soul, and the third the property of the people. But I saw they were all out, out of the wisdom, out of the faith, out of the equity and perfect law of God.

And as the Lord opened these things unto me, I felt his power went forth over all, by which all might be reformed, if they would receive and bow unto it. The priests could be reformed and brought into the true faith which is the gift of God. The lawyers might be reformed and brought into the law of God which answers that of God (that is transgressed) in every one, and brings to love one's neighbour as himself. This lets man see if he wrongs his neighbour he wrongs himself; and this teaches him to do unto others as he would they should to unto him. The physicians might be reformed, and brought into the wisdom of God by which all things were made and created; that they might receive a right knowledge of the creature and understand the virtues of them, which the Word of wisdom, by which they were made and are upheld, hath given them. Abundance was opened concerning these things; how all lay out of the wisdom of God, and out of the righteousness and holiness that man at first was made in. But as all believe in the light and walk in the light, which Christ hath enlightened every man that cometh into the world withal, and so become children of the light, and of the day of Christ; in his day all things are seen, visible and invisible, by the divine light of Christ, the spiritual, heavenly man, by whom all things were made and created (J 28 f.).

This section of the *Journal* then undergoes an ample development concerning one of the three classes mentioned above, the priests, and ends with some important statements related to spiritual hermeneutics and its connection to the recovery of the pre-lapsarian condition:

> But as a man comes through by the Spirit and power of God to Christ that fulfills the types, figures, shadows, promises, and prophecies that were of him, and is led by the Holy Ghost into the truth and substance of the Scriptures, sitting down in him who is the author and end of them, then they are read and understood with profit and great delight.
>
> Moreover the Lord God let me see, when I was brought up into his image in righteousness and holiness, and into the paradise of God, the state how Adam was made a living soul, and also the stature of Christ, the mystery, that had been hid from ages and generations, which things are hard to be uttered and cannot be borne by many. For, of all the sects in Christendom (so called) that I discoursed withal, I found none that could bear to be told that any should come to Adam's perfection, into that image of God and righteousness and holiness that Adam was in before he fell, to be so clear and pure without sin, as he was. Therefore how should they be able to bear being told that any should grow up to the measure of the stature of the fullness of Christ, when they cannot bear to hear that any should come, whilst upon earth, into the same power and Spirit that the prophets and apostles were in? Though it be a certain truth, that none can understand their writings aright without the same spirit by which they were written (J 32-3).

4. From these pages, to my way of thinking, the two basic positions of early Quakerism emerge.

The first concerns spiritual interpretation: it is impossible to read the Scriptures properly without "being in that spirit which gave them forth". [4] This principle allows us to go over the whole of Biblical history, understanding it from the inside, "duly applying them to their own states" (J 31), that is reproducing in oneself the Baptist's state, and that of the Prophet, of Moses, and in the end of Adam: recovering the beginnings through the end, through the new Adam.

Having once been stated at this particular moment of Fox's spiritual evolution, this principle will be repeated over and over again.

> For I saw in that Light and Spirit which was before Scripture was given forth, and which led the holy men of God to give them forth, that all must come to that Spirit, if they would know God, of Christ, or the Scriptures aright, which they that gave them forth were led and taught by (J 33).
>
> I was to direct people to the Spirit that gave forth the Scriptures, by which they might be led into all Truth, and so up to Christ and God, as they had been who gave them forth... These things I did not see by the help of man, nor by the letter, though they are written in the letter, but I saw them in the light of the Lord Jesus Christ, and by his immediate Spirit and power, as did the holy men of God, by whom the Holy Scriptures were written. Yet I had no slight esteem of the Holy Scriptures, but they were very precious to me, for I was in that spirit by which they were given forth, and what the Lord opened in me I afterwards found was agreeable to them (J 34).
>
> ... so that spirit of God must be in them that come to know them again, by which spirit they might have fellowship with the Son and the Father and with the Scriptures and one with another, and without it they cannot know neither God, nor Christ, nor the Scriptures, nor have fellowship one with another (J 136).

5. The second position is of an anthropological character. If the first principle is that in order to read the Scriptures one can and must recapture the spirit in which they were written, the second is that one must, and it is possible to, reaffirm, through Christ the model of innocence and of the lordship of Adam over creation, before the Fall. Between the two assertions there is the closest of connections, the one depends upon the other, and Fox is aware of this. Note the way his argument goes: "Therefore how should they be able to bear being told that any should grow up to the measure of the stature of the fullness of Christ, when they cannot bear to hear that any

---

[4]   Cf. my afterword to R.W. Emerson, *Teologia e natura*, It. transl. M. Lollini (Genova: Marietti, 1991) pp.187-208, where I studied this formula, used by Emerson in his essay *Nature*.

should come, whilst upon earth, into the same power and Spirit that the prophets and apostles were in?".

And note how aware he is that it is a question of specific propositions, showing the novelty of his movement by comparison with the rest: "of all the sects in Christendom (so called) that I discoursed withal, I found none that could bear to be told that any should come to Adam's perfection, into that image of God and righteousness and holiness that Adam was in before he fell, to be so clear and pure without sin, as he was. Therefore how should they be able to bear".

This position marks a break with puritan beliefs, despite the fact that Fox grew up in them, precisely because there is a different anthropological approach. It is not a question of Fox denying the reality of evil and of sin: on the contrary this is where he starts from, as his first experience fully testifies. One only needs to refer to Robert Barclay's *Apology for the True Christian Divinity* (1676, the first theological text in a technical sense, in that it is organized around theses), to realize that the acceptance of the doctrine of the Fall is quite clear (including his opposition to the Socinians and the Pelagians). As a counterweight to it, however, there is the doctrine of the universality and interior nature of the redemption, which is proposed to every one through the "light that enlightens every man", and the Seed present in every man. There is a polemical letter of Fox's in which all this is vigorously set out.

> The deceivers are not worth the setting foot after; and yet ask them for what end Christ came. They will say: "To destroy the Devil and his works". And then ask them if the body of sin and death be not the Devil's work and imperfection. They will say "yes". And so are in confusion. Christ came to destroy the Devil and his works, they say, and yet they must carry them to the grave. People are saved by Christ, they say, but while you are upon earth you must not be made free from sin. This is much as if one should be in Turkey a slave, chained to a boat, and one should come to redeem him to go into his own country; but say the Turks, "Thou art redeemed, but whilst thou art upon the earth thou must not go out of Turkey, nor have the chain . off thee". So you are redeemed, but must carry a body of sin and death about you and cannot go to your father Adam's house before he fell, but you must live in you father Adam's house in the Fall while ye be upon the earth (Ep. 222, in 1662).

6. Fox's background and education, plus many aspects of his personality, can only be understood in reference to puritanism: above all his sense of evil, in ourselves, in the world and in Christianity , the need for purity and for reform, his courage and the absolute independence of his seeking, and the primacy of the Bible. It is not to be wondered at that strenuous attempts have been made to see in the Quaker movement just an extreme expression

of Puritanism.[5] That same decisive phrase for Fox: "There is one, even Jesus Christ, that can speak to thy condition" can and in a certain sense must be read above all against a puritan, or rather protestant, background; it is indeed a protest against every form of religious mediation: "there is *one*".

But as has been rightly noted, the spiritual experience of early Quakerism goes beyond the boundaries of "only Scripture" that define the essential demarcation line between evangelical and reformed positions – not so much in the individual statements as in the basic assertion that both the individual and the community can and must receive the inner expression of that light, of that spirit, that even if present in the Scriptures, would otherwise remain shut up, a dead letter. Douglas Gwyn correctly insists that the eschatological attitude is a defining aspect of the early Quaker movement, which awaits in silence the inner, direct manifestation of Christ the Master, the substance of the Scriptures. "*Even* Jesus Christ can speak...". In other words, "Christ is come to teach his people himself by his Spirit" (J 149). This eschatological experience also explains the richly apocalyptic tone typical of Fox's early visions, manifestations and "openings". It can all be better understood if we bear in mind the role of the apocalypse in primitive Christianity, as Ernst Käsemann has so clearly pointed out.

7. This interpretation, which would place the experience of Fox and the Friends in the archaic framework of the post-crucifixion community, gathered together to await the Risen Lord, is quite fascinating (even if offered within a militant perspective by no means foreign to Gwyn and in general to those who are interested in these questions). And anyway, precisely those texts I have called attention to, and whose relevance appears to escape the more recent interpreters mentioned, do not allow us to accept the above examined solution for long. Those texts, with the two assertions I have just recalled, (or rather one assertion, of a two-sided nature, one anthropological and one hermeneutical), are not entirely to be assimilated to the early Christian eschatology. So let's go back to them once more.

The idea of a mystical ascent, of the reappropriation of Paradise, is certainly in St. Paul (who was personally "caught up into paradise", according to 1 Cor. 12:4), from whom comes the idea that believers in Christ, the New Adam, can in a certain sense regain a paradisal condition (1 Cor.

---

5   Above all in the work of Geoffry Nuttall, *The Holy Spirit in Puritan Faith and Experience* (Oxford, 1946) and in Hugh Barbour, *The Quakers in Puritan England* (New Haven, 1964); cf. Douglas Gwyn, *Apocalypse of the Word* (Richmond, 1946) pp. XVI f.

15). And it is true that Adam, the Lord of Creation, gives things their names, already in the account of *Genesis*. And anyway in Fox's vision, the recovery of Adam's paradisal condition. And it true that Adam, the Lord of Creation, gives things their names, already in the account in *Genesis*. And anyway in Fox's vision the recovery of Adam's paradisal condition – certainly not immediate, but in Christ, and therefore in a more stable and decisive form – is presented in an incredibly concrete way: "The creation was opened to me, and it was showed me how all things had their names according to their nature and virtue. And I was in a stand of mind whether I should practise physic for the good of mankind, seeing the nature and virtues of the creatures were so opened to me by the Lord". A passage of the apocryphal *Wisdom of Salomon* could well be the inspiration behind it: Salomon was given "an unerring knowledge", among other things, also of "the *natures* of living creatures" and of "the *virtues* of the roots". But all this does not belong to Fox's Bible, nor does the last part of the description, exactly: "Great things did the Lord lead me into, and wonderful depths were opened unto me, beyond what can by words be declared; but as people come into subjection to the spirit of God, and grow up in the image and power of the Almighty, they may receive the Word of wisdom, that opens all things, and come to know the hidden unity in the Eternal Being".

We owe to the great liberal Quaker scholar Rufus Jones, in his fine book, *Spiritual Reformers in the 16th and 17th Centuries*, (1914), the most convincing case for Fox's sources:[6] a writer Fox never quotes – that's not his style – but who was circulating in translations just at the time of his early experiences: the mystic Jacob Boehme. The latter had gone through an analogous experience around 1600. In the introduction by the translator John Sparrow to the Forty Questions, (1647), one could read of the possibility of knowing the works of the Creator "in signatures, shapes, figures and qualities or properties". If texts a little while after Fox's vision are taken into consideration (it must be remembered that the *Journal* was written much later), Justice Hotham's life of Boehme of 1653 may be compared (still following Rufus Jones). In addition, in John Ellistone's 1649 introduction to the translation of Boehme's *Epistles* there is an even greater affinity: the knowledge drawn from divine light leads us to know the "different secret qualities and vertues", hidden in all visible things, which can be "applied to

---

6 The classic study by W.C. Braithwaite, *The Beginnings of Quakerism*, (1912) (Cambridge, 1955) pp. 38-41, notes the importance of Fox's vision of Paradise, and refers to Boehme already on the basis of R. Jones, *Studies in Mystical Religion* (1909).

their naturall use for the curing and healing of corrupt and decayed nature". Behmenist correspondences can be seen also in the passage through the sword of fire, and through the "perfume" of Paradise. Likewise the reference to Wisdom, to Sofia, which demonstrate the unity of the created with God, is a typical, constant theme of Boehme's. Even the idea that it is impossible to understand the Scriptures without the gift of the Spirit occurs frequently in Boehme and his English interpreters.[7]

8. R.M. Jones's historical work in now consigned to the usual oblivion of positivistic historiography of a liberal theological tendency. Yet his *Spiritual Reformers* is indispensable in placing the Quaker movement correctly in a context of reform, humanism and mysticism, and as such the work should be reconsidered.

There are however certain aspects of Fox's vision of Paradise that can't be attributed to Boehme's influence, in particular the tendency to draw immediate, practical rather than theological conclusions from his mystical experience, which is a long way from Boehme's contemplative spirit. In the Vale of Belvoir Fox understood that the members of the three professions, – the doctors, magistrates and clergy – were each of them lacking in wisdom, judgment and faith. But he believed that the professions could be reformed, and be led back "into the wisdom of God by which all things were made and created". Fox's concern was therefore to grasp at once the secular relevance of the paradisal vision; it meant the reappropriation of the basic professions, medicine and science in general, the magistrates and government activity, and theology and the ministry, through a single reforming project. About which, in its three aspects, I will make some final observations.

9. Perhaps a classic like Christopher Hill's *The Intellectual Origins of the English Revolution* (1965) may be of use to evoke the atmosphere – in the century of Bacon and Pascal – in which that terrible doubt which assailed George Fox can be placed: "'All things come by nature'; and the elements and stars came over me so that I was in a manner quite clouded with them". Thus we may also remember with Hill, how the extraordinary developments in medical science in that age may explain why Fox, transported to Paradise, asks himself if it wouldn't be the best thing to become a doctor – "practise physic for the good of mankind". William Penn's Preface to the *Journal* may be relevant here, when he writes: "For in all things he acquitted himself

---

7   R.M. Jones, *Spiritual Reformers of the 16th and 17th Centuries* (1914) (Boston, 1959) pp. 221-227.

like a man, yea, a strong man, a new and heavenly minded man, a divine and a naturalist, and all of God Almighty's making. I have been surprised at his questions and answers in natural things; that whilst he was ignorant of useless and sophistical science, he had in him the foundation of useful and commendable knowledge, and cherished it everywhere" (J XLVII). It's a kind of idealisation of Fox, to whom are attributed the features of the New Adam, so central to the Friends' way of thinking, all the more so for those, like Penn, who were moving forward into the new American experience.

10. In the England of Milton's *Paradise Lost* and *Paradise Regained*, of Locke's *Two Treatises of Government*, the arguments concerning Adam's state were fundamental, and ideas of the state of nature and of natural law were decisive for modern political theory and practice. As far as Fox and the early Quaker movement is concerned, the anthropology implicit in the vision of paradise grows at once into a praxis in which politics and mysticism are perfectly in harmony.

The vision in which Fox explains why he must address everyone as "thou" and not take off his hat to anyone comes immediately afterwards (J 36). Fox is imprisoned in 1650 through holding to his vision:

> They put me in and out of the room from the first hour to the ninth hour at night in examinations, having me backward and forward, and said in a deriding manner that I was taken up in raptures, as they called it.
> At last they asked me whether I was sanctified.
> I said, "Sanctified? yes", for I was in the Paradise of God.
> They said, had I no sin?
> "Sin?", said I, "Christ my Saviour hath taken away my sin, and in him there is no sin".
> They asked how we knew that Christ did abide in us.
> I said, "By his Spirit that he has given us".
> They temptingly asked if any of us were Christ.
> I answered, "Nay, we are nothing, Christ is all".
> They said, "If a man steal is it no sin?"
> I answered, "All unrighteousness is sin".
> And many such like words they had with me. And so they committed me as a blasphemer and as a man that had no sin, and committed another me with me to the House of Correction in Derby for six months (J 51 f.)

He calls upon his vision once again in Derby prison when they want to make him an officer in the Commonwealth army, and he replies to their insistence and flattery, about his "virtue", "as they said", maintaining that he "lived in the virtue of that life and power that took away the occasion of all wars" (J 65 f.). In the horrible prison of Derby he feels deeply concerned about the fact that the judges "put men to death for cattle and for money and small things". Spiritually oppressed for this, a vision consoles him: "standing in the will of God, a heavenly breathing arose in my soul to the Lord. Then did I see the heavens opened and the glory of God shined over all" (J 65 f.).

Out of faith in his vision he will write to Cromwell in 1655: "Live in the wisdom of the life of God, that with it thou mayest be ordered to his glory, and order his creatures to his glory" (J 194), and similarly to Cromwell's sick daughter.

11. It is also out of faith in his vision, for the redemption of all marriages after the Fall, that Fox will much later, at the age of 45, marry Margaret Fell, widow of the magistrate Thomas Fell. I would like to end here by evoking the image of the first meeting between Fox and Margaret Fell, which took place in 1652. This vivid scene sums up the themes and methods of early Quaker preaching (here again there is no comparison to the contemplative Behmenist tradition). The words of Fox, his declarations and his questions, take for granted what was said earlier about the two fundamental hermeneutic and anthropological positions of Quakerism; but all this is translated by Fox into two simple questions in which the ancient hermeneutic principles, of the early fathers still more than Behmenist, of reading the Scriptures in the same spirit in which they were written, becomes the productive principle of a new relation between word and deed: "The Bible says: but what canst thou say?".

> And when they were singing before the sermon, he came in; and when they had done singing, he stood up upon a seat or form and desired that he might have liberty to speak. And he that was in the pulpit said he might. And the first words that he spoke were as followeth: "He is not a Jew that is one outward, neither is that circumcision which is outward; but he is a Jew that is one inward, and that is circumcision which is of the heart". And so he went on and said, How that Christ was the Light of the world and lighteth every man that cometh into the world; and that by this Light they might be gathered to God, etc. And I stood up in my pew, and I wondered at his doctrine, for I had never heard such before. And then he went on, and opened the Scriptures, and said, "The Scriptures were the prophets' words and Christ's and the Apostle's words, and what as they spoke they enjoyed and possessed and had from the Lord". And said, "Then what had any to do with the Scriptures, but as they came to the Spirit that gave them forth? You will say, Christ saith this, and the apostles say this; but what canst thou say? Art thou a child of Light and hast walked in the Light, and what thou speakest, is it inwardly from God?".

This opened me so that it cut me to the heart; and then I saw clearly we were all wrong. So I sat me down in my pew again, and cried bitterly. And I cried in the spirit to the Lord, "We are all thieves, we are all thieves, we have taken the Scriptures in words and know nothing of them in ourselves".[8]

---

[8]   From *Wait for the Light. The Spirituality of George Fox*, J. Lampen ed. (London, 1981) pp. 112 f.

3

Emerson and Wisdom
Maternal patterns of knowledge in Emerson's *Nature* (1836)

The end of the section "Language" in Emerson's *Nature* is particularly rich from a theoretical point of view and of fundamental relevance in understanding some peculiarities of transcendentalist language and attitude. Speaking of the correspondence between nature and spirit, or soul, Emerson uses some expressions worthy of careful analysis. Let us first focus our attention on this text.[1]

> It is the standing problem which has exercised the wonder and the study of every fine genius since the world began; from the era of the Egyptians and the Brahmins, to that of Pythagoras, of Plato, of Bacon, of Leibnitz, of Swedenborg. There sits the Sphinx at the road side, and from age to age, as each prophet comes by, he tries his fortune at reading her riddle. There seems to be a necessity in spirit to manifest itself in material forms; and day and night, river and storm, beast and bird, acid and alkali, preëxist in necessary Ideas in the mind of God, and are what they are by virtue of preceding affections, in the world of spirit. A fact is the end or last issue of spirit. The visible creation is the terminus or the circumference of the invisible world. "Material objects", said a French philosopher "are necessarily kinds of scoriae of the substantial thoughts of the creator, which must always preserve an exact relation to their first origin; in other words, visible nature must have a spiritual and moral side".
>
> The doctrine is abstruse, and though the images of "garment", "scoriae", "mirror" &c., may stimulate the fancy, we must summon the aid of subtler and more vital expositors to make it plain. "Every scripture is to be interpreted by the same spirit which gave it forth" is the fundamental law of criticism. A life in harmony with Nature, the love of truth and of virtue, will purge the eyes to understand her text. By degrees we may come to know the primitive

---

[1] I propose here a further analysis of a passage to which I already devoted some pages in my "Postfazione" to R.W. Emerson, *Teologia e natura*, It. trans. by M. Lollini (Genova:Marietti, 1990).

sense of the permanent objects of nature, so that the world will be an open book, and every form significant of its hidden life and final cause.

A new interest surprizes us, whilst, under the view now suggested, we contemplate the fearful extent and multitude of objects; since "every object rightly seen, unlocks a new faculty of the soul". That which was unconscious truth, becomes, when interpreted and defined in an object, a part of the domain of knowledge, – a new weapon in the magazine of power.[2]

Emerson begins in a rather solemn way with *philosophia perennis*. The succession: Egyptians, Brahmins, Pythagoras, Plato, Bacon, Leibnitz, Swedenborg should testify that a relationship between mind and Nature exists and can be known. The flavor of these lines – especially the list: "day and night... acid and alcali" – recalls Swedenborg. A follower of the Swedish theologian, a "French philosopher", the Swedenborgian Guillaume Oegger,[3] is in fact quoted,[4] but his formulation is soon criticized. *Scoriae*, "garment", "mirror": such gnostic terms can satisfy fancy, but they are perceived as "abstruse", because of – I would suggest – the radical dualism they imply. Then, expressing his dissatisfaction with his language (*scoriae*, "garment", "mirror", and similar neo-platonic vocabulary) Emerson feels the necessity of turning to "subtler and more vital expositors",[5] for help, and enunciates the hermeneutic rule already mentioned: "'Every scripture is to be interpreted by the same spirit which gave it forth', is the fundamental law of criticism". The "subtler and more vital expositor" is George Fox.[6] The

---

2   *Nature*, IV, *The Collected Works of R.W. Emerson*, I, *Nature, Addresses and Lectures*, R.E. Spiller-A.R. Ferguson eds. (Cambridge Mass.: Belknap Press, 1971) pp. 22 f.

3   See H. De Lubac, *La posterité spirituelle de Joachim de Fiore*, I (Paris, 1978) p. 264: "Un autre pretre, l'abbé Oegger, vicaire de Notre-Dame de Paris, rompait avec l'Eglise catholique, pour fonder une église swédenborgienne". The *Journals* (1835, V, 66-69) contain a longer quotation from Oegger's *True Messiah* which confirms that Emerson is following it also beyond this explicit quotation.

4   According to the editor, R.E. Spiller of the new *Collected Works*, Oegger, *The True Messiah, or the Old and New Testaments, Examined According to the Principles of the Language of Nature*, trans. by E.P. Peabody (Boston, 1842) which Emerson had in his library (and which was used also by Thoreau): but, on account of the dates, I would suggest that Emerson quoted rather from the manuscript of the translation of *Le vraie Moïse, ou l'Ancien et le Nouveau Testament examiné d'après les principes de la langue de la nature* (Paris, 1829).

5   In *Representative Men*, in the corresponding essay, well worth reading, Swedenborg's philosophy is characterized as "dynamic", but not "subtle".

6   The editor refers to W. Sewell's *The History of the Rise, Increase and Progress of the Christian People Called Quakers*, I (Philadelphia, 1823, 1823). Cf. Emerson's *Journal* 1832, IV, p. 31: "He [G.Fox] taught that the Ss [Sacred Scriptures] could not be understood but by the same spirit that gave them forth". See the Divinity School

result of a deeper insight into the "analogy that marries Matter and Mind" (a few lines further on) can be better appreciated by recalling an ancient, traditional rule of biblical interpretation, and widening its application to Nature. Emerson is suggesting here a movement of thought exactly contrary to that suggested by Oegger, whose declared purpose was to examine the Scriptures "according to the Principles of the Language of Nature". On the contrary, he is suggesting that intertextuality must not only be applied to the relationship between Old and New Testament, but it must also be extended so as to comprehend Nature. Nature then becomes Scripture, he concludes by emphasizing with a quotation from Coleridge, *Aids to Reflection*, the fruitfulness of this "fundamental law", applied to Nature as Scripture.[7]

The difficulty of this passage lies in Emerson's movement from Swedenborg to Fox. It is hard to understand how Fox's authority could be used in favour of Emerson's idealism. I studied the *Journal* of George Fox to check the precise passage in which he states the above-mentioned hermeneutic rule. This idea, and almost the same words, recur many times, but the most significant instance is to be found in the year 1648. Fox tells us of his reading of the Bible. "I saw how people read the Scriptures without a right sense of them and without duly applying to their own states... I saw plainly that none could read Moses aright without Moses' spirit, by which Moses saw how Moses was in the image of God in Paradise".[8] And a little futher on:"This I saw in that Light and Spirit which was before Scripture was given forth, and which led the holy men to give them forth".[9]. The history of this rule can be traced back to primitive Christianity, and particularly to a formula of Jerome's.[10] This section of the *Journal* begins with a vision,

---

Address: "Once leave your own knowledge of God, your own sentiment, and take secondary knowledge, as St. Paul's, or George Fox's, or Swedenborg's, and you get wide from God with every year the secondary form lasts and if, as now, for century, – the chasm yawns to that breadth, that men can scarcely be convinced there is in them anything divine".

[7] The source is *Aids to Reflection*, J. Marsh ed. (Burlington, Vt., 1828) pp. 150-151, *Aphorism XXXVI, Comment*, but here the emphasis is rather on platonic ascension: "Thus all lower natures find their highest Good in resemblances and seekings of that which is higher and better".

[8] *The Journal of G. Fox*, J.L. Nickalls ed. (Cambridge U.P., 1952) p. 31.

[9] *Ib.*, p. 33.

[10] "Quicunque igitur aliter Scripturam intelligit, quam sensus Spiritus sancti flagitat, quo conscripta est, licet de Ecclesia non recesserit, tamen haereticus appellari potest, et de carnis operibus est, eligens quae peiora sunt": *In Ep ad Gal.* 5,19-21, PL 26, 445AB. In the background of Jerome's formulation, there is Origen. And finally there are New Testament texts, like 1 Cor. 2:16: ("He who is spiritual judges

which, rather than literally, should be taken as a demonstration of his reading of the Bible in the first person.

> Now was I come up in spirit through the flaming sword into the paradise of God. All things were new, and all the creation gave another smell unto me than before, beyond what words can utter. I knew nothing but pureness, and innocency, and righteousness, being renewed up into the image of God by Christ Jesus, so that I say I was come up to the state of Adam which he was in before he fell. The creation was opened to me, and it was showed me how all things had their their names according to their nature and virtue. And I was in a stand of mind whether I should practise physic for the good of mankind, seeing the nature and virtues of the creatures were so opened to me by the Lord. But I was immediately taken up in spirit, to see into another or more steadfast state than Adam's innocency, even into a state in Christ Jesus, that should never fall. And the Lord showed me that such as were faithful to him in the power and light of Christ, should come up into that state in which Adam was before he fell, in which the admirable works of the creation, and the virtues thereof, may be known, through the openings of that divine Word of wisdom and power by which they were made. Great things did the Lord lead me into, and wonderful depths were opened unto me, beyond what can by words be declared; but as people come into subjection to the spirit of God, and grow up in the image and power of the Almighty, they may receive the Word of wisdom, that opens all things, and come to know the hidden unity in the Eternal Being.[11]

I think that this page is very useful in understanding Emerson's second reference, to the "more subtle interpreter". Emerson's "purged eyes" seem to echo Fox when he speaks of "pureness, innocence and righteousness". "The primitive sense of the permanent objects of nature", and "every form significant of its hidden life and final cause" recalls Fox: "It was showed me how all things had their names according to their nature and virtue". Again, "So that the world will be an open book" echoes Fox: "the nature and virtues of the creatures were so opened to me", and "the Word of wisdom, that opens all things" (there are other two occurrences of "open"). But, independently of factual coincidences, it is fascinating to discover under Emerson's idealistic position the memory of the Paradisiac myth.

The comparison with the description of the new Adam according to Fox's experience is also useful in understanding Emerson's final words about the "new weapon in the magazine of power" which shall be at hand.

---

all things, yet he himself is judged of no man..."); of course, 2 Cor. 2:6: "the letter kills, but the spirit gives life", and other corresponding Johannine formulations (*John* is particularly important in the explanation of further developments of the "spiritual sense", as in Fox or Swedenborg).

[11] *The Journal of G. Fox,* cit., pp. 27 f.

For Fox too the new knowledge of the sense of creation means the acquisition of a new power: "And I was at a stand of mind whether I should practise physic for the good of mankind, seeing the nature and virtues of the creatures were so opened to me by the Lord". And if here at first sight "power" seems rhetorical, Emerson's use of "power" is in reality much more complex. In "Language", for instance, he writes: "A man's power to connect his thought with its proper symbol, and so to utter it, depends on the simplicity of his character, that is upon his love of truth and his desire to communicate it without loss [...] When simplicity of character is lost [...] and duplicity and falsehood take the place of simplicity and truth, the power over nature as an interpreter of the will is in a degree lost".

Here again Genesis, and Fox 's reading of it, appear in the background. God has given Adam dominion over every living creature (Gen. 1:28) and brings the creatures "unto Adam to see what he would call them: and whatsoever Adam called every living creature, that was the name thereof" (2:19). Thus, there is a human power over Nature, which consists in calling living creatures according to their own names (*Genesis*), in knowing "how all things had their names according to their nature and virtue" (Fox), "in connecting thoughts with their proper symbols". But this is possible only to the man who goes to Nature "with purged eyes", in "simplicity of character", rightly exerting power over her, as the first Adam could do. Nature can resist a man who does not approach her in pureness, or – in terms taken not from the Bible, but rather from Plato's Socrates and from stoicism – a man whose life is not "in harmony with Nature, who does not love truth and virtue". Because Nature too has a power, a subordinate power as "interpreter of human will". Nature has the power to interpret our thoughts and the will and the desire to communicate. If we have power over Nature, a "dominion" which consists first of all in giving names, i.e. in language and thought, in our turn we depend on Nature for the expression of ourselves: language, thought and creativity are possible only if we accept Her as the interpreter of our will, only if in simplicity we submit to Nature when She presents us her creatures, as God did to Adam in Eden. In "Oversoul" Emerson says the same thing: "the insight proceeds from obedience". Not essentially different is the lesson to be found both in Francis Bacon's *Novum organon*, just at its beginning and, of course, in the original transcendentalist attitude, the a priori synthesis in Kant's elaboration. We see here how a theological conception, and a mystical formula[12] can be turned into an

---

12 Again G. Fox, in a letter of 1652: "Stand still in that which is pure, after ye see yourselves; and then mercy comes. After thou seest thy thoughts, and the temptation, do not think, but submit, and then power comes" (Ep. 10).

epistemological axiom.

A further, final step can be taken if we ask the question about the possible foundation of the peculiar attitude toward Nature, which I have defined above as power over – through submission to – Nature. Hypothetically I would make here a suggestion I have proposed elsewhere, which is that of seeing the prototypical situation of this attitude in the mother-child relationship. The body of the mother, and particularly the breast, perceived as a reservoir of infinite power, is the first permanent object of representation for the child. The mother gives a sense to what the child can perceive only with anxiety; she forms and orients his or her desires; she receives his or her perceptions projected on her and returns them to the child in a more elaborate form: her apparatus of thought has structuring effects for the child's mind.[13] This, I would suggest, is the prototype of the Paradisiac situation, in which dominion and obedience interact. This situation, in its turn, is the pattern which we must recall in order to attain the specific quality which the transcendentalist attitude towards Nature possesses.

This attitude can be well expressed through the Biblical, and feminine figure of Wisdom. Let us read "Idealism", a few pages after the passage I began with. Here Emerson speaks of the "intellectual science":

> It fastens the attention upon immortal necessary uncreated natures, that is, upon Ideas; and in their presence we feel that outward circumstance is a dream and a shade. Whilst we wait in this Olympus of Gods, we think of nature as an appendix to the soul. We ascend into their region; and know that these are the thoughts of the Supreme Being: "These are they who were

---

[13] In my "Postfazione" quoted above I applied this pattern to the relationship with the sacred Books: "The body of the mother, the nourishment that comes forth from her, the words of wisdom which accompany and are themselves nourishment and the frustration for the absence of the bosom (Melanie Klein, and especially Wilfred R. Bion) are the fundamental experiences which, strengthened by further contact with a more abstract parental authority, will accompany the child in his growth and will provide rich emotional material which will underlie his future experiences with books, especially sacred Books (where culture admits them). Scripture will be a parental substitute, will be the breast from which to take nourishment, the corpus of pragmatic learning, the words of wisdom, always appropriate, to which one freely submits oneself, in order to grow and find new words for self-interpretation. When, in a much more varied and obscure way, in 'the fearful extent and multitude of her objects', Nature will offer herself, the law suggested by primeval wisdom – power and generation through submission and obedience – will be at hand, still preserving its full validity and truth". I have developed these ideas in an essay on St. Augustine, "Figure materne e Scrittura", *Annali di storia dell'esegesi* 9:2 (1992).

set up from everlasting, from the beginning, or ever the earth was. When he prepared the heavens, they were there; when he established the clouds above, when he strengthened the foundations of the deep. Then they were by him, as one brought up with him. On them took he counsel" (*Nature*, "Idealism", § 4).

The reference to Olympus, the plural "ideas", the image of ascension, as in Diotima's speech in *Symposion*, and in Plotinian (and Augustinian) ecstasy, must not prevent us from recognizing that this is a paraphrase of a Biblical text, Prov. 8:23.27 f., in which Wisdom introduces herself: "I was set up from everlasting, from the beginning...". This Wisdom is the feminine partner of God in the creation (it has long been recognized by specialists as a transposition into the Hebrew Bible of the Egyptian Maat, goddess of Truth-Justice), and she exercises the function of mediator between God and mankind: "...Then I was by him, as one brought up with him: and I was daily his delight, rejoicing always before him; rejoicing in the habitable part of his earth; and my delights were with the sons of men. Now hearken me...» (*ib.*, 30 f.). Identified with the Logos, the Word of God, in John's Gospel, this figure continually reappears in different ways throughout the history of Christian theology and piety.[14] Unmistakably she appears also here although necessarily in a disguised form: Emerson can no longer use Biblical language as his paradigmatic language, as he will explicitly declare in his *Divinity School Address* (1838), and as he had already written in his Journal: "Make your own Bible" (July 21, 1936).

As I said, the function of Wisdom is one of mediation: she "rejoices" to be with God and with men, she shows the unity between them. A similar experience is expressed, for instance, by Fox in the same text quoted above: «...they may receive the Word of wisdom, that opens all things, and come to know the hidden unity in the Eternal Being". And again Emerson, later on, in a very important passage in the first pages of *The Over-soul* , states:

> We live in succession, in division, in parts, in particles. Meantime within man is the soul of the whole; the wise silence; the universal beauty, to which every part and particle is equally related; the eternal ONE. And this deep power in which we exist and whose beatitude is all accessible to us, is not only self-sufficing and perfect in every hour, but the act of seeing and the thing seen, the seer and the spectacle, the subject and the object, are one [...] Only by the vision of that Wisdom can the horoscope of the ages be read, and

---

14 See the interesting pages R.A. Grusin devotes to Theodor Parker, and his idea of God as the "great housekeeper [of the universe], the ever-present mother therein", in *Transcentalist Hermenutics. Institutional Authority and the Higher Criticism of the Bible* (Durham and London: Duke University Press, 1991) pp. 130 ff.

by falling back on our better thoughts, by yielding to the spirit of prophecy which is innate in every man, we can know what it saith. Every man's words who speaks from that life must sound vain to those who do not dwell in the same thought on their own part.

Here, the experience of total unity, of perfect fusion, of complete trust, and more specifically the perception of a space, both internal and external, and of a time, which is out of time, and the equivalence of seeing and being seen, all of these are vividly illuminated when compared with some observations about the mother-child relationship to be found for instance in D.W. Winnicott's *Playing and reality* (1971).[15]

In conclusion: in order to re-evaluate Emerson as a philosopher, alongside the comparison with contemporary philosophy – "finding Emerson and Thoreau to underwrite Wittgenstein and Austin"[16] – I think that the *via regia* consists principally in deepening our perception of the richness of his synthesis between ancient and new, between traditional cultures, above all Biblical culture, and modern insights. To do so, I am convinced that we must re-discover the powerful and flexible instrument he used, the conception of a fundamental, maternal Wisdom, which is an instrument which allows the widest and freest inter-cultural displacements, while fully respecting all diversities.

---

[15] Winnicott refers also to J. Lacan, *Le stade du miroir* (1949), for the idea that the mother appears to the child as she sees the child. Consequently, some light is also thrown on the imagery of finding oneself behind the raised veil, which can be encountered in Schiller, Novalis and, in another form, at the beginning of the chapter "Reading" in Thoreau's *Walden*. I studied this topos in *"Le Sacre Scritture, o Bibbie dell'umanità"* in *Walden di H.D. Thoreau*, to be published soon (a shorter version has already appeared: "'Sacred Scriptures, or the Bibles of the Nations' in *Walden* by Henry David Thoreau", in J. Neusner, E.S. Frerichs, N.M. Sarna eds. *From Ancient Israel to Modern Judaism*, IV [Atlanta: Scholars Press, 1989] pp. 105-114).

[16] So S. Cavell, *In Quest of the Ordinary* (Chicago and London: University of Chicago Press, 1988) p. 25. Cavell has been working for years on at this aspect of Emerson's importance with great cultural perceptiveness.

4

"Sacred Scriptures, or Bibles of mankind" in *Walden* by H.D. Thoreau

In *Walden* the chapter "Reading", placed as it is immediately after the two long preceding chapters "Economy" and "Where I lived and what I lived for" (which are indispensable for defining the reasons for and the procedures of Thoreau's choice), stands out as the first of a long series of brief chapters dedicated to various aspects of his "Life in the woods". There is a philological factor which highlights the importance of this chapter: "Reading", unlike the other chapters, was already in its almost final form in the first version of *Walden*, which was printed in 1854, after at least six revisions.[1] To these pages Thoreau entrusts a series of general theses on reading rather than a plan of specific readings: what a real book is, how to be a real reader, and what real reading is.[2] Thus, we are dealing with genuine hermeneutic theses, which I would like to consider by placing them in a wider context. For this reason, my recent research on ancient hermeneutics and its modern revivals will be useful.[3]

This is a revised version of my "'Sacred scriptures, or the Bibles of the Nations' in *Walden* by Henry David Thoreau", in J. Neusner, E.S. Frerichs, N.M. Sarna eds., *From Ancient Israel to Modern Judaism.Intellect in Quest of Understanding. Essays in Honor of Marvin Fox*, IV, *The Modern Age. Theology.Literature. History* (Atlanta: Scholars Press, 1989) pp.105-114.

[1] Cf. L. Lindon Shanley, *The Making of Walden, with the Text of the First Version* (University of Chicago Press) p. 95: "It is fairly safe to assume that it is practically in its final form here".

[2] In *The Senses of Walden* (New York: The Viking Press, 1972) p. 5, S. Cavell points out that we should use this chapter to understand, first of all, *Walden* itself: "its task, for us who are reading, is epitomized in discovering what reading is and, in particular, if *Walden* is a heroic book, what reading *Walden* is...". My point, as will appear later on, is different (cf. n. 20).

[3] *L'interpretazione infinita. L'ermeneutica cristiana antica e le sue trasformazioni* (Bologna: Il Mulino, 1987). I would like to take a definition from this work: "If interpretation is an art, hermeneutics is the reflective moment which provides it with a theory

1. The solemn beginning of "Reading" transports us immediately out of time, into a special, sacred, mysterious atmosphere.

> In acquiring property, for ourselves or our posterity, in founding a family or a state, or acquiring fame even, we are mortal; but in dealing with truth we are immortal, and need fear no change nor accident. The oldest Egyptian or Hindoo philosopher raised a corner of the veil from the statue of the divinity; and still the trembling robe remains raised, and I gaze upon as fresh a glory as he did, since it was I in him that was then so bold, and it is he in me that now reviews the vision. No dust has settled on that robe; no time has elapsed, since that divinity was revealed. That time which we really improve, or which is improvable, is neither past, present, nor future (p. 402).[4]

The text is rich in autobiografical references and suggests a series of intellectual precursors which should be explored more carefully. There is a reference to the veil of Maya, in Buddhism, there is Platonism, there is perhaps a recollection of Moses' veiled face in Ex. 34 and 2 Cor. 3, there is Swedenborg, there is the evocation of the mysterous inscription in the temple of Isides in Sais, which inspired Schiller[5] and

---

of the text, which is often only implicit, and above all with rules of interpretation".

[4] Quotations from H.D. Thoreau, *Walden* and *A Week on the Concord and the Merrimack Rivers* (abbr. *Week*) from R.F. Sayre's edition (New York: The Library of America, 1985).

[5] According to Plutarch, *De Iside* IX, 354 C, l, the inscription was: "I am all what has been, is and will be: and no mortal ever raised my peplum (cf. also Herodotus II, *Hist.*, 170 f.). Thoreau knew directly Plutarch's text, cf. *Journal*, B. Torrey ed. (Boston 1906) p. 139 (June 14, 1840). On this text, quoted with admiration by Kant in his *Critique of Judgement*, see E.H. Gombrich "The Symbol of the Veil: Psychological Reflections on Schiller's Poetry", in *Freud and the Humanities* (New York: 1985) p. 82, with reference to P. Hadot, "Zur Idee der Naturgeheimnsisse", *Abhandlungen der Akademie der Wissenschaften, Geistes- und sozialwissenschaftliche Klasse* (1982), n.8, pp. 3-33. Schiller returns many times to this topic, since his 1795 poem "Das verschleierte Bild von Sais", where the young man who raises the veil of the goddess dies without being able to say what he saw. According to Gombrich, for Schiller the terrible truth to be veiled, consisted in nothing else than in the animal character of our human nature (p. 92). Schiller's poem certainly influenced Melville in a passage of *Moby Dick*, at the end of chapter LXXVI: "But clear Truth is a thing for salamander giants only to encounter: how small the chances for the provincials then? What befel the weakling youth lifting the dread goddess's veil at Sais?" See *Moby Dick, or the Whale*, L.S. Mansfield e H.P. Vincent eds. (New York: Hendricks House, 1952) p. 770 f. (the first edition had "Lais", which passed into C. Pavese's Italian translation). Melville was acquainted with Schiller's poem through Ed. Bulwer Lytton's translation, "The Veiled Statue at Sais", in *Poems and Ballads*. He bought this book in 1849.

Novalis.[6] All these allusions are intended to establish a certain idea of the relationship between the text and its reader, inviting him to assume, when approaching it, an attitude analogous to that presumed by the ancient way of reading, as "lectio divina", as a spiritual exercise, as a sacred action which transports the reader into the spiritual world. "Being seated to run through the region of the spiritual world: I have had this advantage in books. To be intoxicated by a single glass of wine; I have experienced this pleasure when I have drunk the liquor of the esoteric doctrine": this quotation from Mir Camar Uddin Mast comes shortly after the passage quoted above. And a passage which follows immediately evokes even more consciously the ancient practice of meditation, with its insistence on ascetic separations from the world in order to dedicate oneself to meditation on the Book, paying attention to every single word, seeking a "sensus plenior" which is exemplary for the reader, in such a way that the apparently dead language in which it is written becomes alive, and the only one which is alive.

---

6   Cf. his *Distich* 1798: "Einem Gelang es – er hab den Schleyer der Göttin zu Sais - Aber was sah er? Er sah – Wunder des Wunders – Sich Selbst" ("A man managed to lift the veil of the Goddess of Sais. But what did he see? He saw – miracle of miracles – Himself") (Novalis, *Werke, Tagebücher und Briefe Friederich von Hardenbergs*, H.J. Mähl and R. Samuel eds., I [München 1978] p. 128). The distich must be compared to a pair of passages of Novalis' *The Adepts of Sais*, p. 204 and p. 218 in the same edition. According to L. Schleiner, *Emerson's Orphic and Messianic Bard*, ESQ 25 (79), pp. 191-202, Emerson knew Novalis and the orphic Jesus of his *Hymns to the Night*. It is not possible to demonstrate a direct influence here with any certainty. Thoureau's attitude is nearer to Novalis than to the more negative position of Schiller. His emphasis is rather on the identity of the two subjects who, at a great distance of time, repeat the same enterprise of raising the veil and contemplating the same glory. Maybe Paul's 2 Cor. 3 underlies both Novalis' and Thoreau's text: Moses had to veil his face, to speak to the Hebrews, while the Christian believer can contemplate with boldness (*parrhesìa*) the glory of God, moved by the Spirit who transforms him into the same glory (L.L. Long, "The Bible and the Composition of Walden", *Studies in the American Renaissance* [1979] pp. 309-353, did not see this allusion). A passage of *Week* presents the same image of the veil, but with a different emphasis: "Critical acumen is exerted in vain to uncover the past: the *past* cannot be *presented*; we cannot know what we are not. But one veil hangs over past, present and future, and it is the province of the historian to find out, not what was, but what is" (p. 125). See also in *Week*, "Wednesday": "This is my Carnac [...] Where is the spirit of that time but in / This present day, perchance the present line?" (p. 205). And "Thursday": "The life of a wise man is most of all extemporaneous, for he lives out of an eternity which includes all time. The cunning mind travels further back than Zoroaster each instant, and comes quite down to the present with its revelation" (p. 255).

> The heroic books, even if printed in the character of our mother tongue, will always be in a language dead to degenerate times; and we must laboriously seek the meaning of each word and line, conjecturing a larger sense than common use permits out of that wisdom and valour and generosity we have (p. 403).[7]

It is therefore opportune to review rapidly the essential features of ancient religious hermeneutics, paying special attention to the tradition in which Thoreau can be placed, in spite of his historical and cultural distance.

Ancient Christian hermeneutics, with all their differences between authors, epochs and traditions, and with many features in common with others religious traditions, especially the Jewish tradition, converge above all in their conception of the sacred text. The Bible evidently transcends any other writing. In it, text and history coincide: "narrat textum, prodit mysterium", says Gregory the Great, who synthesizes preceding hermeneutical tradition at the end of the sixth century; animated by the spirit, it constitutes a living, unified and coherent body, which moves with a force, "virtus", and "dynamis" of its own, like the chariot in the vision of Ezekiel, as Gregory himself writes, in his commentary on the Prophet.

Secondly, ancient hermeneutics agree on the definition of the reader of the sacred text. It requires a reader who is also animated by the Spirit, a reader who by reading and interpreting, seeks, through letter and history, knowledge of the "mystery" (as it was then called). Such is the spiritual power, the "virtus" of authentic scriptural contemplation, that it "not only recognizes Sacred Scripture, once it has been created, but would be capable of creating it, if it did not already exist".[8]

From this, thirdly, there is the idea of reading as an act which generates infinite meanings, which spring from connections among the texts, and between the texts and the reader. The biblical universe is thus at the same time infinite and closed (symbolic links to the natural world are possible, but only until the twelfth century, and in subordination to the Bible and with a

---

7   On this "larger sense", see *Walden's Conclusion:* "'They pretend' as I hear 'that the verses of Kabir have four different senses; illusion, spirit, intellect, and the exoteric doctrine of the Vedas'; but in this part of the world it is a ground of complaint if a man's writings admit of more than one interpretation" (p. 373). This text is obviously very important for S. Cavell, *The Senses of Walden* , cit., p.15, cf. n. 20.

8   Gregory the Great, "Contemplatio enim virtus est, non solum per quam Scriptura condita recognoscitur, sed per quam nondum condita conderetur et per quam condita ad Dei voluntatem cotidie disponatur" (*In l. I Reg.* III, 171). Cf. my *L'interpretazione infinita*, p.67, where there is a commentary on the text.

biblical basis) and in this universe there is the reader himself. The final result of reading will thus be the prolongation of the text until it involves the reader in his present time: the text becomes true, it becomes exemplary and normative for the reader and for his community. Its application is not external to its interpretation, but constitutes the necessary final moment of that interpretation: it is *gnosis*, knowledge as the link between contemplation and action, in which contemplation ends.

2. We now come to the examination of the hermeneutic theory underlying "Reading". Even in the hermit's solitude of Walden there is a *lectio divina*, but with what analogies and what differences from the ancient model?

Above all, there is the notion of the sacred text. This is not denied; however, "Scripture" at this point becomes plural, "Scriptures": "the recorded wisdom of mankind, the ancient classics and Bibles", "the sacred Scriptures, or Bibles of mankind" (p. 407 f.).[9] There is not just one sacred text: every people and every tradition has them, and all are admitted into a sort of canon. It is time for anyone who is seeking knowledge to abandon the "silent gravity and exclusiveness" of a person who thinks that his own religious experience is unique and can be referred to a single text. It is necessary "to learn liberality together with wisdom... Zoroaster, thousands of years ago, travelled the same road, and had the same experience and established worship among men; but he, being wise, knew it to be universal". Thus it is necessary for the solitary person, who thinks he is alone in his faith, to "humbly commune with Zoroaster... and, through the liberalizing influence of all the worthies, with Jesus Christ himself, and let our church go by the board" (p. 409).

In a complex passage, preceding that which I have just quoted, Thoreau establishes a distinction between classics and Scriptures, but both types of text are then joined together: one should begin, and then continue to add to a great sacred library, for the sake of humanity:

> That age will be rich indeed when those relics which we call classic, but even less known Scriptures of the nations, shall have further accumulated, when the Vaticans shall be filled with Vedas and Zendavestas and Bibles,

---

9 "Ethnical Scriptures" was a section of the *Dial*, the trascendentalist review, in which Indian, Chinese, Persian texts were published. Cf. also *Week*, pp. 58 f.: "The reading which I love best is the scriptures of the several nations, though it happens that I am better acquainted with those of the Hindoos, the Chinese, and the Persians, than of the Hebrews, which I have come to last. Give me one of these Bibles and you have silenced me for a while".

with Homers and Dantes and Shakespeares, and all centuries to come shall have successively deposited their trophies in the forum of the world. By such a pile we may hope to scale heaven at last (p. 505).

With this last comment, the image of a new Vatican is transformed into a biblical reference: the new universal library will be the real Jacob's ladder, and will succeed where the tower of Babel failed, in reaching heaven.[10]

The sacredness of the text is also the sacredness of language: Thoreau distinguishes between common language and the language used in the Classics and in Scriptures: the ancient masses were able to speak Greek or Latin, but they could not read or understand the great works: they spoke their "mother tongue", but for great texts it was necessary to know a "father tongue, a reserved and select expression, too significant to be heard by the ear, which we must be born again in order to speak" (p. 403). It is necessary to be born again, through a sort of mystic initiation, to be able to understand a language of the classics or the Scriptures.

Here one is struck by the clear affirmation of the primacy of written language over spoken language. Of the dialogues of Plato, who expressed in *Phaedrus* and in the *Seventh Letter* his distrust of the written word, Thoreau specifically says that these "contain what is immortal in him" (p. 408). One is also struck by the argument against the occasional nature of rhetoric, which is opposed to the universality, stability and purity of writing: "The noblest written words are commonly as far behind or above the fleeting spoken language as the firmament with its stars is behind the clouds" (p. 404).[11] I would say that the emphasis here tends to be different from Emerson, who, in the *Divinity School Address* of 1838 protested against "the assumption that the age of inspiration is past, that the Bible is closed" (like

---

10 For Thoreau's eclepticism, cf. R. Sattelmeyer, *Thoreau's Reading. A Study in Intellectual History with Bibliographical Catalogue* (Princeton UP, 1988) pp. 20 ff., who underlines the role of Victor Cousin in Thoreau's education. See more in general G.J. Joyaux, "Victor Cousin and American Transcendentalism" (1955), in *Critical Essays on American Transcendentalism*, Ph.F. Gura and J. Myerson eds. (Boston: Hall, 1982) pp. 327-338. O. Brownson was responsible for making Cousin better known, around 1838.

11 Incidentally, Thoreau rediscovers an ancient image here. As *Isaiah* 34:4 says that in the end the "heavens will be rolled up like a book", Augustine develops in several places the connection between Scripture and the heavenly firmament (*En.in ps.* 103,7-9; cf. *Conf.* XIII, 15, 16 f.) and above all affirms: "However much one may progress in science, he will always find himself underneath that Scripture which God has placed, like a firmament, above all human hearts" (*Ad Orosium*, XI, 14; PL 42, c. 678).

earlier German romanticism);[12] who in *Self-reliance* affirmed that "the highest merit we ascribe to Moses, Plato and Milton is that they set at naught books and traditions, and spoke not what men, but what they thought", and in *The American Scholar* declared of books that "they are for nothing but inspire".[13]

Secondly, similarly to the ancient conception, the reader should be congenial to the text, should be animated by the same spirit:

> To read well, that is, to read true books in a true spirit, is a noble exercise and one that will task the reader more than any exercise which the customs of the day esteem. It requires a training such as the athletes underwent, the steady intention almost of the whole life to this object. Books must be read as deliberately[14] and reservedly as they were written (p. 403).

Here too is a spontaneous restoration of the situation, the *Sitz im leben* of the ancient *lectio* and "spiritual exercises": the study of scriptures requires conformity to the spirit of the text, a decision, an "intention" which is also an act of isolation from others and a continual exercise. One notes the stoic and monastic terminology, the *askesis* (we have already seen how reading requires "wisdom, generosity and valour", p. 403).[15]

But we see, further on, the introduction of a modern, humanistic and universalistic element: one should (and can) learn ancient languages, at least what is necessary to understand the language in which the text is written: this learning is necessarily artificial, because in each case it concerns a "father tongue" which we would not possess spontaneously even if we had the same "mother tongue".

And here, thirdly, is the result: reading. With the text thus perceived,

---

[12] Texts by Novalis ("Who said that the Bible is still closed? Shouldn't we think of the Bible as still growing?"), F. Schlegel, by the young Schleiermacher, in *L'interpretazione infinita*, p. 133.

[13] Cf. H. Bloom: "...the characteristic Thoreauvian swerve towards the authority of books, rather than away from them in the Emersonian manner", *Modern Critical Views, H.D.Thoreau*, H. Bloom ed. (New York-New Haven-Philadelphia: Chelsea House Publishers, 1987) "Introduction", p. 9. For Emerson, a prose-writer was *un orateur manqué*, cf. the pages on Emerson's "Eloquence" in F.O. Matthiessen, *American Renaissance: Art and Expression in the Age of Emerson and Whitman* (New York: Oxford University Press, 1941) I, I, § 2.

[14] "Deliberately": see Matthiessen, *American Renaissance*, I, II, § 3 (on the use of this term in the famous passage of the II chapter, "I went to the woods because I wished to live deliberately...", p. 394).

[15] Cf. P. Hadot, *Exercises spirituels et philosophie antique* (Paris: Etudes Augustiniennes, 1987). Ch.R. Anderson, *The Magic Circle of Walden* (New York-Chicago-San Francisco: Holt, Rinehart and Winston, 1968) insists on more pagan than Christian "ascetical" aspects in Thoreau.

and the reader thus prepared, now comes the meeting between the author of the text and his reader. The reader discovers that he is not alone. In the classics, modern man finds the answers to the questions that he asks: "They are the only oracles which are not decayed, and there are such answers to the most modern inquiry in them as Delphi and Dodona never gave" (p. 403). More fully:

> There are probably words addressed to our condition exactly, which, if we could read and understand, would be more salutary than the morning or the spring to our lives, and possibly put a new aspect on the face of things for us. How many a man has dated a new era in his life from the reading of a book. The book exists for us perchance which will explain our miracles and reveal new ones. The at present unutterable things we may find somewhere uttered (p. 408).

Thus, in every situation, there is a book "for us". It is difficult not to remember the "for us" with which Christian authors evoke Hebrew texts: for Paul, in the *I Corinthians* the events of the Exodus find their meaning "to admonish us, who have arrived at the end of time".[16] Along with this, we remember the "even greater wonders" which Jesus promised that his disciples would perform (*John* 14:12). The reward of reading is thus the acquisition of words of wisdom – "wisdom" is here the key term –: "golden words, which the wisest men of antiquity have uttered, and whose worth the wise of every succeeding age have assured us of" (p. 408). Let us return to the beginning of "Reading": reading, finally, is the appropriation of past experience, to the point of becoming the same person who first had that experience: "It was I in him... and it is he in me".

3. Having sketched the similarities between the two hermeneutical approaches, it is necessary at this point, in conclusion, to highlight the differences, by referring however to elements which have already been mentioned.

First of all, while it is true that the expansion of the sacred text, the open unlimited structure of the canon (to the point of including not only the classics and the scriptures of the past, and not only future works, but also the book of nature itself)[17] occurs through an extensive use of sacred terminology,

---

[16] Cf. Emerson, *History* : "Law was enacted, the sea was searched, the land was found, or the blow was struck, for us... So all that is said of the wise man by Stoic or Oriental or modern essayist, describes to each reader his own idea, describes his unattained but attainable self".

[17] An obvious aspect, which I have not stressed, and which appears in our own

there is no doubt that the general process is one of secularization. It is what Novalis describes, when he narrates how the follower of Sais, lifting the veil of the goddess, discovered under the veil nothing but himself.[18]

Furthermore, this insistence on the aspect of learning the language presupposes the reformed idea of "claritas Scripturae" (that is, its independence with regard to the context of ecclesiastical tradition), presupposes the humanistic upheaval and thus the autonomy of the critical method,[19] and alludes to the first romantic philology, of F. Schlegel, for example: where philology, as precise linguistic research and the search for "intentio auctoris" often coexists happily with the interpretation of the textual segment in a wider connotation, because in the content directly meant by the author "the entire world" is present, as a concomitant representation (thus Schleiermacher).[20] Again, it is the secularization, that

---

chapter: one cannot neglect the study of ancient authors with the excuse that they are old: "We might as well omit to study nature because she is old" (p. 146). This sentence is missing in the first version, where, instead, we find an important variation: books "have to be studied in the same spirit that we study nature. They are only valuable commentaries on her works, never ancient, and never modern" (Shanley, *The Making of Walden*, p. 147). An identification of works of art and works of nature is also missing in the final version (*ib.* , p. 149). But the theme of nature is developed in "Sounds": "Will you be a reader, a student merely, or a seer?", cf. n. 19.

[18] The first version contains the most noteworthy variations, in my opinion, in the entire chapter. The last sentence of the first paragraph "That time which we really improve... is neither past, present, nor future" was at the beginning, and was illustrated as follows: "I might say that the student always studies antiques. In our studies we do not look forward but backward into antiquity with redoubled pauses. Where is that lost first page of history? We have never found the literature that dated from an antiquity sufficiently remote. The most adventurous student seeks the remotest antiquity, the history of a time, as it were, prior to time. Or, if we prefer, such is the Protean character of things, we may say that he always interprets prophecies and oracles, and is interested solely in the future. In accumulating property..." (Shanley, *The Making of Walden*, p. 144). This first version emphasizes atemporality, while the final version highlights self-identification.

[19] Sattelmeyer, *Thoreau's Reading*, speaks of Thoreau as "a bookish man with scholarly instincts", p. 110.

[20] This is the only "larger sense" allowed at present: differently from S. Cavell's interpretation, and in coherence with W. Benn Michaels', I see in the reference to oriental poliseemy (the "four different senses", p. 373, quoted in n. 6) the perception of a no longer superable cultural gap between the ancient and the present way of interpreting: the latter has its pattern in the interpretation of nature, which is necessarily monosemic: "the power of figurative reading is not the only thing Walden teaches us; it also urges upon us the necessity of reading literally, not so much in addition to reading figuratively as *instead of* reading figuratively". In this sense, W. Benn Michaels rightly quotes the beginning of "Sounds" (p. 156): "But while we are confined to books, though the most select

is the criticism and rational recovery of the ancient hermeneutical procedure.

Finally, the encounter between text (with its author) and reader does not occur any more as the construction of symbolic connections (myths such as the allegory of virtue, or the Old Testament as a stock of typologies for the New Testament), but as a conceptual construction at a level which is essentially rational and ethical,[21] or, that is, as the discovery of the permanent validity of certain models, the exemplary nature of certain figures, and the pertinence of certain answers, because the questions are universal, and human nature is fundamentally the same everywhere.[22]

Thus, my task is completed. And yet, that which is most characteristic and fascinating in Thoreau, the extraordinary political intensity of his cultural proposal, has not been mentioned. Thoreau, as is well-known, strongly supports an aristocratic knowledge (note his scorn for popular literature), but rejects an aristocratic model: "Their authors are a natural and irresistible aristocracy in every society, and more than kings and emperors, exert an influence on humanity" (p. 405). And he also rejects the usual model of aristocratic knowledge, opposing this with nothing other than that of the first medieval university: "As the nobleman of cultivated taste surrounds himself with whatever conduces to his culture, genius,

---

and classic, and read only particular written languages, which are themselves but dialects and provincial, we are in danger of forgetting the language which all things and events speak without metaphor, which alone is copious and standard... Will you be a reader, a student merely, or a seer?" ("Walden' False Bottoms," in *Modern Critical Views, H.D.Thoreau*, cit., p. 92; in the same direction J. Carlos Rowe, "The being of Language: The Language of Being", *ib.*, p. 146 f.). On cultural distance, cf. "The Pond in Winter", last paragraph: "... and I doubt if that philosophy [i.e. the Bhagavad-Gita] is not to be referred to a previous state of existence, so remote is its sublimity from our conceptions" (see Matthiessen, *American Renaissance*, I, III, § 2).

[21] On the "pragmatic" character of Thoreauvian reading, cf. *Week*, "Sunday": Pythagoras', Plato's, Jamblicus' "long, slimy sentences are of that consistency that they naturally flow and run together. They read as if written from military men, for men of business, there is such a dispatch in them" (p. 84 = *Journal*, March 28th, 1842, p. 353). One notes again how the opening passage quoted, with its mystical nature, ends with an ethical tone, the ancient idea of spiritual progress: "That time which we really improve, or which is improvable,is neither past, present, nor future".

[22] On universalism see *Week*: "All nations love the same jests and tales, Jews, Christians and Mahometans, and the same suffice for all. All men are children, and of one family. The same tale sends them to bed, and wakes them in the morning" ("Sunday", p. 49).

learning, wit, books, paintings, statuary, music, philosophical instruments, and the like, so let the village do... New England can hire all the wise men in the world to come and teach her" (p. 410). Just before this he had already used this provocative *hire*: "Can we not hire some Abelard to lecture to us?".

But the force of his proposal is in the fact that it comes from someone who speaks, paradoxically, from outside the city and outside the university, and who insists that it is possible to return, in solitude, amongst the trees, to the most ancient and universal idea of knowledge, that in which book and nature are mingled:

> My residence was more favorable not only to thought, but to serious reading, than a university; and though I was beyond the range of the ordinary circulating library, I had more than ever come within the influence of those books which circulate round the world, whose sentences were written on the bark, and are now merely copied (p. 144).[23]

---

[23] Cf. H. Bloom: "Thoreau's crucial swerve away from Emerson was to treat natural objects as books, and books as chunks of nature, thus evading all literary tradition, Emerson's writings not excepted", in *Modern Critical Views, H.D.Thoreau, Introduction*, p. 7. This will also be the reason why he criticized Ruskin, for not having fully accepted the primacy of nature over the Bible. Cf. Thoreau, *Vita di uno scrittore*, B.Tedeschini Lalli ed. (Vicenza: Neri Pozza, 1963) p. 71.
I must finally thank Cristina Giorcelli (University of Rome): she read this paper and made useful suggestions to a simple *amateur* of American literature, as I have remained since the time, many years ago, when we read Matthiessen's *American Renaissance*, together with Pavese's introduction to the Italian translation.

5

Leo Tolstoy's *Cycle of Reading*

1. Tolstoy's last years are characterized by his definitive separation from European culture. It is a divorce that involves his own past works, the works that had introduced him into that culture and made him famous. In 1905 he writes on his *Journal:* "Now the history of my relationship with Europe has been clarified: 1. happiness at being known, modest man as I was; 2. happiness at being as much appreciated as one of themselves; 3. appreciated more than one of themselves; 4. you begin to understand who those who appreciate you are; 5. doubts as to whether they can understand you; the certainty that they do not; 6. you realize that they do not understand anything; that those whose appreciation was to me so dear are stupid and primitive people".

Solov'ëv's final attacks on Tolstoy, his excommunication by the Orthodox Church, the criticism coming from leading figures of Russian culture, from people who had been his admirers in the very recent past, such as Merezhkovsky and Cechov, Tolstoy's refusal to show any solidarity with reformers and revolutionaries at the moment of the Russian-Japanese war and of the so called first Revolution – all these are the expressions of this rupture. But separation and solitude are only one aspect: they are the price he pays for the discovery of new affinities with the great ethical and religious traditions of the rest of the world, and sometimes also, concretely, for new acquaintances, like his friendship with Gandhi, at the end of Tolstoy's life, and at the beginning of Gandhi's political activity.

A pluralistic interest is already present in Tolstoy's culture already at the beginning of the 1880s, that is, at the beginning of the last period of his activity, after his conversion to a form of radical and universalistic Christianity. When we read his letter to Lederle, in 1891, where he speaks of the books he preferred in his sixties and seventies, alongside the Gospels in Greek, the *Genesis* in Hebrew, Henry George, Theodore Parker, Pascal and Epictetus, we find also authors such as Confucius, Mencius and Buddha.

2. This interest very soon expressed itself in the project of a "cycle of reading", comprising – I quote – "Epictetus, Marcus Aurelius, Lao-Tse, Buddha, Pascal, the Gospel. It should be necessary to everybody" (*Journal*, March 15, 1884). It was the idea of a gnomic, or rather sapiential compilation: short texts, from every age and culture, which should serve as testimonies to his ethical and religious convictions. As a precedent for this idea, there had been not only, in earlier years, the experience of his reading-book for children, but also, in the 1870s, his study of "Lives of the Saints" and of the "Proverbs of the Russian People", in Dahl's edition and of the Wisdom Literature (the part of the Old Testament he enjoyed most). This material was organized for daily reading and meditation, according to the stoic, and afterwards Christian model, of spiritual exercises. Tolstoy worked systematically on this book only after *Resurrection*. Helped by relatives and friends he prepared first a collection of "Thoughts of wise men for every day", then he published in 1906 the *Cycle of Reading*, in 2 vols. with a revised edition soon afterwards, *For every day*. Attracted by the idea of a thematic disposition of collected materials, he published a final edition of the collection organised according to themes and sub-themes, such as faith, soul, God, love etc. He called his last work: *Put' zhizni, The way of life*.

Tolstoy's presence in this work is imposing. He chooses the texts, of course, on the basis of his own sensibility. He introduces and concludes each item (every day, or each thematic unity, in *The way of life*), and very often inserts his own reflections.

Personally and with the help of relatives and friends, he translated or rather paraphrased many of the texts. In a provocative, very clear text, meant originally to be a preface to the *Cycle*, but which remained unpublished, Tolstoy explained the criteria behind his translations.

> The works of the great writers were great only because they are necessary and because it is desirable that the largest possible number of people may enjoy the spiritual goodness those writers communicate. And in order that the largest possible public may enjoy this benefit, it is necessary to make these writers accessible, and therefore to make fully clear what is not fully clear. It is necessary to drop what might be difficult or shocking for the contemporary reader[...].
>
> But, some will say, this will no longer be the Gospel, or Epictetus, or Pascal, or Rousseau, but your work. This argument is considered irrefutable in the scholars' world as if all the importance were in him to whom the work is attributed. I believe indeed that Epictetus', Rousseau's and other writers' thoughts, although transmitted with modifications, abridgements, or even additions, will anyway be Epictetus', Rousseau's, and that no harm, but on the contrary much profit can come from the attitude of those who love these thoughts and try to transmit them insofar as they understand them,

changing them so that they could be understood more easily and with more strength by those who think in the same way. All this I have said to explain why I translated freely the thoughts gathered here with a single purpose: to make the book as accessible and useful as possible to the majority of readers. In this way if there are people who intend to translate this book into other languages, I do not suggest they have to look in their own language at the original texts of the English Coleridge, of the German Kant, of the French Rousseau, but, if they really are willing to translate, let them translate from my own text (PSS 42, pp. 470-473).

3. Let us for the moment continue to read the *Cycle*, starting from its first page, from January 1st, in which Tolstoy precisely speaks of reading (PSS 41, pp. 11-13). His introductory sentence runs as follow:

Better the knowledge of a few really good and necessary things, than a second-rate and unnecessary knowledge.

There follow thoughts of various authors, all of them very familiar to Tolstoy (except perhaps Locke), and very often quoted in further pages of the *Cycle of Reading*. I will present them, without stopping to comment on single authors, although a good deal of work could be done on them (some of which I have already done, finding the sources, and placing them in Tolstoy's own context). Here is Ralf Waldo Emerson, from the essay *Books* in *Society and Solitude*. I do not follow for the moment Tolstoy's suggestion, and quote texts in English from the original, noting that his translation does not change it essentially:

Consider what you have in the smallest chosen library. A company of the wisest and wittiest men that could be picked out of all civil countries in a thousand years have set in the best order the results of their learning and wisdom. The men themselves were hid and inaccessible, solitary, impatient of interruption, fenced by etiquette: but the thought which they did not uncover to their bosom friend is here written out in transparent words to us, the strangers of another age (*Society and Solitude, Twelve Chapters*, 1904, p. 190).

Tolstoy might well recognize himself in this portrait of *Society and Solitude*! A passage by Locke follows. The source is the *Essay on Human Understanding*,

We are of the ruminating kind, and it is not enough to cram ourselves over again with a great load of collections; unless we chew over again, they will not give us strength and nourishment (*The Works of John Locke*, III, 1823, p. 241).

It is also worth reading the few preceding lines in Locke's *Essay*: "Those who have read of everything are thought to understand everything too; but it is not always so. Reading furnishes the mind only with materials of knowledge: it is thinking that makes what we read ours". The unmistakable classical flavour of this passage, with its metaphor of reading as digestion, prepares us for the following thought, picked up from Seneca's second letter to Lucilius. The original text is amplified, but recognizable. I translate here from the Russian.

> You must be afraid that reading many authors and books of any kind will bring into your mind confusion and uncertainty. You must nourish yourself only by writers of undoubted value, if you want to draw some profit from them. Too many books distract the mind. Thus, read only books of proven value [lat. "probatos"], and if sometimes you wish to pass temporarily to other works, never forget to return to the first ones.

Then very briefly Thoreau:

> Read the best books first, or you may not have a chance to read them at all ?

This text does not come from chapter 3 of *Walden*, "Reading", but from *A Week on the Merrimack and Concord Rivers, Sunday*, interestingly alongside a quotation from *Bhagavadgita*.

Next, there are two rather long texts by Schopenhauer, from *Parerga and Paralipomena* (24, "Ueber Lesen und Bücher"), very freely elaborated, it seems. The first one:

> One must read books only when the spring of one's thoughts is exhausted, which not rarely happens even to the best of men. But to let one thought of one's own escape before it matures, because of a book, constitutes a sin against the spirit [probably a summary of *Parerga*, § 291].

The second refers to § 295. Its central point is that, faced with the enormous amount of useless, or rather, harmful literary production,

> one is obliged to lose the habit of reading those books that occupy common attention or provoke noise. (the original speaks of: "die Kunst nicht zu Lesen"). Simply speaking, it is necessary to despise those books whose first year of life will be also the last one. One must consider that he who writes for the ignorant will always find a large set of readers, whilst men ought to devote their short existence to making acquaintance with the great masters of all ages and nations, whose richly endowed creative spirits excel and tower over the multitude of bad writers. Only writers of this kind can educate and teach.

A comment again by Tolstoy himself concludes the reading proposed for the first day of the year:

> The difference between material and intellectual poisons lies in this, that most material poisons are repugnant to taste, whilst the intellectual ones, in form of bad books, are often unfortunately attractive.

To complete this complete collection one must go to another page, where one can find Lichtenberg saying:

> What a quantity of useless reading could be avoided by an autonomous reading! Are reading and study really the same same thing? Someone has maintained, not without good reason, that, if the press has allowed a more widespread culture, it has also caused a loss of quality and substance. Reading too much is harmful to thought. The best thinkers I met among the authors I studied were the less erudite. If people were taught how to think, and not only what to think, we could avoid ignorance.

On the same page, an aphorism by Ruskin:

> Mind is strengthened or weakened by reading, exactly as the body with fresh or rotten air.

4. The very ancient gnomic genre to which Tolstoy's *Cycle of Reading* belongs was very widespread in this period. To find examples, it is enough to consult, in the editor Gusev's critical appendix, the list of Tolstoy's sources. There are many works of this kind, English, French, German, and of course Russian. The *Posrednik* (which means *The Mediator*), whose origins lay in the collaboration between Tolstoy and the editor Sytin, produced a number of such compilations, some of them by Tatiana, Lev Tolstoy's elder daughter.

Jeffrey Brook's interesting study, *When Russia Learned to Read. Literacy and Popular Literature, 1861-1917* (Princeton University Press, 1985), shows the context in which this kind of work must be placed. This book is a study of the diffusion of popular books during the 50 years preceding the Revolution. These are the years of emancipation, of urbanization, of industrialization, and of the final attempts at imperialistic expansion, but are also the years in which a positive, cosmopolitan, universalistic perspective makes its way in Russian culture. This is the moment at which, alongside the popular novel, the feuilleton, and other popular genres the gnomic genre flourishes, with the contribution of editors such as *Posrednik*, whose catalogue contained many such collections, drawn from Russian or foreign, ancient or modern sources.

5. The originality of Tolstoy's sapiential collections lies in the fact that for him the unhistorical universalism characteristic of the gnomic genre is no longer ingenuous, collecting maxims from everywhere and from all periods without any criterion, except that of their correspondence with tradition and the common sense of the middle class. Tolstoy's universalism is here deliberate and critical and is applied to the collection of extremely problematic and provoking axioms and must be seen within the framework of the later Tolstoy's spirituality, that is of his expanded and radical Christianity. All this can be already understood from the lines quoted above, with which he himself begins and closes the aphorism of the first page of his *Cycle*. His position is even more evident if we read the introduction to the same page in the further elaboration, in *The Way of Life, Put' zhizni*: "Superstition and deception torment people. One thing alone can free them: truth. We know the truth both personally and through wise and holy persons who lived before us. Thus, in order to live a good and fine life it is necessary to search for the truth both personally and through the wise and holy persons who lived before us". And again: "One of the most effective means in order to know the truth that frees us from superstition consists in the knowledge of all that has been done in the past by mankind to know and to express eternal truth, common to all men".

6. There is here a precise conception, which should be discussed separately. I shall say something about it towards the end of my presentation. But let me now discuss briefly Tolstoy's idea of reading. Its peculiarity consists in the fact that the tradition of religious hermeneutics, and the ancient conception of the sacred book is here re-enhanced, but at the same time secularised.

For Tolstoy, certain books, in some way inspired, come to us with a special timing and strength, responding to our own vital questions. Although fully accessible, these books must be sharply distinguished from all other books, from the bulk of vulgar production. But these books are not only the Christian scriptures, but come from many different sources, transmitting, with the same intensity as the oral word, the thought of the "wise and holy men" who preceded us. The canon which contains them is always open: it is a library that can be always enriched by new contributions.

These books require a selected and enlightened reader who shares their inspiration (Intr. KC: *lyudi odinakogo s nimi ponimaniya*), a reader able to separate himself from the world and to devote himself to the spiritual exercise of self-knowledge (a formula with a long history) through the mirror of scripture. But this exercise does not culminate in an act of faith in the text, which justifies allegorically every detail of it. The relationship with the text – or rather, the texts – is a critical one: it can include historical criticism, it can give the text a clarity it still does not possess, and in any case leaves the last word to the insight of the independent mind of the reader. Reading is no longer a *lectio divina*, a "sacred action", an act of mystical identification with the text. Rather than being inside the text, the reader assimilates it through conceptual elaboration, in line with his own moral transformation .

7. We must be precise, regarding this word "assimilation". Interpretation does not mean depriving a writer of his authorship. Tolstoy wrote, in the preface to the *Cycle* quoted above: "I cannot say that these are thoughts of mine and therefore, although I have somewhat changed them, they remain Rousseau's" (later he cancelled this explanation, probably because he believed it to be superfluous). Concern for history and philology is not at all lacking in Tolstoy's attitude towards the text. He had a remarkable gift for languages, and from the 1870s onwards we see him studying the classics and the Bible in their original languages. His correspondence shows his eagerness for new editions of classics and monographs. In Moscow he attended the largest library and asks the librarian N.F. Fedorov for help, as well as erudite friends, such as V. Stasov and N. Strachov. But Tolstoy aims at accessibility and moral utility in reading, and this could lead him sometimes to simplification and a lack of attention to philological details (especially in his New Testament exegesis). But this attitude was founded upon a deep conviction: at the level of *razumenie*, as he said, which is not the level of exoteric or mystic knowledge, but the level of the instruction necessary for life, there is a substantial concordance, a convergence among authors. The fundamental truths, indispensable for the life of mankind, cannot differ radically from one country (or culture, or time) to another. This makes it possible and legitimate to enter the text, paraphrase it and even omit things considered to be non essential, with the certainty that the interpretation will not be an overturning of the text. Its point, the elements of wisdom it contains will in any case not be lost. For this reason, with his taste for paradox, Tolstoy could maintain: "Let them read me, not Kant in German, or Coleridge in English, or Rousseau in French". This was an extreme formulation of Tolstoy's ethics of reading, whose point consisted in a serious plea in favour of identity and universality.

8. "Eternal truth", "superstition"....: these terms, that we read above, evoke the philosophical and religious theses Tolstoy had begun to expound after 1880, with *My Faith*, and the *Kingdom of God is Among You*, and many other secondary writings, now almost forgotten, but at that time famous and much discussed. Now it is evident that what we have here is not only an idea of reading. "How to read" here, like in the ancient stoic tradition, is strictly connected with "how to converse", "how to live" and "how to die". This way of reading the sources of the past is a result of the conviction, which I have already pointed out, that there exists a fundamental wisdom, common to various cultural traditions, and that this wisdom is the only one worthy of being pursued. This wisdom, in a secularized and multi-cultural world, must be pursued only in a multiplicity of sources, which must be read with the certitude of their fundamental convergence. This conviction he shared with the authors we recalled in the first page of the *Cycle*, Emerson, Thoreau, Ruskin, Schopenhauer, and many others that should be remembered, between the Enlightenment and the Romantic Age, with important classical precedents. The last one is perhaps Simone Weil.

This sapiential idea cannot be discussed here. I have done this elsewhere, indicating some arguments in favour of Tolstoyan critical universalism[1]. Let me only suggest that the notion of secularisation is essential for the evaluation of Tolstoy's religious approach. Unlike Karl Barth's protestant perspective, secularisation, in Tolstoy's view (although he did not use this word) did not mean removing religion from society but blending it positively into the latter, under the form of a radical and universalistic religious ethics. In any case, this idea of reading, which claims to be at the same time a way of life, deserves much more attention. From this point of view the *Cycle of Reading* should be systematically studied as the expression of a courageous ethical project that can begin to speak again to us, through the extraordinary plurality of the voices it conveys.

---

[1]   See my *Tolstoy. Oltre la letteratura*, cit.

6

Oskar Pfister, "Pfarrer in Zürich ", and Lay Analyst

"Oskar Pfister, Pfarrer in Zürich": this is how one of the first lay analysts signed his writings on psychoanalytical subjecs during almost 50 years of activity. According to Ernest Jones, he was the first non-medical analyst, along with a woman, Hermine Hug-Hellmuth, a Viennese specialist in child psychoanalysis. Oskar Pfister (1873-1956), vicar at the Predigerkirche in Zurich, came across Freud's work in 1908 and had been in correspondence with him before meeting him personally. Karl Jung, in turn, had often spoken of him to Freud, as Freud himself mentions in his first letter to Pfister, on January 18th, 1909.

Another of Freud's letters recalls the sensation brought about by Pfister's first appearance in Berggasse 19, on Sunday, April 25th, 1909. A miniature reproduction of the Matterhorn, a present from Pfister, a passionate climber, was on his table, and brought to mind a sense of gratitude:

> It reminds me of a remarkable man who came to see me one day, a true servant of God, a man in the very idea of whom I should have had difficulty in believing, in that he feels the need to do spiritual good to everyone he meets. You did good in this way even to me.[1]

Oskar Pfister came to Berggasse when he was 36. His personality was

---

This text is based on my "Oskar Pfister, 'Pfarrer in Zürich' e analista laico", *Psicoterapia e scienze umane* 1990, n. 3, pp. 3-36 (see also *Revue internationale d'histoire de la psychanalyse*, 1990, n. 3, pp. 129-143).

[1] I quote the correspondence between S. Freud and O. Pfister (*Briefe 1909-1939* [Frankfurt a.M.: S. Fischer Verlag, 1963]) according to the English edition: *Psycho-Analysis and Faith. The Letters of Sigmund Freud and Oskar Pfister*, ed. by H. Meng and E.L. Freud, transl. by E. Mosbacher, [London: The Hogarth Press and the Institute of Psychoanalysis, 1963] p. 24. I shall simply give the date of the letters.

already well formed. His short autobiography, his 1927 *Selbstdarstellung*,[2] gives an idea of his background. After studying theology and philosophy in Basel, Zurich and Berlin (he attended the lessons of teachers such as Hermann Lotze, Richard Avenarius and Friedrich Paulsen), and after a doctorate in religious philosophy, he became in 1902 vicar at the Predigerkirche, the church that had belonged to the Dominican order, the "preachers", before the Reformation and Zwingli. He was troubled both by the sad pictures of sickness, poverty, and moral degradation caused by industrialization, and by the impotence of the theology and the pastoral care of his times. His contemporaries Karl Barth, the great theologian, Albert Schweitzer, the Bible scholar, musician, and physician and Leonhard Ragaz, the Christian socialist, certainly had in common with Pfister, together with social and pastoral concerns, also a very critical view of what Pfister called the "pitiful condition of our theology", "outdated, abstract, scholastic, non-scientific, bewildered"[3]. Barth and Ragaz would pursue the reformation of theology and preaching through the denunciation of the dependence of theology on romantic, positivistic culture and middle-class interests. Pfister's perspective is on the contrary well expressed in an early essay of 1899: his problem is the reconstruction of theology, pastoral care and pedagogy through their encounter with modern science. Acquaintance with Freud's work, in 1908, was for him decisive.

Pfister would later gratefully remember his visit to Freud as one of the most pleasant moments in his life (December 30th, 1923). In any case, from this moment on, the principal events in Pfister's life are connected with his relationship with Freud. Their correspondence – unfortunately only partially published – shows Pfister's unconditional admiration for Freud, and Freud's interest in and appreciation of his Swiss disciple. Freud saw in him an opportunity for the expansion of the psychoanalytical movement into a new context, a long way from the Jewish-Viennese medium in which psychoanalysis had its origins. He moreover understood that pastor Pfister could open interesting perspectives for the application of psychoanalysis to a new field, that of pedagogy.

Pfister, who a few weeks before his visit to Freud, had decided not to take a chair at the Theological faculty of Zurich (that chair would be occupied by

---

[2] "Selbstdarstellung", in *Die Pädagogik der Gegenwart in Selbstdarstellungen* (Leipzig, 1927), especially pp. 161-173.

[3] "Das Elend unsrer wissenschaftlichen Glaubenslehre", *Schweiz.theol. Zeitschr ift* 22 (1905) pp. 209-212, quoted in "Selbstdarstellung", p. 7.

Leonhard Ragaz) had to face violent attacks on psychoanalysis in this period. We can read in Evangelische *Freiheit* Pfister's polemical answer to the attacks of Friedrich Wilhelm Foerster. He published in this period various works: methodological essays and studies in which he applies psychoanalysis to religious history, among which a monograph devoted to Zinzendorf, which Jung admired greatly (1910). An essay in *Imago* in 1912 presents in particular the first results of the application of psychoanalysis to pastoral care (the title is *Anwendungen der Psychoanalyse in der Pädagogik und Seelsorge*) with various reflections on the insufficiencies of both Catholic and Protestant pastoral care. His essay is chiefly devoted to the study of cases met with in pastoral activity: compulsive lying, kleptomania, cruelty towards animals, vandalism, refusal to work, refusal to eat certain foods, eccentric behavior, matrimonial difficulties, abnormal religious attitudes and so on. He opposes corporal punishment and reticence in sexual education. His final considerations are marked by pioneer enthusiasm: "Many people, who, finding themselves in a situation of neurotic compulsion, are and cannot but be but a cause of unutterable suffering for their parents and other people, could recover their health with the help of psychoanalysis and become pleasant and useful persons". At the end of this essay Pfister sets forth the fundamental principles on which the analyst-pedagogue and theologian should draw his of her inspiration: the liberation of the capacity to love. He sees in this a special correspondence with New Testament ethics: "Jesus' commandment, or better, counsel, to love God, one's neighbor, and oneself, shows us the best way to channel the libido: it allows the unfolding of love in its highest quality and exalts personal happiness and collective welfare, especially if the idea of God is understood in its widest and deepest meaning, as the compendium and real foundation of everything that is beautiful, good and true".[4] A few years later, Pfister published his volume on *Psychoanalytical Method*. Freud in his *Preface* set forth an important declaration in favor of lay analysis:

> The practice of psychoanalysis calls much less for medical training than for psychological instruction and a free human outlook. The majority of doctors are not equipped to practice psychoanalysis and have completely failed to grasp the value of the therapeutic procedure. The educator and the pastoral worker are bound by the standards of their profession to exercise the same consideration, care and restraint as are usually practiced by the doctor.[5]

---

[4] "Anwendungen der Psychoanalyse in der Pädagogik und Seelsorge", *Imago* 1 (1912) pp. 56-82, pp. 77-78.

[5] I quote the Standard Edition (abbr. SE) 12, pp. 330-1.

Pfister, in the same book a few pages further on, concluding his *Introduction*, presents a lyrical elaboration of one of Freud's phrases ("psychoanalysis itself is neither religious nor irreligious", February 9th, 1909).

> Psychoanalysis, so maligned and often abused, is neither religious nor irreligious; it not only is consistent with but also presupposes the highest ethical and religious requirements. Analysis has confirmed my conviction that man is not only a sexual creature of the highest order, but also that he truly deserves that variegated spiritual realm and peculiar nobility that the idealist philosophy attributes to him. I certainly could not hide from myself that the sexual life has a much greater importance in our spiritual economy than traditional psychology would like to admit, and in this it goes against the views of a great many poets and other students of mankind. But the most accurate analyses have shown that sexual life is very closely tied to the needs of the soul (*Gemüt*), so that what is purely animal is pushed strongly to the background as of little importance. We do not hide from ourselves the fact that in poetry and even more so in religion love has a predominant role and that Jesus gave a certain form of love as his principal commandment. As Gounod said so well: "the law of life like the law of art lies in Augustine's words:'Love is all'". Why should we be shocked if in mental illness, in dreams, in apparently casual behavior, in short in all the operations that depend on the soul, the influence of love comes to the surface? [6]

These years were years of hardship, in Zurich. In mid-July 1912 there was a 24-hour general strike. "In that calm the demon of civil war was haunting the country" wrote Leonhard Ragaz at that time. Two years later, Lenin would live in Zurich and would attend the library close to Pfister's home.

These were also years of passionate work and production for Pfister, in which he was first acknowledged within the international psychoanalytical movement. The Weimar Congress of the International Psychoanalytical Association in September 1912 was certainly for him an important event. For the last time, everybody (except for Adler) was still there, and Pfister among them, as a picture of the participants shows. But the attacks on psychoanalysis, and Pfister in particular, intensified. His position was extremely delicate, as a church minister and psychoanalyst, who had moreover to face some matrimonial difficulties (he was married to Erika Wunderli). The correspondence between Freud and Jung reflects this situation. Freud appeared to be reluctant to accept Jung's irony about the pastor and was sincerely concerned with his friend's problems. In the same

---

[6] *Die psychoanalytische Methode, Eine erfahrungswissenschaftlich-systematische Darstellung* (Leipzig, 1913) pp. V and VIII.

year 1912 Freud broke with Jung, and Pfister followed Freud. Pfister managed to overcome this difficult period. Jones remembers that when the storm fell on psychoanalysis in the years before the First World War, the only "gentiles" who did not give up were Binswanger, Pfister, and Jones himself.[7] Reciprocal attraction and esteem were very important in maintaining this bond. Jones speaks of Freud's real passion for Pfister: he admired his ethical attitude, his generous altruism and his optimism towards human nature. Moreover the idea of having a protestant pastor as a friend amused him. This did not prevent him from perceiving the excesses of Pfister's "positiveness": "I think that your Analysis suffers from the hereditary vice of virtue", whilst "without a trace of that kind of unscrupulousness the job cannot be done" he wrote to him. But considering that Pfister's activity was more than anything else a pedagogic one, he added: "things are easier for you than for us physicians, because you can sublimate the transference on to religion and ethics, which is not easy for the invalids of life" (June 5th, 1910).

As for Pfister, Freud's friendship and help was extremely important during that period. We do not have Pfister's correspondence of those years: on his request, Freud had to destroy them, with regret, in 1927 (June 1st, 1927). But, in an unpublished letter in 1926, he spoke of his "vehement hunger for love". "Without analysis, I should have broken down long since".[8] The war made the contacts between Freud and Pfister more difficult. The contacts began again, in rather polemical terms, with the letter, in which Freud, in addition to several objections in the field of ethics and sexual theory, asks Pfister the famous question, why the world had to wait for a godless Jew to create psychoanalysis. Pfister replied, as is well-known, with his equally famous "You are no Jew, which to me, in view of my unbounded admiration for Amos, Isaiah, Jeremiah, and the author of Job and Ecclesiastes, is a matter of profound regret, and in the second place you are not godless, for he who lives in the truth lives in God, and he who strives for the freeing of love ("dwelleth in God") (*First Epistle of John*, 4:16)". Considering the larger context in which Freud and his work should be inserted, it is possible to affirm: "A better Christian never was" (October 29th, 1918). Pfister's book on child analysis (1922) [9] expresses deliberately the author's willingness and desire to overcome the conflict that, more or less explicitly, separated him from Freud. The book, he said, was a step ahead for him, because in it he had overcome a number of obscurities which

---

7   E. Jones, *The Life and Works of S.Freud* (New York: Basic Books, 1953) II, III, XV.

8   P. Gay, *Freud. A Life for Our Time* (London-Melbourne: Dent, 1988) p. 181.

9   *Die Liebe des Kindes und ihre Fehlentwicklungen* (Bern, 1922).

had developed in him through Adler and Jung. He admitted that as far as religion, ethics and philosophy were concerned, there were differences (*Unterschied*) between them, but not an abyss (*Kluft*) (April 3rd, 1992).

On Freud's suggestion Pfister did not abandon his most significant book (till that moment), *Die psychoanalytische Methode*, and prepared a revised edition, which would be published in 1924. Conflicts were going to be smoothed over, and with a diminishing of tension Pfister displays in his letters the fullness and intensity of his affection, by words that, although a little embarrassing, probably did not displease his interlocutor.

> It is now nearly fifteen years since I entered your house for the first time and quickly fell in love with your humanitarian character and the free and cheerful spirit (*fröhlich-freien Geist*) of your whole family (December 30th, 1923).
> One gladly takes refuge from the turmoil of Christmas in the quiet of Bethlehem to rest, reflect and meditate, free from dogma and science... There I derive gladness and strength, and science awakens memory, not of deprivation and hardship, but of germinating greatness, succour, and growth (December 23th, 1925).

In 1924 Pfister was able to read, surely with emotion, an appreciation of his own work and a declaration in favour of lay analysis in Freud's *Selbstdarstellung* in 1924:

> Dr. Oskar Pfister, a protestant pastor at Zurich, led the way as a tireless pioneer along these lines, nor did he find the practice of analysis incompatible with the retention of his religion, though it is true that this was of a sublimated kind [...] It is no longer possible to restrict the practice of psychoanalysis to doctors and to exclude laymen from it. In fact, a doctor who has not been through special training is, in spite of his diploma, a layman in analysis, and a non-doctor who has been suitably trained can, with occasional reference to a doctor, carry out the analytic treatment not only of children but also of neurotics (SE 20, pp. 69 f.).

Pfister of course also appreciated Freud's *The Problem of Lay Analysis* (1926): he was only displeased that among "pedagogic applications" he did not think of the "analytic pastoral care".

> As one of your first lay pupils, the book gave me unspeakable pleasure. Only *one* lacuna struck me. You mention educational cases, but not the enormous number of adults who are not ill in the medical sense but are nevertheless in extreme need of analysis [...] I earnestly appeal to you to cast a benevolent glance at the analytic cure of souls, which is, after all, another of your children. Undoubtedly the cure of souls will one day be a recognized non-ecclesiastical and even non-religious calling (September 10th, 1926).

Freud replied that he preferred to avoid to touch the subject, writing in Catholic, conservative Austria (September 10th-14th, 1926). Pfister did not participate in the rich debate on lay analysis which took place in the *Internationale Zeitschrift für Psychoanalyse* and in the *International Journal of Psycho-Analysis,* but he published in the spring of 1926 a booklet on "analytic pastoral care": *Analytische Seelsorge. Einführung in die praktische Psychanalyse für Pfarrer und Laien* (Göttingen 1927). Probably Freud recalled it, when he wrote his *Nachwort* to *Die Frage der Laienanalyse,* concluding the debate on this subject.

> A professional lay analyst will have no difficulty in winning as much respect as is due to a secular pastoral worker. Indeed, the words "secular pastoral worker" might well serve as a general formula for describing the function which the analyst, whether he is a doctor or layman, has to perform in his relation to the public. Our friends among the Protestant clergy, and more recently among the Catholic clergy as well, are often able to relieve their parishioners of the inhibitions of their daily life by confirming their faith – after having first offered them a little analytic information about the nature of their conflicts (SA 20, 255 f.).

Freud was clearly filling the gap for which Pfister in some way reproached him. But this did not mean that he was attributing a scientific value to the specifically *religious* foundation of pastoral care.

In the same year, 1927, *The Future of an Illusion* appeared. Freud had announced it in advance to Pfister:

> In the next few weeks a pamphlet of mine will be appearing which has a great deal to do with you. I had been wanting to write it for a long time, and postponed it out of regard for you, but the impulse became too strong. The subject-matter – as you will easily guess – is my completely negative attitude to religion, in any form and however attenuated, and, though there can be nothing new to you in this, I feared, and still fear, that such a public profession of my attitude will be painful to you (October 16th, 1927).

To which Pfister had replied:

> In music, philosophy and religion, I go different ways from you. I have been unable to imagine that a public profession of what you believe could be painful to me: I have always believed that every man should state his honest opinion aloud and plainly. You have always been tolerant towards me, and am I to be intolerant of your atheism? (October 21st, 1927)

Towards the end of his letter of November 25th, 1928, Freud explained:

> I do not know if you have detected the secret link between the *Lay Analysis*

and the *Illusion*. In the former I wish to protect analysis from the doctors and in the latter from the priests. I should like to hand it over to a profession which does not yet exist, a profession of *lay* curers of souls who need not to be doctors and should not be priests (November 25th, 1928).

To Freud's book, Pfister responded with his *The Illusion of a Future. A friendly discussion with Prof. Freud* (1928). Freud had written to him:

> Such is your magnanimity that I expected no other answer to my "declaration of war". The prospect of your making a public stand against my pamphlet gives me positive pleasure, it will be refreshing in the discordant critical chorus for which I am prepared. We know that by different routes we aspire to the same objectives for poor humanity (October 22th, 1927).

"To aspire to the same objectives": the theme is developed at the end both of *The Future of an Illusion* and Pfister's answer. Privately he wrote to Freud: "You are much better and deeper than your disbelief, and I am much worse and more superficial than my faith" (February 20th, 1928).

Freud by this time was sick and tired: but his intellectual lucidity remained intact, as he wrote to Pfister stoically (February 7th, 1930). One of his last writings was a sort of disavowal (and apology at the same time) of Judaism: *Moses and Monotheism*. He told Pfister about it, with the same frank attitude as at the moment of the publication of the *Future of an Illusion*. Pfister gave no polemical reply to it. Only after Freud's death would he briefly reject this hypothesis (Pfister 1944, 188, n. 25).

His admiration for the "noble Nathan, who is much better than the Christians who are such only by name" (April 23rd, 1932) remained steadfast and unchanged. He expressed it once more to Freud's wife immediately after his death, in a moving letter, rich in personal memories and fragments of correspondence. This letter ends boldly: "Though the unfavourable times are more willing to strike up a dance for the devil of lies that to listen to symphonies of truth, I believe with your husband that 'La verité est en marche'" (December 12th, 1932).

In the same year, and thirty years after their first meeting, in 1939, he retired, leaving the Predigerkirche where he had been pastor since 1902. He was at that time 66, and would have all the leisure time necessary for his major work, *Das Christentum und die Angst* (Christianity and Anxiety), which was to be published in Zurich in 1944.

A photographic portrait, a bust, annexed to his 1927 *Selbstdarstellung*, shows Oskar Pfister in the years of his full maturity. A regular face, with light coloured eyes, a thick moustache, a neat hair-parting: thin hair by that time. The suit is that of a *langweilig befrackten Pfarrer*, the dull dark suit of the parish priest of which he spoke in his letter of December 30th, 1923, but his features are not clerical, and rather betray vigour and firmness: sometime before he had written to Freud of the seventeen books written by him (translations included), and after a year he would again climb the Matterhorn.

Pfister of course sent his *Selbstdarstellung* to Freud, too, who replied, thanking him for it, and "the complementary accompanying poem, which obviously accords with your idea of your outer ego" (April 11th, 1927). This allusion to a poem can be solved by reading, among Pfister's papers in the Zentralbibliotek in Zurich, some playful verses he wrote, dated March 28th, 1927. In the poem Pfister comments on his photograph, ending with the words: "When the curtain falls / the trust will remain: / Truth and Love may continue forever to bloom".

This poem was meant to amuse Freud, but reading Pfister's *Selbstdarstellung* the former seems to find with surprise some evidence that Adler's perspective had a certain influence on Pfister when he evolved his synthesis. His emphasis on the "unity of psychic life" in some way was in contrast to but symmetric with Adler's emphasis on the opposing drive: whilst Freud rejected utterly by that time every simplification of psychic life under the term of "love". Freud was by then sick and irritable and could hardly appreciate the pastor's pervasive vitality, which exalted the pair "truth-love" to which, in advance, he had already opposed another couple, "the grim divine couple, *logos kai ananke*" (April 6th, 1922).

In this second half of my presentation, in which I want to analyse just three major points of conflict between Freud and Pfister, the theme of love must then obviously take first place. As Thomas Bonhoeffer put it, Pfister's work can be characterized as "an attempt to integrate theology, psychology, pastoral care and philosophy into a theory and praxis of love. [10] This perspective emerged immediately as soon as Pfister met Freud and was probably the topic of one of Pfister's first letters, judging from Freud's reply on February 9th, 1909 in which he wrote: "You are aware that for us the term 'sex' includes what you in your pastoral work call love". Pfister emphasizes his point of view in *Imago*: "Jesus' commandment, or better, suggestion, to love God, our neighbour and ourselves, shows us the best

---

[10] Th. Bonhoeffer, "Preface" to Pfister, *Das Christentum und die Angst,* (1944) (Olten and Freiburg i. Br., 1975 II ed.) p. IX.

way to channel libido".[11] In the preface, already quoted, to his *Psychoanalytische Methode* (1913), he recalled Augustine: "love is all". The severe Predigerkirche in Zurich, has in its apse as its only ornament an inscription of Mt. 22:37-39: love is the summing up of the commandments. After the pause between 1913 and 1918, and in reply to Freud's very harsh letter ("a godless Jew"), Pfister quotes the 1st letter of John, 4:16 "God is love". Probably the most penetrating essay he wrote on religious history, *The Development of Apostle Paul*, belongs to this period. He concludes by setting up Paul and the synoptic Gospels in opposition in some way: "To people endowed with great inward freedom, synoptic Christianity is for all times the ideal in which to find the fullest development of their personality, both for themselves and for others; but for inhibited persons, who need a rebirth, Paul is the direct model to whom one must turn, also because Paul refers to the one who was greater than he was".[12] In the same years Pfister reviewed very positively Nachmansohn's essay, which compares the Freudian libido with the platonic eros, and integrates it within his own reading of *Symposion*: Plato was for him a "forerunner of psychoanalysis", and he quoted with enthusiasm Eriximacus' speech in which the task of medicine is precisely defined as "the restoration of love" (January 14th, 1921).[13] Freud considered all this concentration on love as a naive candid simplification of human nature, to which he opposed his theory of the death instinct. Pfister did not accept this, seeing in the death instinct only a diminished vital energy (February 4th, 1930), although Freud immediately objected that the death instinct was an "inevitable assumption" (Febraury 7th, 1930).

Freud's most complete and severe criticism of Christian love, and its claims to universality, can be found in *Civilization and its Discontents*. It is hardly possible that he was not thinking of Pfister when he wrote his pages about "Love your neighbour as yourself", to which he objects not only that this maxim is older than Christianity, but also that it is intrinsically unfair (I cannot love in the same way those who deserve my love and my enemies). He emphasizes the practical contradictions in Christianity, with its intolerance: "After the apostle Paul laid universal love among men as the basis of his Christian community, it was inevitable that the extreme

---

[11] "Anwendungen der Psychoanalyse in der Pädagogik und Seelsorge", *Imago* 1 (1912) p. 78.
[12] "Die Entwicklung des Apostel Paulus. Eine religionsgeschichtliche Skizze", *Imago* 6 (1920) p. 87.
[13] "Plato als Vorläufer der Psychoanalyse", *Zentralblatt für Psychotherapie* 7 (1921) pp. 264-269.

intolerance of Christianity would rise against those who remained outside of it". Freud in his *Moses and Monotheism* would show that, in a certain sense, Judaism was much more universalistic than Christianity, because Judaism had the honour of having transmitted to the whole of humanity the highest ethical expression of Egyptian religion, Aton's monotheism, whilst Christianity had on innumerable occasions betrayed its universalistic program, based on love. Pfister would in some way accept this criticism with his *Das Christentum und die Angst*, "the result of 36 years of study on the essence and the history of Christian love", where the history of Christianity appears as a continual betrayal of love, "as an enormous misunderstanding, as the history of a disease of Christianity".[14]

We now turn to the question of the meaning of lay analysis. As we have seen, Pfister was one of the first lay analysts, but his "laity" was of a quite special quality. He was a clergyman, who vindicated the rights of his profession in terms of pastoral care. On the one hand, he criticized very severely the ineffectiveness of traditional pastoral methods; but, on the other hand, he insisted on the convergence, at least partial, between historical pastoral care and analytical psychotherapy. Thus we have seen his enthusiasm for Nachmansohn's essay on Plato, whom he considers a "forerunner of psychoanalysis". With the same enthusiasm some years later, at the end of the second part of his book (on *Psychoanalysis and Weltanschauung*) he establishes a comparison between Socrates and Freud: "notwithstanding the difference of methods, the analogy is striking".[15] In 1932 Pfister published in *Imago* an essay on psychoanalysis among the Navaho Indians, in which he tries to recognise a form of anticipation of psychotherapy in certain methods of treatment of mental disease among so-called primitives.[16]

Pfister is especially concerned with the relationship between psychoanalysis and the New Testament, devoting his book on *Analytische Seelsorge* of 1927 to this topic. Freud wrote to him that he perceived a "rift, not in analytic, but in scientific thinking which one comes upon when the subject of Christ or God comes up" [clearly by Pfister] and categorically denied any psycoanalytical usefulness to Jesus' saying: "Rise up and walk" (November 25th, 1928).

---

14 *Das Christentum und die Angst*, 2nd ed. (Olten und Freiburg i. Br.: Walter Verlag, 1975) p. XXXIX and XXXVI.
15 *Psychoanalyse und Weltanschauung* (Leipzig/Wien /Zürich, 1928) p. 93
16 "Instinktive Psychoanalyse bei den Navaho-Indianern", *Imago* 18 (1932) esp. pp. 103-4.

Pfister replied indirectly with his long essay in *Imago* on *Neutestamentliche Seelsorge und psychoanalytische Therapie* (1934). Many common elements are pointed out by Pfister, starting from the fact that both New Testament pastoral care and psychoanalytical therapy originate with the aim of eliminating anxiety arising from a sense of guilt .

He concludes:

> One should not oppose heart and mind, on the basis of a formula like: "Pectus facit theologum, intellectus analyticum": they cannot work separately. Analytic psychotherapy is a secularized and scientifically elaborated pastoral care, that in some points coincides with that of Jesus ("Die psychoanalytische Therapie is eine säkularisierte und wissenschaftlich ausgebaute Seelsorge, die mit derjenigen Jesu in manchen Punkten übereinstimmt").
>
> In any case, notwithstanding fundamental differences, between NT pastoral care and analytic psychotherapy, both of which pursue liberation through truth and the restoration of love, there are such surprising analogies that they should not fight against each other like enemies (which has unfortunately been the case until now), but each should consider the other as an ally. As far as they both look for a liberation and a recovery through truth and love, both serve, despite their differences, the same noble cause (1934, p. 443).[17]

Pfister's definition of psychoanalysis as a "secularized and scientifically elaborated pastoral care" helps us to understand the meaning of "lay" analysis and to perceive where Pfister converges with Freud and where he diverges from him. Freud uses substantially "lay", "laie" with the meaning of "non-physician"; but when in the postscript to *The Question of Lay Analysis*, he speaks of analysts as a sort of *weltliche Seelsorgern* there is something more, a special intensity, which is expressed by the underlining. In this context, "laity" becomes an essential attribute of the psychoanalytical discipline as such. This attribute can mean many things at the same time: a high degree of rationality, wide accessibility and a full transmissibility through rigorous didactic programs. All this could have been accepted also by Pfister. But in Freud's perception, "lay" analysis also means its provenance, detachment and autonomy with regard to traditional disciplines such as medicine and pastoral care. Thus he insists with Pfister that his two works, *The Question of Lay Analysis* and *The Future of an Illusion* are secretly linked by their concern to defend analysis from physicians (in the case of the former) and from priests (the latter); the new *weltliche Seelsorgern* "do not

---

[17] "Neutestamentliche Seelsorge und psychoanalytische Therapie", *Imago* 20 (1934) p. 443.

need to be physicians and must not be priests".

These lines are written to Pfister and against him. Pfister cannot accept these final consequences. His formulation, as we have seen, is rather "analysis as secularisation", and by it he emphasizes that analysis is the result of the crisis and the transformation of pre-existing psychotherapeutic procedures, which, notwithstanding all the differences due to the scientific revolution, are still there in modern analysis.

But let us now consider the third aspect of the conflict between Pfister and Freud: the question of the *Weltanschauung*. Psychoanalysis does not need a *Weltanschauung* of its own. Psychoanalysis borrows its *Weltanschauung* from the "universal scientific conception of the world", as Freud asserted in his 25th lesson in *Introduction to Pychoanalysis* (1932) and earlier in a letter to Pfister (February 16th, 1929), in which he added that "this scientific conception is incompatible with religion". This point had emerged ten years before. On January 2nd, 1919 Freud wrote that he would like to accept Pfister's suggestion to speak about his relation to positivism. In 1920 Pfister published his "Psychoanalyse and Weltanschauung", in his volume *Zum Kampf um die Psychoanalyse*. On Febraury 4th, 1924 Pfister, dealing with Ferenczi-Rank's *Entwicklungsziele der Psychoanalyse*, affirmed that psychoanalysis, as such, precisely as analysis, could contribute to, but not create a *Weltanschauung*. He repeats the same thing on November 24th, 1927, and Freud's *The Future of an Illusion* having been just published, this letter represents a sort of sketch of the reply Pfister was preparing for *Imago* in 1928. *The Illusion of a Future. Psychoanalysis and Weltanschauung* was the title of a new book, published in 1928, which contained a new edition of his 1920 "Psychoanalyse and Weltanschauung", and *The Illusion of a Future*. We have already seen how the first part of the book ended with a parallel between Socrates and Freud. We may now cite the conclusion of the second part (published also in *Imago*):

> I am happy that Freud himself fundamentally pursues the same aim as I do: he, by his genial researcher's insight, I, by my modest means. He is driven by his God Logos, which he understands as Intellect (*Intellekt*), "presumably" towards the same aim: – *the love for mankind and the diminishing of sufferance* - as mine, to which aim I am driven by my God Logos, whom of course I understand in the terms of the first chapter of John's Gospel, as divine Wisdom and Love. We are driven towards the same aims, which however I understand as the creation of positive good, internal and external, much more than Freud, who expresses himself in terms that recall Schopenhauer... Profession of faith is not the true criterion of the Christian... John 13:35 presents another criterion: "By this shall all men know that you are my disciples; if you have love one to another". Risking repeating myself, I dare once more, in the light of this word, to affirm that Freud, with his

conception of life and with his life's works precedes many practising Christians who consider him, as he considers himself, a Pagan. Thus, *The Future of an Illusion* and *The Illusion of a Future* come together in a strong faith, whose creed is: "The truth shall make you free" (from *Imago* 1928, pp. 163 f.).[18]

To these words, which in fact corresponded to what Pfister had already written privately to him in 1918 ("A better Christian never was"), Freud replied with the last pages of *Civilization and its Discontents*, with the last lecture of *Introduction to Psychoanalysis*, but also with his *Moses and Monotheism*. Here he proposed a reinterpretation of Judaism, concentrating it into an essence of "truth and justice": the religion of the Egyptian Moses and of the prophets. It was a way of coming closer to Pfister, but also of responding to his reproach (almost 20 years had passed): "You are no Jew, which to me, in view of my unbounded admiration for Amos, Isaiah, Jeremiah, and the author of Job and Ecclesiastes, is a matter of profound regret".

Studying Pfister we realize not only how closely and deeply tied he was to his master, but also that Freud in some way depended on Pfister: in the last years of his life, when his interest returns to the problems that had occupied him in his youth (*Postscript* 1935), the interlocutor and often the adversary, continually present in his mind, is Pfister. Studying Pfister means discovering the proper context of many great Freudian metapsychological themes, the context of a lifelong discussion, in which religious identity and tradition were enormously important. Many general discussions about psychoanalysis and religion could profit greatly from a serious examination of the relationship between Freud and Pfister, in which so many problems of the kind are faced, if not solved, with incomparable seriousness.

Moreover, studying Pfister one is struck by the impressive silence that surrounds this figure, both in theological and psychoanalytical contexts. He is remembered above all because of the edition of his correspondence with Freud, decided by Anna Freud under the "overflowing of feelings" of which she speaks in the Preface of this edition. This edition unfortunately contains very little of Pfister, in comparison to the Freudian material. After a brief interlude, with the conference in Zurich to celebrate the centenary of his

---

[18] "Die Illusion einer Zukunft. Eine freundschaftliche Auseinandersetzung mit prof. Dr. Sigm. Freud", *Imago* 14 (1928) pp. 163-4

birth, and the re-edition of his major works, this silence seems to have returned: his work is *geflissentlich totschweigen*, is "deliberately kept under a silence of death". So said Scharfenberg in 1968 and this judgement can be considered valid up to the present.[19] None of the important reference books on religious historical subjects mentions Pfister (the important encyclopedia *Die Religion in Geschichte und Gegenwart*, 2nd ed., had two items by Pfister, "Freud", and "Psychoanalyse»"both of which disappeared in the 3rd).

This silence, on the theological side, depends on the fact that Pfister belonged to a "critical", "liberal" Christianity, a point of view that allowed him to accept with enthusiasm psychoanalysis and modern science in general. But liberal Christianity, that perhaps reached its peak in 1900 with Adolf von Harnack's famous *Essence of Christianity* , was superseded in the twenties by the neo-orthodox dialectical theology of another Swiss theologian, Karl Barth. Albert Schweitzer underwent the same substantial rejection.

One may also guess the reasons for which Pfister's work was forgotten in a psychoanalytical context as well. His often antiquated and rhetorical vocabulary, his claims of continuity from Socrates to Jesus to Freud, his embarrassing religious apology, his naive encyclopedism, the excessive prolixity of his written publications are obstacles to those who try to approach his writings, except for those who are interested in the history of the psychoanalytical movement. Even in this case, Pfister appears only as a secondary figure and is used to throw still more light on the main protagonists. This is true also of P. Gay's excellent monographs.

In the 1973 Zurich conference, important suggestions (it seems to me, although I am not a specialist) were made to understand Pfister's contribution to psychoanalysis. Thomas Bonhoeffer and Günther Bittner proposed seeing in Pfister the first person who recognised and made therapeutic use of "primary love" (Balint). Bonhoeffer, who started from biographical considerations, insisted on the important "heroic" i.e. narcissistic paradigm in Pfister's attitude to life[20]. Bittner emphasized the objective incompleteness of the tools Pfister had at his disposal, as an analyst trained in the years around 1910, so full of controversies and conflicts. He substantially emphasized "primary love", continued Bittner, but as he avoided metapsychological constructions, he made a compromise between technical language and a language taken from the *Umgangssprache*, drawing

---

[19] *S. Freud und seine religionskritik als Herausforderung für den christlichen Glauben*, (Göttingen 1968), p. 17.

[20] "Das Christentum und die Angst, dreissig Jahre später", *Wege zum Menschen* 25 (1973), esp. pp. 441 -2.

on ordinary pastoral and pedagogic practice, and spoke simply of "love" in a way no psychoanalyst – except Lou Andreas Salomé – ever dared to do. His therapeutic intuition did not correspond, however, to an adequate definition of religion.[21] According to Thomas Bonhöffer, in his preface to the new edition of Pfister's *Das Christentum und die Angst*, "he placed – i.e. explained – religion in too tardy Oedipus structures",[22] whilst, still according to Bonhöffer, who recalls E. Erikson, we should rather to this purpose resort to the oral stage and "primary trust".

There is one final point to be made regarding Oskar Pfister's search for a synthesis. There was a risk in this, that Freud sometimes reminded him of: "It looks to me as if you want a synthesis without a previous analysis" (October 9th, 1918). The most important fact seems to me the stress he put on the necessity of the insertion (*Einbeziehung, Einfügung, Ergänzung* etc.) of psychoanalysis into a more complete historical and theoretical framework, in a *Weltanschauung* that psycho-analysis *per se* cannot create or, as he said once, in quite candid terms, into a philosophy "in accordance with the nature of mankind and the world" (November 24th, 1927).

Was this simply the effect of his apologetic concern to reconcile science and faith and to subordinate psychoanalysis to theology or philosophy? Or was it rather, as I would suggest, an attempt to place psychoanalysis on a line of continuity with the history of psychotherapy, seeing *Seelsorge* as prehistory of psychotherapy? The following proposal arises out of Pfister: to see "the making of psychoanalysis" not from the point of view of the paradigm of discontinuity and absolute novelty, but rather from that of continuity (the *nihil sub sole novi*, "nothing new under the sun", that Freud applied in his *Moses and Monotheism*). Or, more exactly, from the point of view of secularisation as Pfister meant it, as the positive transformation and assumption into modernity of ancient *Weltanschauungen*. From this point of view we may even wish to discuss whether Freud's life should be only "a life for our time". We could on the contrary recall Pfister's claim (dropping his naive apologism, "a better Christian never was…") to insert Freud's work in a greater context: "which is as necessary", he continued, "as the synthesis of the notes is to a Beethoven symphony".

---

21 "Oskar Pfister und die 'Unfertigkeit' der Psychoanalyse", *Wege zum Menschen* 25 (1973) esp. pp. 468 and 472-4.
22 "Preface" to *Das Christentum und die Angst*, p. XII

7

Moses, the Great Stranger

1. The question of the relationship between Freud and Judaism can be examined from two distinct but inseparable points of view: psychoanalysis as a "Jewish science", and Freud's personal attitude towards Judaism. In recent years there have been important historical contributions to both topics.

Among these, we must acknowledge our gratitude to Peter Gay's works: his excellent biography, preceded by his shorter but important *A Godless Jew.*[1] In the latter book Peter Gay sets out the position which forms the basis of his larger work. He discusses Anna Freud's famous statement, concluding the inaugural lecture for the S. Freud Chair at the Hebrew University in Jerusalem: psychoanalysis "has been criticized for its methods being imprecise, its findings not open to proof by experiment, for being unscientific, even for being a 'Jewish science'. However the other derogatory comments may be evaluated, it is, I believe, the last-mentioned connotation which, under present circumstances, can serve as a title of honour".[2] His conclusions are clearly expressed a few pages further on: "In the light of this copious record, it takes a certain audacity to discover an impact of the Jewish mystics on Freud, and it is not surprising that there have been few serious attempts to construct such a pedigree" (p. 130). "The claims for the Jewishness of psychoanalysis based on its materials or its intellectual inheritance have proved to be without foundation [...] Freud, I conclude, was a Jew but not a Jewish scholar" (pp. 147-8). Freud's *Moses and Monotheism* confirms this thesis: "When Freud's loyalties to Judaism and to science

---

[1] P. Gay, *A Godless Jew. Freud, Atheism and the Making of Psychoanalysis* (New Haven and London, 1987); *Freud. A Life for Our Time* (New York, 1988), It. trans. *Un ebreo senza Dio. Freud, l'ateismo e le origini della psicoanalisi* (Bologna: Il Mulino, 1988) with a foreword by P.C. Bori, pp. 9-21.

[2] "Inaugural Lecture for the Sigmund Freud Chair at the Hebrew University", Jerusalem, *International Journal of Psycho-Analysis* 59 (1978) pp. 145-145.

clashed, Judaism would have to give way" (p. 151).

Yosef Hayim Yerushalmi has devoted his latest work specifically to *Freud's Moses*.[3] His book is open to many conclusions, "except for the depth and intensity of Freud's Jewish identity and commitment, and a rejection of any interpretation that would regard *Moses and Monotheism* as a repudiation of that identity or even ambivalence toward it, this book does not attempt to reach closure on any of the themes of which it treats" (p. XVIII). In this sense, one of his polemical targets is Marthe Robert[4] and her thesis that *Moses and Monotheism* is an attempt at disaffiliation from Judaism (Paul Ricoeur spoke of an "exorcism"). Consulting Freud's manuscript gives the author the chance to observe that "especially when one belongs oneself to that people" ("zumal wenn man selbst diesem Volke angehört"), has been added to the original first sentence of the book, which simply read in 1934 "One will not easily decide to deny a nation its greatest man, because of the meaning of a name»" and became "To deny a people the man whom it praises as the greatest of its sons is not a deed to be undertaken lightly, especially when one belongs oneself to that people" (p. 7). But Peter Gay is also subjected by Yerushalmi to serious criticism. Having "maintained that although Freud's Jewish identity may have been personally important to him, it had no relevance to his creation of psychoanalysis" seems to Yosef Hayim Yerushalmi "an essentially ahistorical approach", "curious in an eminent social and intellectual historian" (p. 116). Showing the possibility of gaining an insight into Freud's Jewish education, beyond his own readiness to admit it, is one of Yerushalmi's important achievements: his splendid analysis of Jakob Freud's Hebrew inscription to the Philippsohn Bible is a very good example of this. In this perspective, *Moses and Monotheism* appears as an act of "deferred obedience" (p. 77).

Ilse Grubrich Simitis' work, devoted to *Moses and Monotheism: Freud's Moses as Tagtraum*[5] is a short, fascinating essay, which the utilization of *Der*

---

3 *Freud's Moses: Judaism Terminable and Interminable* (New Haven and London, 1991). This book was preceded by "Freud on the 'Historical Novel': from the the Manuscript of Moses and Monotheism, *The International Journal of Psycho-analysis*, 70 (1989) pp. 375-393.

4 *From Oedipus to Moses: Freud's Jewish Identity*, tr. Ralph Manheim (Garden City, 1976 [orig. 1974]). E. Rice, *Freud and Moses. The Long Journey Home* (New York, 1990) shares Yerushalmi's concern, showing how deep were S. Freud's Jewish roots, and concluding (p. 179) that "the first and last chapters of his life were Jewish".

5 *Freuds Moses-Studie als Tagtraum. Ein biographischer Essay* (Weinheim: Verlag Internationale Psychoanalyse, 1991) preceded by "Freuds Moses-Studie als Tagtraum", *Psyche* 44 (1990) pp. 477-515.

Mann Moses' manuscripts makes even more precious. The essay offers a reconstruction of the original, catastrophic event which took place in Freud's mother's life, as well as in his own life – the absence of the mother!– at the age of two years: the death of his brother Julius, and at the same time the death of one of his mother's brothers, who had the same name. These events constitute the original trauma – a modification and change of object ("Objektveränderung and Objektwechsel") in Freud's psyche which nevertheless formed the basis of his enormous creativity and independence of thought, of his *Für-sich sein* (pp. 38-9).

The Nazi persecution was perceived by Freud as a replication of those original traumatic events, to which he opposed his *Der Mann Moses*. "With the materials of the past, that is with the familiar Tora reading of his childhood Freud tried to build the image of a reassuring future: in the fate of *Moses and monotheism* he could convince himself how a troublesome doctrine, full of claims, could not only escape disappearance, notwithstanding political persecution and repression, but return reinforced after a long interval (p. 28). More precisely, *Moses and Monotheism* as a "daydream" had two functions, according to Ilse Grubrich-Simitis. The first one was to defend psychoanalysis: the discourse on monotheism, with its harsh polemical emphasis on mortality, on scientific theory against magic, on invisibility – is in reality a discourse on psychoanalysis. The second function is, in the moment of resistance to persecution, the identification of Freud with Moses, the law-giver, the prototype of justice, and, at the same time, the response to one of the most important themes of anti-semitism: the Egyptian Moses had elected the Jewish people (pp. 55-6).

2. This growing attention to Freud's *Moses and Monotheism*, from its unpublished manuscript to its psychological genesis and motivation, has not yet led to a corresponding evaluation of its theses. The original introduction to *Der Mann Moses, ein historischer Roman* [The Man Moses, An Historical Novel], never published by Freud, confirms indirectly the need for such substantial evaluation.

Yosef Yerushalmi, right at the beginning of his book, hastens to dismiss the question of the correctness of Freud's historical theses. The book "has been rejected almost unanimously by biblical scholars as an arbitrary manipulation of dubious historical data, and by anthropologists and historians of religion as resting on long outmoded ethnological assumptions. Both these strictures, I hasten to add, are quite correct, and the details, available in the literature, need not concern us here". Yerushalmi does not propose to read *Moses and Monotheism* "merely as psychological autobiography", but to explore "its conscious intentionality", that is as a conscious, "public statement about matters of considerably wider consequence – the nature of Jewish history, religion and peoplehood, Christianity and anti-Semitism – written at a tragic historical juncture" (p.2).

As for Ilse Grubrich-Simitis, she deliberately adopts the psychological point of view: "Freud himself – she states – emphasizes that his conclusions rest only on *psychological* probabilities and lack objective evidence" (p. 19): thus Moses can only be considered as a "daydream". Ilse Grubrich-Simitis refers to the beginning of the second essay of *Moses and Monotheism*, which contains exactly this admission. This passage must be compared with *Moses and Monotheism*, III, 2, A. "Our way of proceeding consists in accepting, from handed-down material, what seems useful to us, in rejecting what is not of use, and in putting together the single pieces according to psychological probability [*nach der psychologischen Wahrscheinlichkeit*]". Such a method, he states, "gives no assurance that truth will be found". But why, then, should such work be undertaken? Because, "greatly mitigating [*wenn man… weit… mildert*] the rigour of the claims of a historical-psychological research [*eine historisch-psychologische Untersuchung*], it will be possible to clarify problems which have always appeared worthy of attention and which as a consequence of recent events impose themselves again on the observer" (I translate very literally). But does this mean that Freud gives up every claim to *historical* truth for his reconstruction?

The problem Freud is trying to clarify is evidently that of the origin and essence of Judaism, and consequently the problem of the origin and essence of contemporary anti-Semitism. If the first solution is that it was "Moses who created the Jew" (as he wrote to Arnold Zweig on September 30th, 1934)[6] a full reply could be found only in a historical inquiry specifically about "the Man Moses", and this reply could be satisfying only as far as historically true, or at least historically probable.

That's why he declares that he considers his work first of all as a "pure historical study" [*reine historische Studie*], as he defines it at the end of the second essay. Its purpose is to demonstrate the truth of the general *historical* thesis contained in *Totem and taboo* in the specific *historical* case of Jewish monotheism. Certainly he doubts whether he succeeded in this demonstration: his work, he says at the end of the second preface to the third essay, looks to his own critical sense like a dancer balancing on the tip of one toe. But his conclusion is that the analytical interpretation of the exposure

---

[6]   S. Freud-A. Zweig, *Briefwechsel* (Frankfurt, 1968) pp. 102 f.

myth and, on the other hand, Sellin's conjecture about the death of Moses are a sufficient support to "cast the dice" and decide the publication of *Moses and Monotheism.*

Ernst Sellin's book, *Mose und seine Bedeutung für die israelitisch-jüdische Religionsgeschichte* (Berlin, 1922) was really decisive for Freud, as Yosef Yerushalmi points out: "Indeed, the correlations to *Moses and Monotheism* are so striking that we must wonder if Sellin's work merely confirmed Freud's prior intuitions or whether it was the reading of the book that triggered his own thinking. Beyond the slaying of Moses, Freud found in Sellin the historicity of Moses and the purity of monotheism; a hidden link between Moses and the rise of Christianity through the expectation of his messianic return; the parallel between the murder of Moses and that of Jesus; above all, the survival of Moses' teaching and the memory of his murder as subterranean traditions ("in complete silence" – *in aller Stille*) that reemerged after a lapse of centuries" (pp. 26-7). Sellin's book is a *historical and exegetical* essay, and is the basis for Freud's own historical essay.

Another historical work is Hugo Gressman's *Mose und seine Zeit* (Göttingen, 1913), to which Freud thought of devoting a "Critical appendix" (*Kritischer Anhang*) which was eliminated in the final version. This appendix – I am using Yerushalmi's quotations from the manuscript which is not yet published – contained some reflections on the historical novel. Gressmann's reconstruction "is only a historical novel, no more certain that the one constructed by us". And at the beginning: "I did not know that it would be so difficult to compose a historical novel. Now that it is completed, my conscience demands that the standard of more sober historical writing apply to it" (p. 24).

This last reflection lies at the basis of Freud's final rejection of the historical novel genre. In his introduction to the *historischer Roman* he planned to say: "That which one can obtain by means of this technique can also be called a kind of 'historical novel', since it has no proven reality, or only an unconfirmable one, for even the greatest probability does not necessarily correspond to the truth. Truth is often very improbable, and factual evidence can only in small measure be replaced by deductions and speculations". When Freud abandoned the idea of a historical novel, he specifically decided that, notwithstanding all the difficulties, he could not weaken his work by deliberately classifying it with a term that, in any case, having to do with "fiction and invention" [*Erdichtung und Erfindung*] could be associated with "the blemish of error" (I quote from Yerushalmi's translation, p. 17). He wanted his work to be accepted as historical truth – a desperate claim, certainly – because historical truth, as a scientist, was his basic concern.

Let me pass now for a moment to a more personal reminiscence. The evaluation of the historical basis of Freud's argument about Moses has always been a central concern, and as far back as 1975 I was approached by the editor Boringhieri, in view of my specific competence as biblical scholar, for the translation of the first two essays of *Moses and Monotheism*. While preparing its footnotes I decided to try and check Freud's exegetical and historical sources by consulting his personal library in London, at 20, Maresfield Gardens. I realized that it was important to see the manuscript of the book, as it was evident from the Freud-Zweig correspondence that Freud wrote something different from what had been published afterwards. With Anna Freud's permission, I had the opportunity to work among Freud's books in December 1976. In December 1978 I was allowed to study the manuscript of *Moses and Monotheism*, and, with the direct help of Anna Freud, and the permission of the Freud Copyright, to publish in an Italian historical review the introduction to the unpublished historical novel. This short essay was preceded by one devoted to books on the history of religions in Freud's library and a second one, *Freud's Moses: towards a first historical evaluation.*[7]

As I was saying, historical concern was at the basis of my work on *Moses and Monotheism*, from its beginning. On February 2nd, 1976 I wrote to Anna Freud: "I am trying to reconstruct Dr. Freud's historical sources, to understand his argument and the evidence alleged in its real value, rather than looking for his ultimate concern and psychological motivations, as for instance M. Robert does. As far as I know, it is the first time such a thing has been done. I am convinced that this book has not yet received the attention it really deserves, and has to be studied first of all as it presents itself, as a *real historical* work". Anna Freud understood perfectly my historical approach to her father's book. I keep a letter from her, after our first visit to 20, Maresfield Gardens, in which she says, among other things: "I know my father would be pleased to see his book on *Moses and Monotheism* really appreciated". It was January the 10th, 1977, in the Summer of the same year that she would pronounce her address at Jerusalem University.

---

7   "Materiale storico-religioso nella biblioteca di Sigmund Freud: alcuni rilievi sul catalogo", *Annali dell'Istituto storico italo-germanico in Trento* 1 (1975) pp. 281-289, now in *L'estasi del profeta e altri saggi tra ebraismo e cristianesimo* (Bologna:Il Mulino, 1989) pp. 223-236; "Il 'Mosè' di Freud: per una prima valutazione storico-critica", *Sic. Materiali per la psicoanalisi*, n. 6, settembre 1976, pp. 21-37, now in *L'estasi del profeta*, pp. 179-222; "Una pagina inedita di Freud. La premessa al romanzo storico su Mosè", *Rivista di storia contemporanea* 7 (1979) pp.1-16, now in *L'estasi del profeta*, pp. 237-258.

Notwithstanding these extraordinarily encouraging words, and although they sounded like a request to do still more for this real appreciation of *Moses and Monotheism*, after my three essays, after 1979, I did not go on, for various reasons. Peter Gay's excellent biographical books, and the publication of Ilse Grubrich-Simitis' and Yosef Yerushalmi's very accurate and rigorous works, enriched finally by the use of *Moses and Monotheism* manuscripts, are for me a reason to return to the subject. More generally, *Moses and Monotheism* itself seems to be returning to the attention of a wider public.

3. An appreciation of the historical content of *Moses and Monotheism* is possible only a) if we accept the essential element of its theses, and not its unnecessary details and b) if we are critically conscious of the ideological paradigm of the absoluteness and exclusiveness of revelation which prevents the admission of any substantial comparison and genetic connection among traditions and denies the possibility of any substantial contradiction inside the religious tradition.

Very briefly, Freud's book contains three theses. 1) The Egyptian origin of Moses and Monotheism; 2) the tragic fate of Moses, and 3) the dualism: the partial adoption of the yahvistic cult and legalism and the return of pure monotheism through the prophets. Now, I do not think that his first thesis falls if we cannot – and we cannot – argue with absolute certainty from the name "Mose" and from the exposure myth in favour of the Egyptian origin of Moses. I think that the *essential element* is in recognizing an Egyptian monotheism as an important precedent to Jewish monotheism, and admit the possibility of historical dependence of the second on the first. Aton religion was characterized by the exclusive belief in one God the creator, the rejection of anthopomorphism and images, of magic and afterlife. Freud almost forgot K. Abraham's essay on this subject[8] and did not quote it, because it did not contain the essential element he needed, which in fact he found in James Henry Breasted, *The Dawn of Conscience* (New York, 1933). He read and annotated this book, very much as I was able to verify, and certainly Breasted's thesis on the connection between the two monotheisms was as decisive as Sellin's book. To this position, which had important precedents both in Hellenistic times and in the Enlightenment,[9] there are

---

8   K. Abraham, "Amenhotep IV (Ichnaton). Psychonalytische Beiträge zum Verständnis seine Persönlichkeit und des monotheistisches Atonkultes", *Imago* 1 (1912) pp. 334-360.

9   See my *L'estasi del profeta*, p. 195-205, and in Yerushalmi, *Freud's Moses*, p. 5.

objections, which insist on the undeniable difference between the two religions. Some biblical scholars recognize the possibility of this dependence, like Cazelles: "Les vues épurées de celui-ci [Amenophis IV] peuvent avoir contribué à disposer le jeune scribe [Moses] à recevoir la révelation".[10] I think the essence of Freud's position is contained in Breasted's book, which does not imply a demonstration of the Egyptian origin of Moses, but a genetic connection between the two conceptions. The difficulties over admitting this connection depend, according to me, on what I defined above as "the ideological paradigm of the absoluteness of revelation", which prevents Christian (Protestant and Catholic), Jewish, Muslim scholars, notwithstanding the immense amount of erudition very often displayed in their work, from accepting and reflecting on the fact of isomorphism even when this phenomenon is extraordinarily apparent.

As for the second point, Sellin was a serious scholar, and his conjecture on *Hosea* 12:14-13:13 is interesting, and makes good sense.[11] He reads: "Ephraim provoked him [not: God, but Moses] bitterly... When Ephraim provoked discord [instead of 'spoke trembling'] he bore them [not 'he exalted himself'] in Israel, and he expiated in Baal [Peor] and died". V. 12. 15b can now be read with reference to the death of Moses: "Therefore shall he leave his blood upon him and his reproach shall the Lord return upon him". But it is difficult to accept such an enormous fact as the slaying of Moses simply on the basis of a good conjecture. What can be said – and, according to me, this is the *essential element* – is that there is an important Biblical tradition (and I mean first of all *Jewish* tradition) about the conflict between the prophet and the people and about the tragic fate of the prophets. It can be also said that in the Deuteronomistic source Moses is presented as a suffering mediator, that he can be likened to the suffering servant of God in deutero-Isaiah and that extra-Biblical rabbinical literature insists on the expiatory features of his death.

As for the third point, most of the objections to Freud are over his psycho-Lamarckism, i.e. on his phylogenetic explanation of the survival of the memory of Moses' legacy and tragic death. Ilse Grubrich-Simitis points out a meaningful lapsus which reveals how Freud himself was uncertain about this question (pp. 40-1) and emphasizes the psychological basis of this

---

[10] H Cazelles, *Moïse, Dictionnaire de la Bible, Suppl.* 5 (1957) col. 1308-1337, esp.1322; in *Autour de l'Exode* (Paris, 1987) the same author no longer touches on the problem; see my *L'estasi del profeta* (pp. 13 and 195-6).

[11] E. Sellin, "Hosea und das Martyrium des Mose", *Zeitschrift für die Alttestamentliche Wissenschaft* 46 (1928) pp. 23-33; see *L'estasi del profeta*, pp. 205-9.

phylogenetic position. Yerushalmi (p. 31) quotes *Moses and Monotheism*: the archaic heritage "comprises not only dispositions but subject matter – memory traces of the experience of earlier generations" and comments: "At this point even the most ardent and loyal admirer of Freud can only whisper to himself, 'Certum, quia absurdum est'". But the *essential element* in this story is not psycho-Lamarckism. Freud was convinced that there was a double origin to Judaism, which could explain a contradiction between the pureness of the religion of the Decalogue, and its many other legal and cultic institutions. This particular explanation, according to me and to many others, is not demonstrable but the essential element is the assumption that a tradition can contain at its origin a contradiction that remains present in its life in a hidden way, and comes out only later, at a certain moment: the essential element lies precisely in the idea of a dualism immanent in the history of Judaism.

This could be a very brief formulation of the three theses contained in *Moses and Monotheism*. But I must repeat my initial warning: to appreciate these theses, in any formulation, we must be free from the paradigm of the exclusiveness of revelation and the absolute integrity of tradition, and capable, on the contrary, of sharing Freud's enlightened and liberal way of considering religious matters which he learnt in his first university studies (as the correspondence with the friend of his youth Silberstein shows).[12] According to his own later formulations, at the centre of this sensibility there is, negatively, "the overcoming of magical thinking and the rejection of mysticism", and positively, the ideas of a religion as "this-wordliness" "truth-justice" and of "spirituality" (*Geistlichkeit*).

It must also be added here that these theses are also not easy to accept for those who belong to the Christian tradition. We know Freud's harsh conclusion about Christianity: "The Christian religion did not maintain the height of spiritualization to which Judaism had soared. It was no longer strictly monotheist, it took over numerous symbolic rituals from surrounding peoples, it re-established the great mother-goddess and found room to introduce many of the divine figures of polytheism only lightly veiled, though in subordinate positions. Above all, it did not, like Aton religion and the Mosaic one which followed it, exclude the entry of superstitions,magical and mystical elements which were to prove a severe inhibition upon the intellectual development of the next two thousand years. The triumph of Christianity was a renewed victory of the Ammon

---

[12] S. Freud, *Jugendbriefe and Eduard Silberstein, 1871-1881* (Frankfurt am Main, 1989).

priests over Ikhnaton's God" (III, 1, D). This may be difficult to accept. But here again, this judgement can be understood and appreciated only if we can share at least for a moment the perspective of a sort of radically imageless and secular religion (and radically secular Judaism), consisting in Truth-Justice.

This perspective was at the centre of Freud's last concerns, not only because it coincided with that essence of Judaism which he had been long looking for, but also probably because he believed that it should be the ultimate perspective of psychoanalysis, as a modern form of therapy of the soul. As Yerushalmi puts it, in his innermost heart he believed that "psychoanalysis is itself a further, if not final, metamorphosed extension of Judaism, divested of its illusory religious forms but retaining its essential monotheistic characteristics" (p. 99). We can accept this way of saying it, with one correction. If we remember that Freud said: "it is honour enough for the Jewish people that it has kept alive such a tradition and produced men who lent it their voice, even if the stimulus had first come from the outside, from a great stranger" (II, 7), we should see the "title of honour" of "Jewish science" only in a wider context, as said of something that brings a message which, while particular (and Jewish) in its origin, is universal in its essence.

Index

DATE DUE

			Printed In USA